Software in
Safety-related Systems

Software in Safety-related Systems

Edited by

Brian A. Wichmann
National Physical Laboratory, UK

B C S **WILEY**

JOHN WILEY & SONS
Chichester • New York • Brisbane • Toronto • Singapore

Other Wiley Editorial Offices

John Wiley & Sons, Inc., 605 Third Avenue,
New York, NY 10158-0012, USA

Jacaranda Wiley Ltd, G.P.O. Box 859, Brisbane,
Queensland 4001, Australia

John Wiley & Sons (Canada) Ltd, 22 Worcester Road,
Rexdale, Ontario M9W 1L1, Canada

John Wiley & Sons (SEA) Pte Ltd, 37 Jalan Pemimpin #05-04,
Block B, Union Industrial Building, Singapore 2057

British Library Cataloguing in Publication Data

A catalogue record for this book is available
from the British Library

ISBN 0 471 93474 7

Production Editing and Typesetting by Edgerton Publishing Services,
Huddersfield, on behalf of the British Computer Society
Printed in Great Britain by Courier International Ltd, East Kilbride

TABLE OF CONTENTS

FOREWORD vii

EDITOR'S PREFACE.. ix

IEE/BCS JOINT STUDY REPORT

Software in Safety-Related Systems... 1
(*A detailed table of contents is given on page 3*)

DRIVE REPORT

Review of Current Tools and Techniques for the Development
of Safety-Critical Software.. 145

EDUCATION AND TRAINING FOR SAFETY-CRITICAL
SYSTEMS PRACTITIONERS 177

A DEVELOPMENT MODEL FOR SAFETY-CRITICAL
SOFTWARE 209

INT DEF STAN 00-55

The Procurement of Safety Critical Software in Defence
Equipment 225
(*Each of the two parts of this standard carries its own page numbering; a full
table of contents is given at the beginning of each part*)

FOREWORD

Under its Royal Charter, The British Computer Society has a responsibility to advise policy makers, design teams and users of any hazards which may arise from the use of protection and control equipment which embodies computers. There are many applications in which the use of information technology enhances the protection to the public. For example, the automation of the flight controls of civil aircraft for safe landings in fog.

Each such technological advance creates new problems which the industry concerned must solve, sometimes at great cost. High integrity computer software for life-critical applications is very expensive, costing 10 to 100 times as much as code for less demanding regimes. The underlying computer hardware becomes more costly too, since redundancy is usually required to ensure 'non-stop' operation. In harnessing computers to systems which are critical to the preservation of human life, the protection of the environment and related commercial issues, we make heavy demands on the design teams involved, their senior managers and the regulatory authorities. The latter include bodies such as the UK Civil Aviation Authority and the Nuclear Installations Inspectorate.

If the Information Technology and Electrical Engineering industries are to use processors and software to enhance safety and reliability, a number of key points must be addressed:

1. The adoption of rigorous international and national Standards, instantiated for specific industries, for the specification, design and verification of safety-critical computer-based equipment.

2. Rigorous international and national Standards for the overall Quality Assurance of the finished product, to check that all the specialised requirements of the safety community have been met, alongside the other criteria which should apply to vital computer systems, such as data security.

3. The use of Hazard Analysis to ensure the Prime Contractor, any sub-contractors and the end-user all agree on the hazards implicit in the system in question, including those arising during any in-service modifications of the equipment.

4. The adoption of rigorous, approved software development environments, including the use of validated compilers, with appropriate certificates from internationally recognised Test Houses, and the provision of audit functions to enable skilled external assessors to study the integrity of the software.

5. Provision of rigorous configuration control of the design of all critical electronic hardware, including mechanisms for external audit, to ensure that company Standards are being maintained.

6. Application of both static and dynamic methods of testing and analysis to all software, both in the environment of the host computer and within the final, target hardware.

7. Adoption of standards and qualification of all staff who work in any professional capacity on the design or modification of safety-critical systems, and the provision of training to enable scientists and engineers to reach the requisite level of skill.

This Report addresses all of these issues and makes positive recommendations, both for managers and technical experts alike. By combining several contributions in a single volume we believe that we are providing a valuable primer for all those engaged in safety-critical Information Technology.

W J Cullyer
Chairman, BCS Safety Critical Systems Task Force
University of Warwick
February 1991

EDITOR'S PREFACE

It is a pleasure to bring together in one volume a number of contributions to the debate on Safety Critical Computer Systems. Although these contributions are very different in style and content, they all add to our understanding of the issue. Hopefully, the debate can then continue from a better perspective.

The first contribution is the IEE/BCS Study Report which was commissioned by the Department of Trade and Industry. This provides a consensus professional view of the area, and is an excellent starting point. Although this was published by IEE sometime ago, this is the first time it has appeared in book format and hence provides a reference source.

The second contribution is a review of current tools and techniques that was prepared for the CEC-funded DRIVE project. Although DRIVE is a project specifically for the automotive industry, this study clearly has wider applicability and therefore its inclusion in this volume is appropriate.

One of the activities of the BCS in response to concerns about safety-critical software has been the formation of a working group on the Education and Training aspects led by Professor John McDermid. The major contribution of this group is the report which is contained in this volume.

The last but one contribution is a personal one by the Editor. This should be regarded as merely a contribution to the general debate rather than a final 'solution' to the issues of software development in this area.

Finally, a major development in the UK has been the decision by the Ministry of Defence to produce a specific standard for the development (and procurement) of safety-critical software. This has created greater awareness of many of the issues, and some controversy over the use of 'Formal Methods'. Hence the inclusion in this volume of the 1991 version of this Standard is particularly welcome.

The Editor wishes to acknowledge those who have contributed to the production of this volume. This includes Dr John Kershaw (RSRE) and Dr Ian Spalding (Praxis) who read and checked the entire manuscript, and Mr G O'Neill (NPL) who has played a large part in preparing the material for printing. The NPL contribution has been funded by the Department of Trade and Industry Software Quality Unit.

B A Wichmann
Chairman, BCS Specialist Group on Safety Related Systems
National Physical Laboratory
September 1991

IEE/BCS
JOINT STUDY
REPORT

Software in
Safety-Related Systems

A report prepared by
a joint project team of
The Institution of Electrical Engineers
and
The British Computer Society

TABLE OF CONTENTS
OF IEE/BCS REPORT

EXECUTIVE SUMMARY 5

PREFACE 9

1. INTRODUCTION.. 11

2. TECHNICAL BACKGROUND 13

    A. Introduction to Safety-Related Systems 13
    B. Benefits of Programmable Electronic Systems 15
    C. Problems Associated with Programmable Electronic
       Systems 17
    D. Methods of Tackling Safety-Related Software 19

3. LEGAL LIABILITY FOR SOFTWARE IN
    SAFETY-RELATED SYSTEMS... 27

    A. Introduction 27
    B. Criminal Liabilities 27
    C. Civil Liabilities.. 29
    D. Protective Measures 32

4. ANALYSIS OF THE INFORMATION GATHERED..................................... 35

    A. Introduction 35
    B. The UK Situation.. 35
    C. International Developments... 39

5.   CERTIFICATION 41

      A. Introduction and Summary... 41
      B. Background 42
      C. Sources of Concern 43
      D. Approaches to Certification 45
      E. Conclusions 50

6.   THE WAY FORWARD 53

      A. Introduction, Discussion and Rationale 53
      B. Recommendations 55

APPENDICES

      A. BASIC CONCEPTS... 61
      B. OVERSEAS STUDY 69
      C. DTI GRANT SCOPE... 83
      D. DEFINITIONS 87
      E. ACRONYMS.. 93
      F. BIBLIOGRAPHY AND REFERENCES 97
      G. IEE/BCS OPEN CONSULTATIVE MEETING 105
      H. FULL ANALYSIS OF RESPONSES TO
          QUESTIONNAIRE.. 109
      I.   LIST OF CONTRIBUTORS.. 143

EXECUTIVE SUMMARY

1. The study is concerned with software in safety-related systems. Safety is defined as the likelihood that a system does not lead to a state in which there is danger to human life or the environment (2.1). The Study was instigated by consideration of the ACARD report and assisted by a grant from the Department of Trade and Industry (Preface and Chapter 1).

2. The objective was to identify and describe current regulatory requirements for, and issues relating to the certification of, the design and approval of safety-related systems employing software, in the UK and internationally; to assess overlaps, inconsistencies and gaps; and to make recommendations on actions required for public safety (Preface, 1).

3. The work was directed and undertaken mainly by a group of senior members of the Institution of Electrical Engineers and the British Computer Society. The bulk of the UK information was provided by a larger working party of representatives from industry and other authorities. In order to ensure maximum consultation, two open national consultative meetings were held. The report thus reflects the considered views of professionals in the IT manufacturing and supply industry, in purchaser and certification agencies, as well as in academia, and it records where conflicting views arose (Preface, 2 and 3). Background material on the existing situation in Europe and in the United States was obtained by means of a sub-contract placed with The Centre for Software Engineering Ltd (Appendix B).

4. Technical considerations regarding benefits (2.18) and problems (2.27) led to the identification of the need for a Technical Framework, whose characteristics are outlined (2.47). A Safety Lifecycle which fits within that framework is discussed (2.50).

5. Legal liability is both Criminal (3.3) and Civil (3.20). Criminal liability is based on the Health and Safety at Work Act (1974) (3.4) and the Consumer Protection Act (1987) (3.12). Civil liabilities are divided into contract (3.19), and tort and product liability (3.24). Protective measures such as insurance are outlined (3.29). The legal position is currently uncertain due to a number of untested cases (3.2) and doubts about European Directives (3.7, 3.26, 3.27). Note that none of this constitutes legal advice.

6. Certification may relate to organisations, individuals, products and/or the production process and its tools (5.2). The advantages, disadvantages and requirements for software certification are considered: there is concern that within organisations certification rather than the proper achievement of safety may become the goal. Certification requires objective quantitative measures: much of safety can

only be assessed using qualitative subjective judgements (5.3). The current position and the issues relating to each certification category are discussed (5.21).

7.   A number of key concerns which underlie the recommendations have been identified (6.14).

Recommendations

8.   The establishment of means for the continuous review of the overall position to ensure both the dissemination of appropriate knowledge as it becomes available and its use as the basis of a programme of certification. This could be achieved by continuing the Project Team, with payment of fees to the specialists from private industry (6.15).

9.   The establishment of an awareness programme to ensure that all involved with safety-related systems including non-engineering professionals in other fields are aware of all the activities in the field, of their responsibilities, and of the factors involved in achieving safety. Consideration should be given to the production of a newsletter. An extensive publicity campaign will be needed (6.16).

10. The dissemination of information about the use of methods of assessment of safety-related software. Realisable detailed recommendations overcoming problems with divulgence of commercially sensitive information may result from further discussions (6.17).

11. The establishment in the UK of a scheme to monitor the introduction of programmable elements in safety-related systems. Active participation by the Health and Safety Executive is likely and legislation may be required (6.18).

12. The development of a technical framework and the adoption of a Safety Lifecycle as a procedural framework for all safety-related systems. This could be undertaken as an independent study or by the Health and Safety Executive (6.18).

13. The development, through a research project, of definitions for quantitative parameters to be used as measures of safety integrity (6.21).

14. Numbers used to categorise systems should be presented only as 'claim limits' based on engineering judgement. Those making such claims must be able to justify them. Research should be undertaken to enable more rigorous quantification (6.22).

15. The technical and procedural frameworks should be adopted via International Electrotechnical Commission (IEC) standardisation to align Europe with the wider international community; they should be given as much force and authority as possible. Standards developers should take cognisance of existing and developing IEC standards (6.23).

16. The focus of attention should not immediately be on the development of certification systems; rather research and development should be undertaken to achieve needed levels of knowledge and to assess the usefulness of certification and how it may best contribute to improved safety assurance. Established certification practices should be continued (6.25).

17. Organisations should, when developing standards, distinguish between generic requirements, industry- and application-specific requirements, and procurement procedures. Within the UK, industry should be encouraged to develop a pan-sector code of practice starting with the adoption of the Safety Lifecycle (6.27).

18. All those involved in the Safety Lifecycle should be competent with respect to their safety-related work. Organisations which supply or operate systems should be responsible for nominating competent persons to identify hazards and ensure that appropriate action is taken. For the most critical systems there should be at least one named competent person with overall responsibility (6.28).

19. Financial liability should lie with the organisation rather than the individual engineers (6.32).

20. The required education, training and experience should be determined and courses made available at post-graduate, post-experience level (6.31).

21. The principles of System Safety Assessment Reports and of independent safety assessment are recommended (6.33).

22. A programme of research (6.35) funded through a Science and Engineering Research Council Interdisciplinary Research Council to:

    (a) analyse previous experience to avoid repetition of earlier errors;

    (b) determine the contribution to safety integrity of different factors individually and in amalgamation and in particular circumstances; develop means for quantifying these;

    (c) refine the technical framework;

    (d) study architectural forms and their appropriateness for particular applications;

    (e) establish and if possible quantify the benefits of diversity of systems, software and hardware;

    (f) investigate testing; statistical inferences drawn from experience; complexity, its measurement, and its relationship to other measures.

PREFACE

1. The work entailed in the preparation of this report has been partially supported by a grant made by the the Department of Trade and Industry to the Institution of Electrical Engineers, working jointly with the British Computer Society. The objective of the study was to identify and describe current regulatory requirements for the design and approval of safety-related systems employing software, both in the UK and internationally, to assess the overlaps, inconsistencies and gaps, and to make recommendations on any action deemed to be necessary in the interests of public safety. The review of the regulatory aspects was to be carried out in liaison with the Health and Safety Executive and Ministry of Defence. Certification issues were to be covered as part of the study of the regulatory framework.

2. The information is presented primarily for two groups (a) software engineers without experience of safety-related systems and (b) safety engineers without experience or knowledge of software. Within those groups there are both managers and practitioners.

3. The work was directed and undertaken mainly by a Project Team consisting of a group of senior members drawn from the IEE and the BCS. The bulk of the UK information was provided by a larger Working Party of representatives from industry and other authorities. The membership of the Project Management Team and the Working Party is listed in Appendix I. By this means the Project Team took into account a very wide range of views. The background material on the existing situation in Europe and in the USA was obtained by means of a sub-contract placed with The Centre for Software Engineering Ltd. Its findings are recorded in Appendix B to this Report.

4. To ensure maximum consultation, two national consultative meetings were held to discuss drafts of the Report. Comments at those meetings and written comments on the drafts have all been taken into account.

5. The Report thus reflects the knowledge, experience and opinions of professionals from a wide range of environments: the IT manufacturing and supply industries, purchasers and users, standards and certification agencies, and academia; and both large and small organisations. Although, as will be seen, there are areas in which views expressed were not consistent, the final outcome represents the considered views of the Project Team.

6. The report can claim only to attempt the documentation of the currently prevailing circumstances surrounding the development and control of safety-related software in the UK, in Europe and in the USA. The techniques of system design and

software design, and the testing and proving of both systems and software for safety-related applications, are all in the process of evolution, and further discussion and development of the regulatory environment will be essential as the situation changes over the years.

7.   During the course of the Study, various related items were produced or were underway and were taken into account:

(a) a new chapter of the STARTS handbook (now incorporated in Ref. 102);

(b) the HSE Safety-Related Software Study (Ref. 56);

(c) the work on software safety of the International Electrotechnical Commission (Refs 67 and 68);

(d) Ministry of Defence Draft Interim Standards 00-55 and 00-56 (Refs 77 and 78).

In the case of the first two, the Project Management Team believes that the findings of this Study does not or will not vary significantly from their contents.

8.   The study could not have been undertaken without the help of, and the supply of material from, a large number of organisations and individuals. The Project Team thanks them for their help.

1. INTRODUCTION

1.1   The use of computers in safety-related systems is becoming more and more widespread. In many cases software affects the safety of the complete system, and hence could endanger human life. Unfortunately it is not yet possible to provide guarantees that software is error free, particularly when the systems are complex or highly sophisticated. Further the degree of trust which we can justifiably place in the software is often much less than that which we can place in other aspects of a system. Thus it is necessary to establish techniques and standards for the development of safety-related software so that it is possible to have at least as much confidence in the software as in other aspects of a system, e.g. mechanical or electronic components. The vital role of software was highlighted in the ACARD report on *Software: a vital key to UK competitiveness* (Ref. 2), and this has led to a number of studies of the use of software in safety-related activities.

1.2   A survey paper on the software aspects of safety-related systems formed a major section of the IEE's response to the ACARD report. Proposals to the DTI were attached to the response, aimed at the resolution of some of the problems which had been outlined. The response from the DTI proposed a programme of work to be carried out jointly by the IEE and the BCS, stating that this should be complementary to the work currently in hand by the HSE. A list of the aspects to be covered, agreed by the DTI, is given as Appendix C and this report represents the major conclusions from that work.

1.3   The proposals envisaged studies leading to recommendations in the areas of a regulatory framework, professional certification and professional liability. On the regulatory aspects, a description of the current situation in terms of standards and codes of practice as well as legislative requirements, both in UK and internationally, was produced as a starting point for the work (see Chapter 5).

1.4   An aim in studying the current situation was to identify any overlaps, inconsistencies and gaps in the coverage of such standards and regulations. Further, information was sought on trends in established practice, and any unnecessary divergence between civil and military standards. It was found that conditions and requirements varied significantly between the different application sectors, and that there was potential benefit from harmonisation across industry sectors. Further, initial feeling was that regulations and legislation in this field should be no more onerous than for other engineering disciplines and that there should not be an over-reliance on formalism.

1.5   The impact of the new product liability legislation was to be considered, and compared with the old conditions when there was a necessity to prove negligence. In pursuance of public safety the certification of systems engineers, systems assessors, supply organisations and products might all be necessary to some degree. One certification problem is to make sure that it is the individual who is being assessed rather than the course of training that he had taken.

1.6   The current work grew out of the responses to ACARD made separately by the two Institutions. However, in order to ensure a fair representation of industry views a panel of experts was formed, and an open consultative meeting was held prior to finalisation of this report. We believe that this report now presents the views of informed professionals in the IT manufacturing and supply industry, purchaser and certification agencies and academia.

1.7   Chapter 2 contains a discussion of the technical background, and refers in particular to a Technical Framework, a Safety Lifecycle, and to System Safety Assessment Reports. Chapter 3 is concerned with legal liability, both criminal and civil. A major part of the Study was a survey of existing practices; the responses are analysed in Chapter 4. Chapter 5 identifies and discusses the various approaches to certification, and reviews the advantages and disadvantages of each. Chapter 6 contains recommendations. These are preceded by a summarising discussion of the rationale underpinning them. In the course of the study there arose a number of topics into which research is needed. These are listed at the end of the chapter.

1.8   Appendix A contains a discussion of the basic concept of safety and explains how this is inevitably accompanied by uncertainty. The international scene was the subject of a related study whose results are included in Appendix B. Definitions, Acronyms, and a Bibliography are included in Appendices D, E, and F. The bibliography includes, but is not limited to, documents examined during the study. Appendix G contains concluding remarks from the first Consultative Meeting. Finally, Appendix H has full details of survey responses.

2. TECHNICAL BACKGROUND

A. Introduction to Safety-Related Systems

2.1   Safety is the likelihood that a system used in a particular operational context does not lead to a state in which human life or the environment are endangered. A safety-related system is one by which the overall safety of a process, machinery or equipment is assured. Examples range from a trip-switch which disconnects power from a lathe if anyone approaches too closely, to the flight-control and engine management systems for a modern airliner. In giving these definitions, we are aware that they are wider than others, such as those proposed by the Health and Safety Executive. It has to be realised that for many terms widely used in the area there are no generally accepted (and precise) definitions.

2.2   Assurance of safety stems from:

   1.   Identification of individual hazards;

   2.   Assessing the risk associated with those hazards.

The safety-related system is thus that system encompassing all components that are related to a particular hazard. The computer-based part of the system, generally referred to as the Programmable Electronic System (PES) part of the safety-related system, is that subsystem that seeks to control or reduce the risk associated with any particular hazard.

2.3   The safety of a system is a system-wide issue, and the safety of any subsystem (for example, computer control system) cannot usefully be considered in isolation from the total system. This is because the system design may include aspects which ensure that a failure of a particular subsystem cannot cause the unsafe behaviour of the total system.

2.4   It is therefore necessary to identify the level of adequate safety and develop each subsystem to standards which assure, so far as is reasonable and practical, that the required level is reached for the system as a whole.

2.5   In addressing safety issues relating to the use of PESs, it is necessary to adopt a 'systems approach' as it is the functioning of the overall system which is relevant to preventing accidents or incidents. A system in this context extends from the equipment sensors, or other input devices via data highways or other communication paths, to the equipment actuators, or other output devices. The human beings who operate safety-related systems must also be regarded as part of those systems.

2.6   In this context, the personnel responsible for the use and operation of the system, whether in a supervisory capacity or directly in manipulating controls, should be regarded as elements in the system which are potentially capable of causing accidents or incidents. (Certification of individuals is discussed in Chapter 5.)

2.7   If the safety-related system requires human intervention for its operation, the human factors aspects, e.g. clarity of data presentation and complexity of input, must be given adequate consideration.

2.8   To achieve a required level of safety, it may be necessary for there to be more than one safety-related system. This produces (potentially) a four-level hierarchy of safety-related systems, subsystems, and sub-subsystems:

1.   the 'total' system, some of the subsystems of the total system may not be safety-related;

2.   a subsystem encompassing all those parts of the system which are safety-related;

3.   each *individual* safety-related sub-subsystem;

4.   the software element within each safety-related sub-subsystem.

Safety-related systems, subsystems and their components can also be categorised within the technical framework described in paragraphs 2.47*ff*.

2.9   For serious risks, more than one designated safety-related system may be required to achieve the necessary level of safety. The 'systems approach' therefore involves addressing all the systems in the hierarchy and all the elements within a system (including software).

2.10   It should be noted that there may be a number of quite separate and independent safety-related systems. Different industries sometimes refer to different levels of the hierarchy when they use the term 'safety-related system'.

2.11   The software which affects safety is not only the software which is the *product* of the software engineering process, but is also the software which is used as a *tool* in the process. Further, safety may not only be affected by the *tool* itself, but also by the *use* of that tool. Statements that a particular tool has been used should not necessarily be taken to imply greater safety, because, misused, it may have had the opposite effect.

2.12   Safety-related systems perform, by definition, safety-related functions. It is desirable to keep separate those functions which are safety-related, and those which are not. In practice it may not be possible to separate the safety-related functions from other general functions to be performed by the overall system.

2.13   In some sectors, safety-related systems can broadly be divided into control systems and protection systems.

2.14   Control systems cause the system to operate in the desired, manner. Protection systems deal with defined fault conditions and generate the correct outputs to mitigate hazardous consequences or prevent a dangerous failure. Control systems and protection systems are both designed to respond to signals from the equipment and/or an operator. (**Note:** Various arrangements of control and protection systems are used. Examples include (a) combined control and protection, (b) separate control and protection and (c) continuous control for safety. Arrangements (a) and (b) are used where there is a 'safe state' and (c) where there is no readily available 'safe state', and continuous control is required to maintain safety. A control system may not always be designated safety-related but usually a protection system will.)

2.15   System failure leading to an accident can result from random failures or systematic failures. Random failures are those which typically result from a variety of normal breakdown mechanisms in hardware, and whose reliability (e.g. failure rate) can often be predicted in a quantified manner with reasonable accuracy. By definition, all those failures which cause a system to fail and are not due to random failures are called systematic failures and can arise:

1.   as a result of errors or omissions in the system requirements specification;

2.   as a result of errors or omissions in the requirements specification for the hardware and software;

3.   as a result of errors in the design, manufacture, installation, or operation of the hardware;

4.   from failures due to errors or omissions in the software at any point in the Software Lifecycle.

2.16   Software induced system failures are classified as systematic failures. Safety integrity refers to both random hardware failures and systematic failures. A safety-related system has to withstand, to a degree which results in acceptable levels of safety integrity, both types of failure.

2.17   Unlike random hardware failures, systematic failures cannot be predicted in a quantified manner to any acceptable degree of accuracy. This point is central to the whole question of assessing the level of safety integrity achieved using programmable electronic systems. There is evidence to show that as the level of complexity increases the proportion of systematic failures increases. (It should be noted that 'random' and 'systematic' are used with their particular connotation in statistics. When something is 'random', the probability of its occurrence can be estimated; this is not true if it is systematic).

B. The Benefits of Programmable Electronic Systems

2.18   Programmable electronic systems have many advantages including the following.

Functionality

2.19   Programmable computers are powerful. They can monitor a large range of inputs, perform complicated calculations, drive many outputs and all at high speeds. This power allows fine control which can be used to operate a system near to its optimum efficiency and without the need for the large operating margins required on cruder systems.

Safety

2.20   The ability of programmable electronic systems to process a large range of variables provides *potential* for increasing the level of safety beyond that which could otherwise be achieved. For example, benefits can arise from:

1.   the ability to perform proof checks on critical components at time intervals significantly shorter than would otherwise be the case;

2.   the potential to provide safety interlocks of almost any degree of sophistication;

3.   diagnostic programs and condition monitoring which may be used to analyse situations and give warnings of impending problems;

4.   the ability to compare actual conditions on the plant or equipment being controlled with the 'ideal' model conditions;

5.   the ability to provide better information to operators and hence improve decision making affecting safety;

6.   the use of advanced control strategies to enable people to be removed from hazardous or hostile environments;

7.   the use of appropriate software designed techniques may help to minimise the problems which arise from complexity (compare paragraph 2.28).

Cost

2.21   The cost of realising a given set of functions is likely to be much lower with a programmable computer than with any alternative mechanisation. Hardware resources are shared between functions thus giving a very efficient utilisation. Microprocessors are cheap components relative to others and the cost of realising additional functions is low. Similarly the cost of change for systems using software, even with all the necessary controls, is generally low compared to the alternative of hardware changes involving new designs, new components, additional testing, installation changes, etc.

Visibility of Implementation

2.22   Given the satisfactory operation of the hardware element, the functionality of the computer system is determined by the software. Software engineering techniques are available to assist in ensuring visibility and completeness of specified requirements, and in the design phase. Used properly, these provide visibility and traceability beyond that normally associated with hardware.

Reliability

2.23 The level of reliability achieved from digital devices operating in appropriate environments is high. The high levels of integration achieved in current devices have reduced component counts significantly and led to corresponding reductions in system failure rates.

2.24 Many of the methods for improving system reliability are applicable to programmable electronic systems. Thus architectures such as multiple redundancy, monitoring standby channels, segregation and diversity can be used to ensure that the software elements are operating in a sound system structure and benefit from the improvements such architectures give.

Ease of Change

2.25 Whilst the ease of changing software can be overstated, it remains true that major functional additions can be made to a software-based system without any significant hardware changes. Provided that adequate growth capacity is incorporated in the original system, it is possible to improve system functionality and performance at a fraction of the cost of hardware changes.

Re-usability

2.26 In certain circumstances it is possible to re-use software algorithms, designs and even code. When re-usability is possible it improves software quality by taking advantage of maturity and reduces costs by reducing new development work. Thus re-use leads to improved (and known) safety integrity.

C. Problems Associated with Programmable Electronic Systems

2.27 Programmable electronic systems used in safety-related applications raise several difficulties for the systems engineer and assessor. These problems are discussed below.

Complexity and Unpredictability

2.28 The failure modes are complex and not always predictable. Systems incorporating software are inherently very complex. A module of 100 lines of code may contain tens of thousands of possible paths. The power of computers allows many inputs, rapid sampling of inputs, complex calculations, and detailed operator displays: these can all add complexity to the safety-related systems (Ref. 102).

2.29 As a result of this complexity, design errors are a major factor in the overall failure rate of systems. The errors may be faults in the specifications, or failures of the software to meet its specification; in either case it is not currently possible to forecast accurately the probability of errors being made and escaping detection before delivery of the system.

2.30 Complexity, in combination with the need for assessment, may result in increased costs. This is discussed in the STARTS handbook (Ref. 102).

Limitations of Testing

2.31   It may be possible to undertake statistical testing. However, this requires that a set of test data is available which is guaranteed to correspond to the operating environment. This is not usually the case; even when it is, a very large number of tests are required. In general, to substantiate that the probability of a system failure on demand is not more than 1 in N, approximately $7 \times N$ tests will be required. (This assumes a Poisson statistical model which would give 99% confidence in the claim. However, this may be an unrealistic assumption for the types of errors found in software.)

2.32   Under other statistical assumptions, or if faults are detected and corrected during testing, numbers of tests much greater than this will be needed. (Examples modelled by the Centre for Software Reliability of City University, UK, have demonstrated a requirement for the $7 \times N$ tests in the above example to be increased to approximately $100 \times N$. These techniques are obviously not appropriate for systems which are required to have extremely low failure probabilities.)

2.33   In summary, it is difficult and often impossible to quantify the probability of failure of complex safety-related systems incorporating software. This is a major limitation to the use of software in such systems. Because no method of quantification has been widely accepted, software assurance has been based on procedures and standards which describe the methods to be used in the design, implementation and maintenance of software.

Programmable Electronic Systems Have Complex Failure Modes

2.34   Many current-day computer systems do not protect software or data against corruption by a fault elsewhere in the software. Consequently the failure condition which results from a fault may be far removed from it.

2.35   Microprocessors, and other LSI components too, create problems. Their behaviour is usually not specified clearly and completely, and different batches may display different behaviour.

Software Failures May Leave No Evidence

2.36   Because software faults are design faults, the software after a failure will usually be the same as the software before. It is likely to be extremely difficult to locate the exact cause of a failure, and some software-induced failures may be ascribed to 'operator error'. This problem can be reduced by using techniques such as audit-trails of the execution paths and error-condition files. The use of these techniques is not universal practice, but it is very useful.

Dependency on Other Products

2.37   Even 'correct' software may execute incorrectly if the compiler, linker, loader, operating system, or microprocessor are incorrect. In general, compilers, linkers, loaders, and operating systems (or other libraries of run-time routines) are very complex and contain faults.

Competence

2.38   For the reasons given above, software has to be designed and assessed differently from hardware (although Application Specific Integrated Circuit (ASIC) design raises many of the same problems as software). Systems engineers need training to understand these differences, and there are dangers in assuming that their experience of hazard analysis and probabilistic safety assessment will carry across without modification to programmable systems.

Summary of Problems

2.39   The design and assessment of complex safety-related systems is inherently difficult, time-consuming and expensive. There are no panaceas for these difficulties; the technical advances in software engineering using formal methods and quality assurance have brought benefits (Ref. 45), but there will always be major areas of uncertainty. There is no current prospect of a major breakthrough which will remove the need for experienced engineering judgement in developing safety-related systems and it is therefore essential that engineers keep their complexity to an absolute minimum, so that the level of safety integrity claimed for a system does not exceed the level which we are confident we can achieve.

D. Methods of Tackling Safety-Related Software

Safety-Related Software

2.40   Safety-related software is defined as: 'Software which forms part of a safety-related system'. To identify safety-related software, it is first of all necessary, in the systems approach, to identify the safety-related systems. If one of those relies on software, then that software is, by definition, safety-related. (**Note:** The term safety-critical software is often used synonymously with safety-related software. For example, one organisation uses the term safety-critical software to mean software which in event of its failure will lead, with certain qualifications, to loss of life. Safety-critical software comes within the scope of the term safety-related software but is a more narrowly defined term.)

Level of Risk

2.41   Risk is defined as: 'The likelihood of a specified hazardous event occurring within a specified period or in specified circumstances.' The concept of risk has two elements; the frequency, or probability, with which a specified hazard occurs; and the consequence of it. In any particular application, there will be a level of risk that could be deemed 'tolerable'. (**Note:** What is deemed 'tolerable' will depend upon many factors. Of particular importance will be the legal criteria in the particular case in question. Considerations concerning 'tolerability' are outside the scope of this document.)

2.42   For situations where the level of risk, without precautions, is not tolerable, there is a need to ensure that the applied safety-related systems reduce the risk to a tolerable level.

2.43   The risk level for a specific situation, which may be stated either qualitatively or quantitatively (e.g. that the specified hazardous event shall not occur with a frequency greater than 1 in 10^4 years), will need to be translated into engineering terms in order that the design of the safety-related systems can proceed. This approach then allows an engineering solution to be adopted for the design of the safety-related systems. See Figures 2.1 and 2.2.

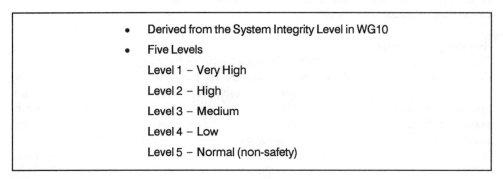

Figure 2.1 Software Integrity Levels

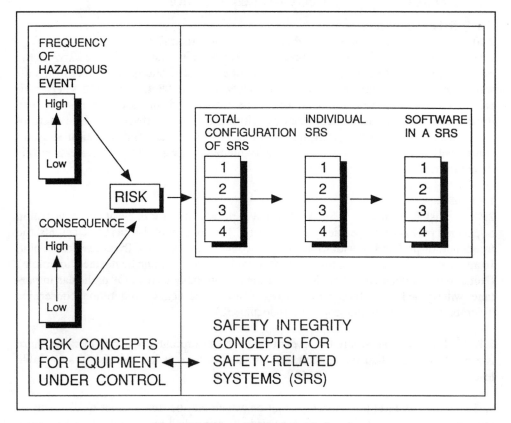

Figure 2.2 Risk and Safety Integrity Levels

System and Software Integrity Levels

2.44   Once the risk level has been translated into engineering terms for the design of the safety-related systems to proceed, the requirements for each system, within the total configuration, can then be specified. The contribution of each safety-related system is determined, in engineering terms, and any associated software in that system must be of appropriate integrity to meet the specified requirements. To cater for the overall risk levels found in practical applications together with the variety of system configurations and their number, there will be a wide spectrum of safety integrity requirements for individual systems. This means there is a need to have available a number of software integrity levels so that an appropriate level can be matched to the required individual system integrity level (Refs 3, 22, 56, 68).

2.45   Using this approach it can be seen that:

1. To determine the required safety integrity level of software, it is first of all necessary to determine the required safety integrity level of the system of which the software forms a part.

2. The level of integrity required by any one safety-related system depends upon the contribution of that system, within the total configuration of safety-related systems, in meeting a given risk tolerability level.

3. The generic software requirements developed for a specific software integrity level are able to be used irrespective of the sector.

4. The software safety requirements which have been developed for a particular level of software safety will apply to all software at that level, irrespective of the particular application or industrial sector for which it has been developed.

Commonality of Approach

2.46   Historically, even at a generic level, different sectors have developed different strategies for the design and assessment of safety-related systems. However, given the complexity of modern systems and the trend for manufacturers to supply equipment across several sectors, it makes sense, from both the economic and safety viewpoints, for safety-related systems to be, wherever possible, specified and designed on common underlying principles.

Elements of a Technical Framework

2.47   From the various initiatives being undertaken there are a number of common threads upon which a common approach could be developed. The following sets out the elements of a technical framework. It is recognised that the management framework is equally important (as are the regulatory issues which can be viewed as part of the management framework).

2.48   It is suggested that a generic framework adopts a systems approach which:

1. addresses the hierarchy of safety-related systems;

2. separates the overall required risk level for the plant or equipment, which is application specific and involves legal, social and economic judgements, from the safety integrity requirements of individual safety-related systems which are used within that plant or equipment;

3. addresses all elements (both hardware and software) within a system;

4. addresses both systematic failure and random hardware failures;

5. establishes a number of safety-integrity levels for both systems and software – these integrity levels would be the mechanism for linking the software to the system of which it forms a part;

6. takes account of all phases from identification of hazards through to maintenance of the operational system(s).

2.49   This model involves classification of systems and subsystems based on levels of:

1. risk for the equipment under control;

2. safety integrity for individual safety-related systems;

3. safety integrity for the total configuration of safety-related systems;

4. software integrity for the individual safety-related systems.

Safety Lifecycle

2.50   There is thus the need for a common generic framework for safety-related systems and, within that, for safety-related software. This should be sufficiently general to take into account the principal requirements of all the various industrial sectors. General guidelines based on this framework would apply to all sectors. Further guidelines would be required (a) at the industry-sector level and (b) at the level of specific applications within a sector. A Safety Lifecycle Model that encompasses the above concepts is shown in Figure 2.3 (Refs 67 and 68). With reference to Figure 2.3 it will be noted that the Safety Requirements Specification is separated into Functional Requirements Specification and the Safety Integrity Requirements Specification.

2.51   The Functional Requirements Specification identifies which functions of a system are safety-related and in what ways. It is not concerned with the appropriateness of particular integrity levels.

2.52   The Safety Integrity Requirements Specification begins with the functions identified in the Functional Requirements Specification; it specifies, for each of those, the required safety integrity level.

2.53   In Figure 2.3 assessment is not shown as a separate item: it will be an element within each phase. For each phase, a set of 'deliverables' will be specified; for each deliverable the relevant actions will be specified. Also for each phase, tests and the means of their performance will be specified.

2.54   It will also be necessary to set up mechanisms to ensure that information is communicated between those responsible for different phases of the Safety Lifecycle, and that such communication takes place whenever the information is affected by change.

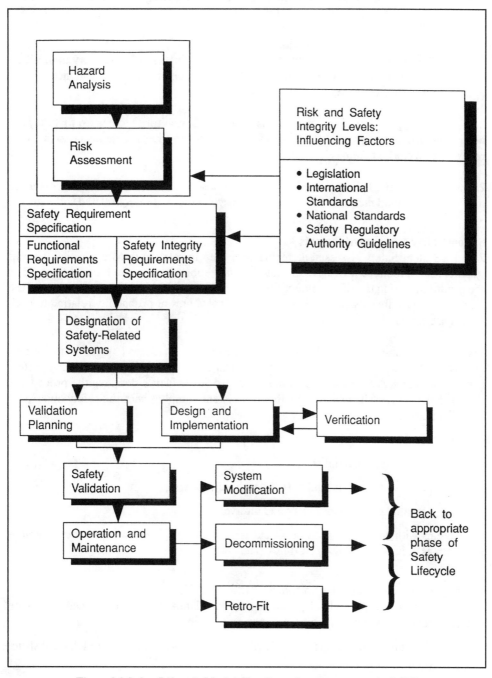

Figure 2.3 Safety Lifecycle Model. For discussion, see paragraphs 2.48*ff.*

Prescribed Methodology for the Safety Lifecycle

2.55   Once the system aspects have been defined the method of developing the system can be formulated. This will take the form of standards for procedures to be applied to all the various phases of the Safety Lifecycle. These standards may range from international standards such as ED12A/DO178A (Ref. 94) through national standards such as Mil Std 2167 (Ref. 33) through to company procedures.

2.56   The procedures are formulated by some combination of regulatory authorities, purchasers and suppliers. They tend to reflect best current practice and need to be updated regularly if they are to remain relevant.

2.57   The application of the procedures needs to be monitored to ensure that they are being followed and to provide feedback of instances where they are deficient so that corrective action can be taken.

2.58   Such methods have served well over the last ten or more years and remain the only widely accepted method of controlling the development of safety-related software.

System Safety Assessment Reports

2.59   System Safety Assessment reports are used in relation to safety-critical aircraft systems for compliance with JAR 25.1309. Similar reports are used in other sectors. They are produced during the development lifecycle. Such a report identifies the hazards of the system, and describes its safety features. Numerical values of probability relating to each hazard are assigned as safety objectives.

2.60   The Assessment includes analysis of the effects of failures (single, combinations, and dormant failures) both for normal operation and for degraded operation when performance is at limits. A successful assessment will provide evidence detailing the procedures used and the test results which show that the system complies with the safety objectives; and will identify:

1.   operating limitations;

2.   emergency procedures;

3.   permitted unserviceability (get-you-home modes);

4.   essential maintenance tasks and intervals.

For systems with software, the Assessment is supported by a Software Accomplishment Summary as defined in ED12A/DO178A (Ref. 94).

Techniques for Safety-Related Software

2.61   The current methods of producing safety-related software are based on a wide variety of techniques but some elements are:

1.   the application of structured analysis to generate a visible, modular construction;

2. diversity in design, implementation and maintenance to avoid failures due to common mode errors;

3. the use of formal methods to improve the verifiability of the specification and the translation into algorithms;

4. strong configuration control to ensure that changes are authorised by the designated engineers and that all the prescribed processes have been carried out;

5. software quality assurance to monitor that the prescribed methods have been applied and that the resulting records are checked;

6. re-usability of established software components;

7. independent design review.

The Use of Standards

2.62   Although standards are necessary in acquiring and giving assurance about safety, their existence is not of itself sufficient for such assurance. They must be adopted and applied, and application must be done with the objective of promoting safety, rather than merely achieving compliance with the standards(s).

2.63   The legal position and role of standards is dealt with at various places in Chapter 3, which also covers the status of European Community directives.

Maintenance and Modification

2.64   The maintenance and/or modification of safety-related systems creates further requirements, as any change to any one component invalidates checks and tests carried out at any previous time, and requires a further round of inspection and testing. These requirements reinforce points made elsewhere about the need for proper specification of requirements, for documentation and for competent personnel.

3. LEGAL LIABILITY FOR SOFTWARE IN SAFETY-RELATED SYSTEMS

A. Introduction

3.1   This chapter outlines what is believed to be the current position with regard to the legal liabilities of the designer and supplier of software. The chapter deals firstly with criminal and secondly civil liability. Its contents in no sense constitute legal advice. Those likely to be affected by them should seek advice.

3.2   While the Study was in progress, a number of legal actions have been raised. Their outcome may affect the situation with regard to the responsibilities of individual employees and those of employers. Both civil and criminal liabilities are involved.

B. Criminal Liabilities

3.3   UK criminal law relating to product safety is divided into two groups: that dealing with safety at work, based largely on the Health and Safety at Work etc. Act 1974 (HSWA); and that dealing with consumer safety based largely on Part II of the Consumer Protection Act 1987 (CPA).

Health and Safety at Work etc. Act 1974
3.4   The Act places a duty on employers to ensure, so far as is reasonably practicable, the health, safety and welfare of their employees (Section 2). It also requires employers and the self-employed to ensure, so far as is reasonably practicable, the health and safety of other persons who may be affected by their undertakings (Section 3). It places a similar duty on manufacturers, designers and suppliers of articles for use at work in respect of the people who use those articles (Section 6). Failure to comply with these duties is a criminal offence and penalties can range from fines to imprisonment. It is the duty of the Health and Safety Commission to make appropriate arrangements for the purposes of the Act, while the Health and Safety Executive (HSE) enforces the legislation. The Act empowers the Secretary of State to make health and safety regulations, which are normally proposed by the Commission.

Guidance and the Application of Standards
3.5   The Commission can also issue, with the consent of the Secretary of State, Approved Codes of Practice (ACOPs) which give practical guidance on how to comply with the Act or Regulations. ACOPs have a legal status – they are admissible in evidence and if a defendant had not complied with an ACOP he would have to prove that he had complied with the law in some other way.

3.6   The HSE also produces booklets, leaflets and guidance notes which may contain detailed technical specifications, quantitative guidance, and reference to standards. This guidance has no legal status as such, although it is widely recognised as setting desirable standards.

3.7   The application of standards is different in product sectors covered by European Directives on safety. In general, products complying with a harmonised European Standard (CEN/CENELEC) are deemed to comply with the corresponding directives, and also with any relevant national legislation. A number of Directives concerning safety at work are being prepared, but none of these has yet been implemented, and none of them will deal with software or PESs as a separate issue.

Duties on the Designer, Manufacturer, Supplier or Importer of Safety-Related Systems
3.8   Provided plant incorporating a safety-related system is designed for use or operation at work, Section 6 of the HSWA will apply. The designer, etc. will have to ensure, so far as is reasonably practicable, that the hardware and any software in the PES provides for safe operation of the system. This includes any necessary research, testing and examination. Any information which is necessary for the safe operation of the system must also be provided.

3.9   It is not necessary to repeat tests and examinations carried out by other persons in the supply chain. For example, the manufacturer of a system need not repeat tests already carried out by the producer of the software, but he needs to ensure that the testing or validation is adequate, and he must avoid using versions for which the testing is not valid.

Duties on the Writers and Suppliers of Software
3.10   Whether the software is supplied as part of a system or provided as a separate package, Section 3 of the HSWA will apply, and there is a responsibility to ensure that use of the software will not expose any people to health and safety risks. As in Section 6, the supplier must carry out or arrange for any necessary testing of what he supplies, to the extent that is reasonably practicable, and he must provide his customers with any necessary information so that their use of it can be safe.

Duties on the End User
3.11   Under Section 2 of the HSWA, an employer has to provide, so far as is reasonably practicable, safe plant and safe systems of work for his employees, as well as adequate training and information. In respect of PESs this will require reasonable tests and checks on in-house programming, and information and training for system operators.

Consumer Protection Act 1987
3.12   Section 10 of Part II of the CPA 1987 makes it a criminal offence to supply any consumer goods which do not comply with the 'general safety requirement'.

3.13   Non-compliance with the general safety requirement is when a person supplies, offers to supply or possesses for supply, consumer goods which are not reasonably safe having regard to all the circumstances. The circumstances which will be taken into account in determining whether goods are reasonably safe or not include:

1. how the goods are marketed, their 'get-up', what marks are on the product and what warnings or instructions are given;

2. whether any standards have been published which might apply to the goods in question;

3. whether there were any means by which the goods might reasonably have been made safer, taking into account the cost of so doing and the extent of the additional safety provided.

3.14   The standards referred to in paragraph 3.13 are 'any standards of safety published by any person...'. The courts may therefore take into account, in determining whether the general safety requirement has been met, not only standards produced by ISO or BSI, or harmonised European Standards, but those produced by particular industries and other bodies. The importance placed on any given standard will naturally depend upon the importance credited to the issuing organisation.

3.15   It is however a defence under section 10 of the Act for the supplier to show that the feature of the goods leading to the charge is directly due to compliance with requirements imposed by law or by European Community obligations, or that the feature of the goods in fact complies with the relevant safety regulations or with standards of safety approved by the government under such safety regulations.

3.16   This section of the Act does not apply to goods intended for export, to second-hand goods, or to retailers, if they had no reasonable grounds for believing that the goods failed to comply with the general safety requirement.

3.17   'Consumer goods' are defined as 'any goods which are ordinarily intended for private use or consumption' but excluding a number of products, such as water, food, gas, drugs, tobacco, motor vehicles and aircraft. Hang gliders are specifically included. The exclusion of motor vehicles takes out the main class of consumer product in which software is beginning to be used in a safety-related way.

3.18   The marketing of safety-related software in goods which are within the scope of Part II of the Consumer Protection Act seems to be some way into the future: nevertheless, the existence of these criminal sanctions is a factor which producers need to bear in mind. Section 11 of the Act is also relevant.

C. Civil Liabilities

3.19   **Contract**: Apart from any express terms of the Contract, under the Sale of Goods Act 1979, there are two relevant statutory implied terms where a sale is made by way of business. The first (Section 14.2) is that the goods supplied are of *merchantable quality*. Such goods are defined as goods which are 'as fit for the purpose or purposes for which goods of that kind are commonly bought as is reasonable to expect having regard to any description applied to them, the price (if relevant) and all the other relevant circumstances.' The second (Section 14.3) is that of *fitness for purpose*, and applies where a purchaser has, either expressly or by implication, told the vendor any particular purpose for which the goods are being bought. In this case, the implied condition is that the goods are reasonably fit for that purpose, even if the purpose is not one for which such goods are commonly supplied. This requirement does not apply where the circumstances show that the purchaser does not rely, or that it is unreasonable for him to rely, on the skill or judgement of the seller.

3.20   In non-consumer cases only (i.e. cases where the goods are not of a type ordinarily supplied for private use or consumption) sellers may attempt to contract out of the provisions of the Sale of Goods Act, but any such attempt is subject to the test of reasonableness as set out in the Unfair Contract Terms Act 1977.

3.21   There is a degree of overlap between the two implied conditions set out in 3.18 above, but the important point is that both the concepts of *quality* and *fitness for purpose* are present in the contract of sale. In the case of software, whether embedded in a product, or used to control a system, failure of the software to function correctly would probably mean that it was not fit for its purpose, and the supplier of the software would accordingly be liable for breach of contract. Other contracts such as hire and supply may contain similar provisions: in these cases the Supply of Goods and Services Act 1982 is relevant.

3.22   The responsibility of a professional design engineer to his employer or his client is to exercise reasonable care and skill in accordance with the normal contemporary standards of his profession. If, despite the exercise of such care and skill, the outcome is unsuccessful, the engineer will not normally be in breach of his contractual duty. An exception to this will be where there is a term (express or, in suitable circumstances, implied) in the contract between the designer and his client that the design will achieve a certain purpose. Failure in this case will amount to a breach of contract.

3.23   There are instances where the engineer will be under contract to design *and supply*. Here the duty is that of supplying goods which are of suitable quality and fit for their purpose, as in paragraph 3.19 above.

3.24   **Tort and Product Liability:** If a 'person' (which includes a corporate body) is injured or his property or goods are damaged or destroyed as a result of another's negligence, or breach of duty, he can recover damages in a civil action for tort. (The extent to which economic loss arising from the damage or destruction can be recovered is at present uncertain.) To prove negligence, the plaintiff has to prove that he was owed a duty of care, that there there was a breach of that duty, and that the loss or damage was a direct result of the negligence. Quite often, these are not easy to prove, and in consequence many injured persons have received less than full compensation. For example, although the law of negligence has   developed considerably over the past 25 years, generally in favour of those making claims, if a software designer could show that he exercised the standard of skill normal to his profession and acceptable at that time to his peers, it is unlikely that he would be found negligent. A great change in product liability however, was made by the

Consumer Protection Act 1987, which was intended to enact the European Directive on Product Liability of 1985.

3.25   Part 1 of the Act provides that people injured, or suffering loss to their private-use belongings, as a result of the failure of a product to provide the safety that people generally are entitled to expect, are to be compensated as of right by the producer of the product without having to prove negligence. A statutory limit on damages (£275) operates. However, there is no provision in the Act for compensation for any consequential *economic* loss suffered as a result of the injury or damage. It is clear that embedded software produced by the manufacturer of a product will attract liability just as much as the hardware. Software produced by another party which is embedded in the product or is used for the design of a product is perhaps a more complex matter. Depending on all the facts of the situation, including the extent to which it was reasonable for the manufacturer of the product to depend on the software's correctness, the software producer may be liable in the same way as the supplier of a defective hardware component. (It is important to note that rights under Part 1 of the Consumer Protection Act extend to people at work, and to people injured by unsafe products used at work.)

The International Dimension
3.26   **European Community**: Under the Civil Jurisdiction and Judgments Act 1982, which enacts in the UK an EC Convention of 1968, plaintiffs in a civil case can bring their claim *either* in the state where the plaintiffs are domiciled, *or* where the defendants' branch, agency etc is domiciled (if the dispute arises out of the operations of such a branch or agency), *or* 'where the harmful event occurs'. This latter may be either where the original act giving rise to the damage occurred (the place of manufacture of the defective product) or where the actual damage occurred (the place of injury). There are distinctions between tort cases and their rules, and contract and consumer cases and their rules, which in the interests of brevity are not made here. The Convention is assigned to give more precise indications of where persons or companies might sue or be sued. Companies could find that they become involved in litigation in other EC countries as well as the UK. (**Note**: In the foregoing the reference to a state applies to European Community countries only. However, the 'domicile' of a company will not necessarily be the country where it has its registered office or where it was incorporated: it might be taken as the state where its central management and control is exercised.)

3.27   A plaintiff may indulge in 'forum shopping': that is, of the several jurisdictions available to him, he may decide to go for the one where he considers he may have the best chance either of winning or of getting the highest possible damages. He will consider such factors as the relative levels of damages customarily awarded in the various countries, how long it takes to bring cases to court, the levels of costs, and the availability of witnesses. One other important aspect is the extent to which member states are likely to permit the recovering of purely economic loss. In cases of product liability he will also consider the extent to which different countries have derogated from the Directive with respect to imposing a maximum level of damages, and the development risks defence. Although these factors are of relevance to the plaintiff when choosing jurisdictions, insofar as the law permits this, nonetheless English courts may not necessarily regard them as crucial in their determination of the issue of which court is the appropriate forum for the case.

3.28   **USA:** In the United States of America, on the other hand, the rules, such as they are, are totally different. A company with manufacturing, marketing and distribution operations in the USA will be subject to the stringent US laws of warranty, tort and strict liability, and the very heavy levels of damages often awarded by American juries with all the concomitant problems of obtaining insurance cover. The position of a company which exports products to the USA through a wholly owned subsidiary which, however, has no assets, or of a UK company whose components are used in US-manufactured products is different again and, indeed, differs from state to state.

D. Protective Measures

3.29   Insurance against civil claims is obviously essential. However, it is becoming increasingly difficult to obtain adequate professional indemnity insurance or public liability cover at a reasonable premium rate, particularly in 'high risk' areas.

3.30   One of the defences against liability under Part 1 of the Consumer Protection Act is the so-called 'development risks defence' or 'state of the art defence'. This states that the manufacturer may not be liable if 'the state of scientific and technical knowledge at the relevant time was not such that a producer of products of the same description as the product in question might be expected to have discovered the defect if it had existed in his products while they were under his control'. It will be far from easy to succeed in this defence.

3.31   In determining whether the safety of a product is such as persons generally are entitled to expect, 'all the circumstances shall be taken into account'. Among the circumstances included in the Act, are 'the manner in which, and purposes for which, the product has been marketed . . . and any instructions for, or warnings with respect to, doing or refraining from doing anything with or in relation to the product' and 'what might reasonably be expected to be done with or relation to the product'. Warnings and instructions as to the uses to which software should or should not be put will therefore be useful, but will not provide a complete defence if there is in fact a programming error in the software which causes damage. However, if the software supplier can prove that warnings and instructions were disregarded, then the partial defence of contributory negligence will be available under the Consumer Protection Act, thus reducing the amount of damages awarded.

3.32   In addition, the proper use of warnings and, perhaps, instructions that the customer should test the software if it is to be used in certain situations, may also help where the software producer, and his customer (e.g. the supplier of a complete system) are jointly and severally liable to the injured party. In that situation the court will apportion liability between the software producer and the producer of the system in such manner as is 'just and equitable' under the Civil Liability (Contribution) Act 1978. Putting some responsibility on the system supplier may be helpful to the software producer in such a case.

3.33   Software suppliers should aim to organise their activities so that they are able to define the level of responsibility which they are prepared to accept for a given software product. This implies an efficient software quality assurance system; something that few suppliers yet have. Nevertheless, such systems are needed. If possible, they should also carefully define the purposes for which the software should or should not be used. However, a warning that it should not be used for certain purposes might lead to problems: such a warning could not cover all the possible applications in question (present and possible) and the omission of one potentially hazardous application could, by inference, be taken to mean that the product was suitable for that application. A more general warning, on the lines of 'this product should not be used for control application where malfunction could prove hazardous' might provide a defence, but any such limitation would have to be reasonable otherwise it could be seen as attempting to shift the burden of responsibility from producer to user to an unjustifiable extent.

4. ANALYSIS OF THE INFORMATION COLLECTED

A. Introduction

4.0   Two major data collection exercises were undertaken for the study. To gather information on the UK scene, an open-ended questionnaire was distributed. Details of the responses are included in Appendix H; the results are analysed in Section B of this chapter. Information about activities in the UK and Europe was gathered during visits undertaken by staff from CSE Ltd, under contract from DTI. Their report is included as Appendix B, and its contents and conclusions form Section B of this chapter.

B. The UK Situation

4.1   In order to ascertain the 'state of play' in the UK across the wide diversity of industries and activities dealing with safety-related systems, a request for information was circulated to over fifty specialists working in avionics, nucleonics, process control, industrial control, railways, road transport, medical instrumentation, the petroleum, gas, coal, steel and automotive industries, software houses, and consultancy.

4.2   It was requested that the information be in line with the following structure, to aid the analysis of responses:

1. Name, address and telephone number of respondent.

2. Type of industry, definition and coverage.

3. Relationship with industry (e.g. designer, supplier, purchaser, inspectorate, consultant).

4. Legal framework and application; supervisory agencies.

5. Classification of hazards.

6. Current practices – regulations, codes of practice, standards (national, European, international and *de facto*), guidance notes and common practice. (State mandatory levels, scope of application, possibilities for conformity assurance.)

7. Certification – method, application and coverage; accountability, signing off responsibilities.

8. Quantified Risk Assessment (QRA) – methods used and application.

9. Insurance position.

10. Terminology and definitions.

11. Techniques in use for hardware and software development, such as risk containment systems, formal methods, animation and simulation, tools, languages.

12. Particular concerns in the industry.

13. Future developments in the use of safety-related systems.

14. Comparative activities, regulations and methods overseas; overseas contacts for further information.

4.3   Thirty-three responses were received and analysed. The full analysis is contained in Appendix H. The following sections contain an overview of this analysis.

Regulations and Supervisory Agencies

4.4   Civil Aviation provides the only example of an internationally recognised system for safety assessment and certification with Europe closely following the model for airborne systems developed in conjunction with the USA Federal Aviation Agency. The CAA, as the UK authority, is responsible for the certification of aircraft and also for ground-based systems. The suppliers take the responsibility for declarations that the designs meet the required safety levels. RTCA/EUROCAE document DO 178A/ED 12A *Software Considerations in Airborne Equipment and System Certification* (Ref. 94) provides guidelines for the acceptance of software.

4.5   The Nuclear Installations Inspectorate of the Health and Safety Executive requires licensees to make a safety case for computer-based protection and safety-related control systems. The case is then judged against the Inspectorate's Safety Assessment Principles and Consent to operate the facility is given if it reaches an acceptable level of safety. In support of their safety case, licence applicants can develop their own safety criteria. For example, the CEGB have drawn up *Guidelines for the use of Programmable Electronic Systems for Reactor Protection* for trial use (Ref. 22).

4.6   In British Coal, all electrical and computer systems (including software) are assessed by the Headquarters Technical Department under their Electrical Acceptance Scheme and BS5750 is a requirement for all major suppliers.

4.7   In British Rail, the generic design of safety systems is certified by the Director of Signal and Telecommunications Engineering on completion of the type approval procedures implemented by that department's Development Section. Each individual installation is signed off by the Regional or Project Engineer concerned.

4.8   The process and manufacturing industries, in general, rely on self-assessment in meeting the various specialised Acts of Parliament, reinforced by the Health and Safety at Work Act. There is no certification of installations by HSE inspectors although installations are subject to routine inspection and reported violations and accidents are investigated.

4.9   In the context of software, the automotive industry is gradually becoming organised internationally with regard to standards and regulations. The wider impact of microprocessors is now beginning to be seen, with the advent of their use in braking, suspension and engine controls.

4.10   For medical equipment, the Department of Health has no requirements with legal or mandatory status. Existing voluntary schemes take no specific account of software. In the USA, where medical devices are legally regulated, the Food and Drug Administration has published draft guidelines for reviewers of computer-controlled medical devices (Ref. 44). In Germany, some test houses have developed test procedures.

Hazard Analysis
4.11   Industries subject to the Control of Industrial Major Accident Hazard Regulations require 'safety cases' to be made for certain sites. In these, plus other major industrial sites, a number of well established techniques for hazard analysis and quantified risk assessment are frequently used as a basis for system design and also in order to provide sufficient evidence to convince any assessors of the capability of the design to meet the required safety criteria. These techniques include:

- Failure Mode and Effects (Criticality) Analysis FME(C)A

- Fault Tree Analysis

- Event Tree Analysis

- State diagrams

- Sequence diagrams

- System Modelling by simulation.

4.12   In process control systems used in the chemical manufacturing and offshore petroleum industries, the HAZOP (Hazard and Operability) survey technique developed by ICI (Ref. 61) is widely but not universally used. In manufacturing and those industries overseen by Health and Safety Executive Inspectorates the checklist approach of the HSE *Guidelines for Programmable Electronic Systems* (Refs 51, 53 and 54) is being taken up to provide a sound basis. These guidelines are now being extended for use in particular industries, e.g. the recently published HSE document on Industrial Robot Safety (Ref. 52), the draft guidelines prepared by the Institution of Gas Engineers (Ref. 65) and the guidelines by the National Association of Lift Makers (Ref. 82).

4.13   The medical instrument industry carries out FME(C)A techniques in some cases, but there are no DHSS guidelines requiring such an approach.

Software Design Techniques
4.14   The avionics, civil nuclear and defence industries lead the field in the application of new software tools and techniques (e.g. Refs 36 and 58). These include formal specification methods, animation, structured design methods, SPADE and MALPAS static analysis tools (Refs 20 and 81), SPADE-PASCAL program validation, and in-house developed

simulation, verification and validation tools. However, the extent of the use of these is not easily assessed. Training in such techniques is costly; the cost of training could be a limiting factor for small companies and the risk of losing expensively trained experts is ever present.

4.15   Certifying and enforcement authorities can play a standardising role by specifying certain techniques but there is, as yet, no common agreement on the methods to be standardised. No fully integrated tool-set exists or is likely to exist for some years.

4.16   A number of respondents reported using software design diversity as a means of reducing common/mode failures in parallel redundant control systems. For example, L M Ericcsons of Sweden, in their railway signalling system, have used two different computers programmed in different languages by separate teams. British Rail, in their solid state interlocking (SSI) redundancy technique, use three microprocessors in a '2 out of 3' mode, with some diversity features to eliminate common mode failures (Ref. 80).

Certification
4.17   Where relevant British or International product design standards exist, these are widely used as contractual requirements or in voluntary statements of compliance by suppliers. However, there are very few, if any, which adequately cover the use of software. One of the most advanced examples, DOD-STD-2167 (Defense System Software Development), has been revised to DOD-STD-2167A (Draft) (Ref. 33) after a relatively short existence. (Incidentally, this standard requires tailoring by the contracting authority to match the severity of the requirement.) There are a number of good guideline documents available, compliance with which is being required in some industries. Examples are the internationally accepted RTCA/EUROCAE DO 178A/ED 12A *Software considerations in airborne systems and equipment certification* (Ref. 94) for civil aircraft development, and the HSE Guidelines for programmable electronic systems for industrial applications.

4.18   Compliance with process standards for software Quality Management Systems such as BS 5750 (= ISO 9001), AQAP 13 is being increasingly required and is tending to have a harmonising effect on management practices throughout industry. Although the cost of compliance may be rather high for the very small software company, the beneficial effect of being subjected to a management audit by an independent competent body must be considerable.

4.19   There are numerous examples of more general regulations concerning the safety of equipment and personnel in the wider sense, and these have covered almost every area of activity. Certification against these, either by contracting authority or by a third-party test agency, is practised in the major industries. Reported examples of personal accreditation are the Designated Engineering Representatives (DERs) appointed by the USA Federal Aviation Authority; these may be company (rather than the FAA) employees tasked with the assessment of (and the responsibility for signing off) the safety impact of engineering details on behalf of the FAA. (It may be that designated senior executives in some UK industries fulfil a similar role.) The accreditation of test houses by NAMAS in the UK has a similar requirement for the naming of key qualified individuals responsible for signing off test reports.

Scope of the Review

4.20   The review has only covered known areas of activity. It is believed that there are many instances of developments being undertaken which use microprocessors or VLSI logic in safety-related situations without an understanding of the hazards and the essential design techniques required.

C. International Developments

4.21   The conclusion from this study, reinforced by comments in the US literature (Ref. 97) is that there is little activity in this field in the countries visited, and at best only a concern that some activity should be needed. There is some awareness in the USA of the UK activities.

4.22   For the moment, the main developments to be observed outside the UK are international in nature, especially work undertaken by the IEC (Refs 67 and 68). These activities follow patterns of thinking reflected in other parts of this report, because they are directed by Committees chaired by US representatives who have been part of the Project Team.

4.23   In summary, it appears that the UK has more to offer other countries than to learn from them. It is desirable to ensure that the lead which the UK has developed can be exploited.

4.24   In general, the results of the Overseas Study (Appendix B) and the recommendations it contains support the recommendations of this study given in Chapter 6.

5. CERTIFICATION

A. Introduction and Summary

5.1   Certification is the provision of a record that something complies with or conforms to the provisions of a standard, code of practice or similar document. Appendix A contains a discussion of the basic concepts of conformance and certification of safety-related elements in systems.

5.2   Certification may be related to:

1. Organisations who provide the products. Certification may relate to the organisation as a whole (the company); to a part (Department) within an organisation; or to a particular sub-unit (an ad-hoc Project Team). It might be long-term and cover several products; or short-term related to a particular (group of) product(s).

2. Individuals/professionals/personnel who contribute to the provision of the products. Certification may be long-term (with a requirement for updating); or short-term, relating to a particular role within a Project Team. Certification may also relate to individuals and organisations who use the product; safety may depend on their ability to understand and use it. These may conveniently be referred to as operators.

3. Processes and tools used to produce the products. Processes in the context of software refer to methodologies and techniques used in specification, design and testing. Tools are generally items of software which may be used in the design process (e.g. CASE tools); tools also refer to software such as operating systems which will form part of or be inextricably connected with the product. A 'safe' system will require that the supplier and the user establish, document and follow appropriate procedures, including documenting adherence to those. It will also of necessity require the employment of bought-in tools, e.g. test equipment and programming languages.

4. Products: the system and/or its components. The need for precision as to what (part of a) product certification relates to, is discussed in Section D.

5.3   The intention in this chapter is to consider:

1. current practices in different application sectors and by different regulatory authorities;

2. the extent to which certification could contribute to safety;

3. limitations on the value of certification;

4. problems concerned with introducing requirements for various types of certi-
    fication and the costs/benefits of imposing new regulations;

5. technical issues (e.g. to what extent software design be considered separately
    from that of the total system).

5.4   Section B provides general background information; Section C examines certification in relation to organisations, individual personnel, processes and tools, and to
products. Section D compares these and Section E presents conclusions.

B. Background

Proposals for Certification Relating to Software

5.5   Recommendations made in the Finniston and ACARD reports (Refs 43 and
2), the potentially serious nature of software failures recorded for some safety-related
applications, and studies carried out at NPL and elsewhere have resulted in suggestions
that some form of certification may help to reduce the risk of incidents caused wholly
or partly by software. The Finniston report recommended that

> where special considerations justify statutory licensing of specific areas
> of engineering practice the requirements of the appropriate regulations
> should be based upon a new statutory register of 'qualified engineers'.

It has been suggested that safety-related software is one such area, and that certification
may be desirable for individuals practising in the development, production, operation or
maintenance of safety-related programmable electronic systems. Alternatively certification
might relate to the organisation, the processes used and the product produced.

5.6   Arguments for the introduction of certification relate to:

1. the enforcement of good digital design practices throughout industry;

2. the awareness that this would create;

3. the promotion of an infra-structure to support professional responsibility;

4. the enforced creation of a pool of highly trained, competent software
    engineers who could operate across application areas.

5.7   Disadvantages include:

1. that here is a danger that effort will concentrate on what can be certified
    against objective conformance criteria, at the expense of considering 'real-
    world' factors which cannot readily be quantified, but which are at least as
    important;

2. the cost of introducing and maintaining such practices;

3. the effect this would have on UK competitiveness in world markets;

4. the practicality and value of certain forms of certification;

5. the fear of creating restrictive practices.

5.8   Any proposed certification scheme must take into account:

1. that safety impinges equally on software, hardware and systems considerations;

2. that certification of organisations may reduce the risks involved in the design of safety-related equipment but cannot ensure an adequate level of safety has been achieved;

3. similarly that product conformance certification cannot provide a guarantee against design faults;

4. the need to ensure that in certifying individual personnel, proficiency, experience and other personal qualities, as well as formal educational qualifications, are taken into account;

5. to ensure the possibility of adequate redress, certification practices should not transfer responsibility from an organisation to individuals;

6. the likelihood that the issues facing different applications must be solved using different approaches in order to maintain competitiveness;

7. the need for compatibility with future European standardisation;

8. where commonality of certification standards is required categorisation of software integrity levels may be necessary.

Current Certification Practices

5.9   Current regulatory systems are application-based, and so vary widely from industry to industry. Thus there is voluntary regulation in medical engineering, regulation through the insurance agencies and the HSE in the process and transport industries, and system certification through independent agencies in the avionics and nuclear industries. With the exception of a few highly specific tasks, the approach used throughout British industry is to approve equipment at the systems rather than at the component level. Evidence of subsystem and component quality is however often required to construct the case for system approval. Existing regulatory agencies and enforcement authorities are listed in Table 5.1.

5.10   The BCS has formed a register of qualified software practitioners. It has however fallen into disuse, possibly because of lack of enforcement, difficulty in administration or lack of benefits to users.

C. Sources of Concern

5.11   Proposals for certification relating (particularly) to software have arisen from the following considerations:

Quality of Software Engineering Practices

5.12   There is evidence that inadequate software engineering practices are used throughout industry and that most practising software engineers are inadequately

Table 5.1 UK Safety Regulatory Authorities (as at 10.8.89)

Civil Aviation Authority

Department of Energy:
  Petroleum Engineering Division
  (Off-shore Installations)

Department of the Environment:
  Inspectorate of Pollution

Department of Transport:
  Vehicle Standards and Engineering Division
  Vehicles and Component Approval Division
  Vehicle Inspectorate Executive Agency
  HM Railway Inspectorate

Health and Safety Executive:
  Hazardous Substances Division
  HM Factory and Agricultural Inspectorate
  HM Inspectorate of Mines and Quarries
  HM Nuclear Installations Inspectorate

Ministry of Defence:
  Director General –
  Defence Quality Procurement Executive

Note: This is not an exhaustive list.

trained to work in safety-critical applications. This gives rise to concern as to whether safety-related systems may contain software which is inadequate for its purpose. Certification, if it encourages good practice, is seen as a means of increasing confidence.

Differences in Regulating Regimes across British Industry
5.13   Different application areas operate under different regulatory regimes. In addition system risk classification differs widely and there is no agreement across industry about required levels of safety.

5.14   Levels of safety integrity will be tabulated in the forthcoming international Standard on Software for Computers in the Application of Industrial Safety-Related Systems (Ref. 68). The levels proposed in the draft are shown in Figure 2.1.

Public Concern
5.15   If there were to be an increasing number of accidents attributable to software this would create a climate of public opinion demanding certification. The software engineering industry should anticipate such demands.

Legal and Professional Accountability
5.16   There are concerns related to the legal (criminal and civil) liabilities of engineers designing and producing software. These matters are dealt with in Chapter 3. There is also an IEE guidance document (Ref. 64).

Responsibility for Software Failures

5.17   Whereas wear- and time-related factors dominate hardware failures, faults in software are predominantly due to human errors in specification and design, so that freedom from fault is largely influenced by the competence of project managers, designers and systems engineers. This appears to enhance the appropriateness of the certification of the individuals concerned with software specification, design and testing.

Complexity

5.18   It is believed that software designs often involve a level of complexity which makes them impossible to comprehend. It is appropriate that software engineers are alerted to this problem (and to the inadequacy of current methods of assessing complexity), and to the risks involved in assumptions about levels of software integrity: the certification process may assist in this.

5.19   Additionally designers have a responsibility to advise management when unacceptable levels of complexity seem likely to arise and to make them aware of the associated problems. Certified status may help to provide designers with an appropriately supportive environment.

Currency of Techniques

5.20   Certification (and, more precisely, a requirement to maintain certified status through continuing education and training) should result in awareness (at least) of new techniques (and their advantages and disadvantages), and may help to ensure that such techniques are used where they are appropriate.

D. Approaches to Certification

Certification of Organisations

Current position

5.21   Formal certification of organisations for safe design practice is not widespread in industry, although in some industries lists of approved organisations are maintained. Means of securing such approval includes audit of the quality procedures by the customer, or else by an independent authority. Certification of test facilities is undertaken with the objective of ensuring that the test facility is competent to test against well-defined measurable acceptance criteria.

5.22   Certification of the quality system operated by an organisation is becoming accepted industry practice. It is seen as a means not only of reducing product risk, but also of reducing the number of audits required as part of the tendering process. There are established quality standards supported throughout Europe and NATO.

Issues

5.23   The use of certification to demonstrate company competence in specification, design and testing through assessment of organisational schemes is broadly in line with Quality Approval schemes already in use in British industry and in other industrial nations. For this reason certification of organisations may be easier to introduce than other forms of certification and is less likely to reduce UK cost competitiveness. Such

schemes, however, impose a significant operating overhead in terms of company structure, qualification of key personnel, provision of specific tools and facilities, and operation of prescribed procedures. Whilst the overhead may be supportable by large organisations, it may prove burdensome to those which are smaller. As an alternative in these
cases, suitable procedures could be carried out during contract negotiation. They would
be the responsibility of key personnel from the customer. The question then arises as to
whether safety should be the matter of negotiation between customer and supplier.

5.24   Certification of an organisation rather than of individuals has the advantage of
independence from the characteristics of individuals. A good organisation is likely to mod-
erate and influence individual attitudes and may compensate for lack of individual training
and experience. In particular, approved procedures with an organisation may compensate
for lack of experience and competence on the part of junior members of staff.

5.25   Furthermore, organisational certification may be more relevant than personal
certification. Task and environment-related factors (such as competing work-place imper-
atives) may be more important determinants of product quality than the personal competence, etc. of individuals.

5.26   Objections to the organisational approach are based on the view that such
schemes are of doubtful utility in practice. For example it has proved difficult to formalise
requirements for 'good' development. Although basic principles are understood it is difficult to devise and apply objective assessment criteria. As a result it is generally accepted
that the development process should be resilient to failures, rather than that any part of it
should be perfect. Since it is difficult to prescribe the content of design reviews, assessment for certification tends to be limited to whether reviews are held, rather than whether
they are effective. Moreover, where a design approach based on quality standards is used,
the quality systems manager may be powerless to enforce procedures with the result that
schemes based on quality assurance are often reduced to monitoring the application of
techniques rather than enforcing the use of the 'best' techniques.

Certification of Personnel
Current Position
5.27   Practice concerning certification of personnel varies greatly. At one extreme certification of the individual is required: examples are welders, radiographers, pilots, doc-
tors, colliery engineers and civil engineers involved in dam construction. Some other
industries issue approvals of key personnel, which form part of an organisation's overall
approval. For example the CAA will approve the chief designer and quality manager, but
make it the responsibility of the organisation to select other staff, including software
engineers, against approved procedures.

5.28   Key technical and quality assurance personnel may be nominated in contracts.
The CEGB requires that a nominated authorised engineer provides a signature for release
of a product, which may only be given after independent assessment of the product has
taken place. Loss of the authorised signatories requires reapproval if the contract can continue. Approval of individuals is carried out against a broad assessment of qualifications
and experiences. Other industries operate voluntary schemes whereby approval and

nomination of key members of staff is carried out during contract negotiation at the discretion of the interested parties.

5.29 In some situations 'Permit to Work' or 'Right to Practice' systems are successful. These have been shown to be enforceable and can be policed. Individual responsibility is assumed if a system is deliberately abused.

Issues
5.30 It may be agreed that while the main responsibility for the system or product must rest with the supplying organisation, part of the responsibility should rest with the individuals involved, in addition to their normal professional and ethical responsibility. This would provide motivation to use best practice and to take all reasonable precautions to ensure a safe product. It would also encourage the development of the appropriate approach and personal qualities, such as competence, experience and motivation, which are believed to have a considerable effect on the quality of the final product and on quality standards. Certification may have the effect of ensuring the provision of relevant initial training.

5.31 The major arguments for certification of personnel are:

1. the quality of the product is dependent on a practical skill which is characteristic of the individual

2. the product of their work is such that it cannot be adequately tested in a non-destructive fashion.

5.32 There are counter-arguments. With regard to point 1 above, development of software is usually a team activity and indeed it is considered poor engineering practice to be dependent on an individual. With regard to point 2 software can be tested, although the extent to which exhaustive testing can be carried out is dependent on practical constraints. However, even where it is possible to have a system of approval of software as fit for purpose within a safety system, there may still be a case for certification of the individuals who would give that approval. Since it is likely that approval would continue to be carried out on an industry-based context this would give rise to a requirement for certified industry-based assessors.

5.33 It was suggested by some Working Party members that only chartered engineers with suitable experience could be recommended for work in safety-critical applications. Since not all Chartered Engineers have suitable experience however, a special grade of safety-critical software engineer would be created. This is considered to be contrary to the recommendations of the Engineering Council which require that an individual chartered engineer should only carry out work for which he is suitably qualified.

5.34 In practice, personnel certification schemes have been found to have the following disadvantages:

1. A formal system must be set up to establish and re-assess the right to practice; rigid enforcement is required and the procedures must cater for all eventualities to avoid exceptions to, and abuse of, the system.

2. Scarcity of suitably qualified staff may lead to difficulties of attitude which in turn lead to inflated salaries and the reluctance to operate on a callout basis; protective practices and preferential pay rewards may be encouraged; adequately qualified staff may not be available when required; and there may be problems associated with constructing a properly balanced team.

3. The need to ensure continuing education without interruption to project requirements can be difficult to accommodate, particularly if there are limited training facilities.

4. The cost of training and licensing practices may be high; of necessity this will require high fees which may discourage the use of certified personnel or consultants.

5. Certification does not take account of personal attitudes, which are acknowledged to play a major part in promoting software quality.

5.35   Explicit objective criteria are required to prevent abuse of a scheme for certifying individuals. Formal educational qualifications seem to be the only criteria which meet this requirement. However in most occupations such qualifications are not, on their own, considered adequate grounds for certification; and other desirable qualities, such as those relating to personal characteristics, are not amenable to objective assessment. Additionally if there is a system of levels of criticality and engineers are certified for individual levels, then a requirement is created for a national or international agreement on what those levels are. Finally certification in relation to specifically software issues is not necessarily enough. Safety-related matters may extend beyond the software and its design. In some situations organisations are unaware of the safety-related implications of particular functions. Dependent on environment and the particular appointment, these suggest that a range of competencies beyond software design skills are appropriate to certification.

5.36   Personal competence may become a public issue to the extent that it may not be acceptable to rely on informal or self-regulating procedures (particularly supplier/customer/contractor agreements) in high-risk areas. It may become the public perception that self-regulation is open to abuse by less responsible organisations; it is in any event difficult to justify. Very small organisations may be inadequately supported. Market forces do not necessarily provide appropriate pressure to ensure that individuals in the design team have satisfactory attitudes towards quality in their work. In this respect placing some degree of liability on the persons concerned may increase motivation to maintain safety standards. Public concern should not be allowed, however, to override engineering judgement in making the informed selection of the best engineering practices.

Certification of Processes and Tools
Current Position
5.37   Certification of a few highly specific processes is carried out in industry, principally where post-inspection of the product would not reveal failures in process quality. Examples are 'clean-room' and test-house processes where objective criteria can be used to measure process quality. The major part of industrial activity relies on approval of processes as part of organisational approval. In some cases, track record, maturity and evidence of a population of good quality products are considered as evidence of acceptable process quality.

Issues
5.38   The principal issue for certification of software engineering processes and tools is that of practicality. In particular, the extent to which software tools, such as compilers and configuration management tools, and CASE tools can be certified is questionable. Many of the tools involve highly complex software developed over several years which may not be amenable to verification using existing technology. The cost of certification of general tools for use in a limited market may be prohibitive, so that there is no incentive for suppliers to produce tools for the design of safety-related software. The practicality of providing fully proven computer hardware and software, adequate to support industrial needs such as the PLC market is also questionable. Faults in microprocessors may vary from batch to batch, for example, and the difficulties associated with securing conformance of industrial components from major suppliers may prove insurmountable.

5.39   An issue which complicates process certification schemes still further is that the use of software tools is not limited to the software industry so that any certification scheme would have wide ranging effects on British industry. For example non-software components such as braking systems are designed using software tools which cannot be guaranteed fault free. In these cases validation through modelling is often carried out. In at least one case, however, the risks entailed have led to a semiconductor manufacturer seeking injunctions to prevent a product being used in medical electronics.

Certification of Products
Current Position
5.40   Certification of components is carried out by suppliers to indicate that their product has been shown to meet the requirements of particular standard(s). Type testing and trials are used in some applications, but have the disadvantage of being time consuming, paper intensive and costly processes which may not ensure that a component will be adequate for a particular configuration. The number of hours of trouble-free operation is used in some areas and has been proposed as a method of software acceptance, on the basis that more aspects of the system will be tested over a longer time interval. Quality control is used to increase the level of confidence in a product, although practical experience suggests that it is difficult to prevent the use of inferior components.

Issues

5.41   It has been suggested that product certification might provide shorthand evidence of conformance, at least in an application specific context. Hardware certification is undertaken by product testing and by monitored rectification. Software, however requires certification of the design and this may only be effective in a structured organisation and supportive environment.

5.42   A major issue for the certification of software products is whether the software can be isolated from the system of which it is a part, and, indeed, whether such approval has any significance for the safety of the system. In particular the required design safety characteristics will be dependent on the application and will be determined by the acceptable levels of risk for that application.

5.43   The question of what constitutes adequate software testing must also be addressed in order to develop product certification schemes. Testing may be concerned with, for example, logical correctness, verification against a formal mathematical specification, conformance against a plain-English statement of requirements, testing for unexpected modes of operation and weaknesses in specification, and failure modes assessment. Combinations of testing philosophies may be required to demonstrate that safety properties such as defensive programming and self-test, as well as temporal aspects are adequately exercised.

5.44   Responsibility for the safe use of a product lies with the prospective operating organisation, however, to demonstrate that they are capable of safe operation and that the system has been developed adequately for the intended mode of operation. This is in keeping with conventional, contract-based authorisation, whereby the prime contractor has total responsibility for the product and must demonstrate that he has adequately discharged his responsibilities to the customer to the satisfaction of both parties.

E. Conclusions

5.45   The principal arguments for the introduction of certification are the need to enforce good digital design practices throughout industry; the awareness that this would create; the promotion of an infra-structure to support professional responsibility; and the consequent creation of a pool of highly trained competent software engineers who would operate across application areas. The principal concerns relating to the introduction of such measures are the cost of introducing and maintaining such practices; the effect this would have on UK competitiveness in world markets; the practicality and value of certain forms of certification; and the fear of creating restrictive practices.

5.46   Safety depends on all of systems, hardware and software. Concern for safety, and consideration of certification, must not, therefore, be concerned exclusively with software.

5.47   Although many industrial representatives on the Working Party were not supportive of general forms of certification, there is mixed support for some forms of regulation, and in particular for self-regulation, or regulation through contractual customer/supplier agreements. The means of regulation will require careful consideration however, if it is to be relevant and cost-effective for the wide diversity of industrial applications and needs.

5.48   Organisational certification is of benefit in reducing the risk arising from the design of safety-related equipment, but does not ensure that an adequate level of safety has been achieved. Options for certification of organisations include the adoption of existing quality standards, use of such standards supported by contractual agreements, licensing of test facilities, and introduction of rigorous codes of practice, either on an industry by industry basis or (preferably) throughout industry. Further investigations would be required to identify criteria which may be used to assess adequately the practice and competence of individuals occupying key positions. Differences in the requirements of and practices in differently sized organisations may need to be addressed, although this does not imply that smaller firms might have a lesser safety requirement.

5.49   Product conformance tests cannot provide a guarantee against software design faults, but may be used to ensure that accepted best practice is applied throughout industry. Whilst testing is essential, it becomes more difficult when the product is or involves software, since it is impossible to test a complex system exhaustively for faults which could occur only following a very rare sequence of events. Mathematical proof and formal methods as a means of overcoming some of the deficiences in testing have limitations, particularly when not used in conjunction with design techniques.

5.50   An issue which impinges on the need for adequate development practices is that for some types of software product, certification testing may not even be possible unless the development process has been carried out in a particular manner. For instance it may not be possible to verify logical correctness with a formal mathematical specification unless appropriate mathematical representations are used during development. The effects of these constraints should be considered.

5.51   Given the difficulty of testing software, the proposal has been made that the engineer should be judged and awarded a 'right to practice'. The danger of certification based on education and training alone, however, is that it is only of indirect benefit in assessing proficiency because competence arises not only from knowledge, nor from knowledge and experience combined, but also from personal qualities. Some aspects of the first two may be measurable, but the third is best judged by peer-group assessment and is difficult to evaluate equitably. Introduction of assessment schemes for persons with responsibility for giving approvals, however, may be possible within the existing application-based regulation framework. Verification does not require an in-depth knowledge of the specific application, although this will be required for validation, hazard analysis and risk assessment. For this reason the introduction of new technologies may be easier to accommodate for assessors, though there will be a need for updating and awareness training. Peer group assessment and track record are the only means of assessing management proficiency.

5.52   Despite the possibility of personnel certifications it is essential that the main responsibility for operational safety should be placed upon the user organisations since these are alone likely to have resources to make adequate compensation for the conse-quence of failure. In order to provide for adequate redress of injured third parties it is important to ensure that new certification practices should not transfer responsibility from an organisation to individuals.

5.53   Generic software engineering standards, not related to specific industries, would be beneficial to British industry as a whole. They would permit the use of soft-ware and software development facilities so as to reduce costs and provide flexibility in meeting new and possible urgent requirements. However, the use of such standards, rather than international industry-based standards, may reduce the ability to compete internationally. Moreover issuing industry-based standards means that the users will have knowledge of the application of systems and be able to make realistic assessments of failure modes and their effects. As there are existing regulatory bodies, any new pro-posals should conform to existing regulatory structures.

5.54   As a prerequisite to achieving common standards across industry, definition of different safety levels is required. This would also be needed for future European stan-dardisation.

5.55   Proposals for certification would require careful study and full account would need to be taken of any European directives which might be issued, although it is likely that these will be very broad and unspecific.

5.56   The overall effect of the introduction of new regulations on industry requires careful consideration. The introduction of design certification would be a major change. To make individuals legally responsible for design errors or failures would be a major and significant change from custom. There is a limit to the speed at which new prac-tices can be implemented; sweeping changes to regulations might have the effect of delaying particular changes which are particularly desirable. This relates to the question of third-party certification *vis-à-vis* certification by the customer. In particular the cus-tomer has the ability to adapt to specific cases and to respond to technological trends more readily than can official bodies.

5.57   It is concluded that good practice based on training, experience and common sense will, for the foreseeable future, continue to make an important contribution to product safety. Some degree of functional conformance testing, recognised by certifica-tion, may be justified and it is for consideration in what areas it is best applied. Product certification should entail a combination of the auditing of the development programme for objective evidence of adequate design practices, in conjunction with the software tests and a 'practical proof' of the finished product.

6. THE WAY FORWARD

A. Introduction, Discussion and Rationale

6.1   This chapter presents our conclusions and the rationale on which they are based.

6.2   At the outset of the study it was recognised that many industrial sectors already have their own approaches to control of the development and operation of safety-related systems. These are based on practical experience of the safety concerns of the particular applications in those industries. Any additional measures for the control of programmable electronic systems should be integrated with existing practice in each sector.

6.3   It was therefore envisaged that, rather than attempt to introduce totally new software controls independent of industry practice, the first step should be to propagate the best of existing practice which exists in some sectors across other sectors through a process of harmonisation. It was intended that the first step should be to identify undesirable 'gaps and inconsistencies', looking across a wide range of sectors.

6.4   Harmonisation would then proceed by extension to industry sectors which do not have any established approach of their own. In this way, the introduction of new procedures to sectors which do not have anything significant in place at present would make good use of the body of practice which already exists in other sectors. It was thought that the analysis necessary for harmonisation, and the resultant structuring of a procedural framework, would provide a distillation of existing practice in a form which would be much easier to carry across to additional sectors.

6.5   In broad terms, all of this still stands. However, during the survey and summary analysis of existing practice carried out in the study, it was initially found difficult to describe existing practice in such a way that comparison could be made across sectors. This was primarily because of the lack of a common structure, or indeed any structure in many cases, for the practice in different sectors. It was found necessary to develop and then impose a structure based on a 'development model' for safety-related systems. We refer to this as the 'Safety Lifecycle': it is illustrated in Figure 2.3 and discussed in Chapter 2, sections 2.48*ff*.

6.6   It is now recommended that this model should be the starting point for harmonisation. The model provides a generally applicable framework for procedural, terminological, and technical harmonisation, identifying the common, or commonly acceptable, features of specific procedures. (The importance of terminology must not be under-estimated: recognition of differences and different usage is often critical to progress on other fronts.)

6.7   Even if procedural integration is eased by harmonisation in this way, there are still other problems with the introduction of new procedures into existing bodies of practice across a range of sectors. These are: the difficulties of interpretation of any new requirements; of understanding what was intended by them; and of recognition of their appropriateness under a variety of circumstances, in the varied contexts of different practices in different sectors.

6.8   We therefore recommend that an attempt be made to try to understand and reconcile these different contexts, by establishing a classification of system types and attributes. Based on this classification there would be a greater likelihood of consensus on the relevance and appropriateness of different specific techniques for design, development, construction, and operation of different types of system or subsystem. This could then lead to guidance on techniques to be adopted for particular situations. The establishment of such a classification is addressed within the recommendation for development of the technical framework.

6.9   Two options exist within this general approach. We considered a specific-to-general method involving choosing examples from a small number of sectors, and developing a model which would be gradually extended by drawing on an ever-wider range of sectors. We preferred however to start with a general model intended to achieve a wide-ranging solution because we felt that this leads to an earlier recognition of fundamental principles.

Relationship with European and International Standardisation
6.10   The difficulty with a pan-sector approach for some industrial sectors is that their more pressing concern is with international (and industrial-sector-oriented) harmonisation, which affects their ability to compete in international markets. While this does not preclude a UK initiative intended to extend across industrial and application sectors, the potential problems must be recognised. No obstacles should be put in the way of those industrial sectors attempting to serve both home and overseas markets.

6.11   It is important also that the UK should press for harmonisation across Europe, in particular in the European Community.

6.12   It should be noted that while there is potential for disharmony as between EC (i.e. CENELEC) and international standardisation activities (for which the principal organisation is the IEC), the intention of CENELEC is to adopt the relevant IEC standard when one is available. This makes it important that there is UK participation in standard making within Europe and internationally.

Awareness
6.13   During the study it has become clear that a major factor affecting safety is a lack of awareness on the part of individuals and organisations of how and to what

extent their work is safety-related. A number of recommendations have been made with the intention of overcoming this. These have been made largely with reference to the UK because they can be implemented more readily on a national basis. Implementing them should additionally provide a competitive edge for UK industry.

6.14   These considerations taken together have resulted in the identification of key concerns, namely

1. the need to ensure that whatever measures are taken will make a genuine contribution to safety and not be merely superficial;

2. lack of awareness of the safety aspects of software and systems;

3. lack of the appropriate body of knowledge needed if requirements for safety assurance are to be stipulated, giving rise to the need for programmes of research;

4. the need to develop appropriate procedures which will improve safety assurance;

5. the need for personnel who are competent;

6. the need to ensure proper safety assessment;

7. recognition of European and wider international dimensions.

B. Recommendations

Continuation and Review

6.15   We recommend that a mechanism be established to enable **the overall position to be reviewed continuously**; with a particular brief to ensure that as appropriate knowledge becomes available it is disseminated; and if possible used as the basis of a programme of certification. This could be achieved by continuing the Project Team, in which case it is likely that its budget will have to allow for the payment of fees to the specialists from private industry. (The study itself has already had an effect and both Institutions have already taken steps which will ensure the continuation of some aspects of the work, but the programme envisaged will require more concentrated effort than can be achieved on a purely voluntary basis.)

Awareness Programme and Dissemination of Information

6.16   We recommend the **establishment of an awareness programme** to ensure that all those responsible for or concerned with safety-related systems (professional engineers, technicians, management and others) are aware of the national and international activities in this field, their responsibilities, and the factors involved in achieving safety. We note that, to achieve maximum effect, this should be directed beyond the engineering community, and be addressed to professionals in other fields who may use computers in particular applications without appreciating the safety-related aspects of their work. The programme should for the large part be of an introductory and tutorial nature. This recommendation will in many cases be implemented through channels already established, some of them as a result of the study itself. The professional organisations will continue to develop their programmes. Consideration should be given to the production of a newsletter. To reach an appropriately wide audience an extensive publicity campaign (*Is **your** software safe?*) will be needed.

6.17   We recommend the **establishment of a means of disseminating information** about the use of methods of assessment of safety-related software. How this might be achieved has not been determined. Difficulties have been foreseen because divulgence of commercially sensitive information may be involved. We believe that discussion of the issue by a group based on the Working Party may help to resolve matters and produce realisable detailed recommendations.

6.18   We recommend the establishment in the UK of a scheme, spanning all industry and application sectors, to **monitor the introduction of programmable elements** in safety-related systems. With any rapidly emerging and evolving technology there arise diverse approaches to its use, and diverse views and opinions on the most appropriate way to control its use. The intention of this scheme would be to collect, analyse, and disseminate real experience. As in paragraph 6.14, the means of achieving this has not yet been established, and requires further investigation, which is likely to require active participation by the HSE. It is considered that legislation may be required.

Safety Lifecycle and Technical Framework
6.19   We recommend **adoption of the Safety Lifecycle** (paragraphs 2.48*ff*) as a procedural framework for all safety-related systems.

6.20   We recommend the **preparation and development of the technical framework** discussed in paragraphs 2.45*ff*. This work could be undertaken as an independent study by a broadly based group or by the HSE.

6.21   We recommend that **definitions** be developed for the **quantitative parameters to be used as measures of safety integrity**, e.g. probability of failure on demand and mean-time-between-failure. This work would be appropriate for a research project.

6.22   We recommend that where **numerical values** are used to categorise systems, they should be used and represented as 'claim limits'; and we recommend that those making such claims should be expected to be able to justify them. Such justification may for now be based on engineering judgement, rather than precise prediction. We recognise that there is at present little scientific basis for the numeric quantities used. We recommend that research be undertaken to enable more rigorous quantification.

Standards and Requirements for Their Implementation
6.23   We recommend that the combination of **the frameworks should be adopted via IEC standardisation** with the intention that Europe should not diverge from the wider international community. These IEC Standards should be given as much force and authority as possible. The relevant section within DTI should make recommendations to this effect (e.g. they might be deemed to be required under an EC directive).

6.24   We recommend that those developing **standards in the UK should take cognisance of the existing and emerging IEC standards**.

6.25   We therefore recommend:

1.   that the **focus of attention should not immediately be on** the development of certification systems;

2.   that **research be undertaken** to achieve the necessary levels of understanding – research topics are listed in paragraphs 6.35*ff* of this chapter;

3.   that further study be undertaken to **assess the usefulness of certification**, and to identify both the particular forms of certification including organisational accreditation and the procedures which are most likely to improve safety assurance; – see also Ref. 100;

4.   that established certification practices, following BS 5750 (ISO-9001) (Refs 15–19), or other industry or application-based code should be continued.

6.26   We recommend that when developing standards, organisations should **distinguish**

1.   **generic requirements**;

2.   industry- and application-**specific requirements** which prescribe how the generic requirements are to be met;

3.   **procurement procedures**.

British Standard 0 (Ref. 12) contains a discussion.

6.27   We recommend that within the UK, **industry should be encouraged to develop a pan-sector code of practice**, starting with the adoption of the Safety Lifecycle. (This is not, technically, the same as 'self-regulation' which has a more restricted usage, applying when third-party, perhaps statutory, regulation is delegated to industries or industrial organisations.)

Competence

6.28   We recommend that **all those involved** in any aspect of the Safety Lifecycle **should be competent** with respect to the safety-related aspects of their work. (A potential model for a definition of competence exists in the *Ionising Radiations Regulations Code of Practice* (Ref. 50); see also ACOP 71.)

6.29   We recommend that **organisations** which supply or operate systems **should be responsible for nominating competent persons** to have responsibility for identifying hazards and ensuring that appropriate action is taken at all stages of the Safety Lifecycle. As many such persons should be nominated as are required to give assurance of safe practice.

6.30   We recommend that **for the most critical systems** there should be **at least one named competent person with overall responsibility** for the safety in operation and maintenance of that system (see paragraph 2.5).

6.31   We recommend that the content of the **education, training and experience elements** to fulfil the requirement for competence of all personnel be determined. Steps must be taken to ensure that this content is included in syllabi and training schemes. This requirement relates not only to professionals whose prime responsibility is safety, but also to technicians and management, and to those for whom safety concerns are only part of their duties or responsibilities. This recommendation may be achieved by agreement between the professional bodies in collaboration with industry. Courses should be at post-graduate, post-experience level (Ref. 11).

6.32   We recommend that **financial liability should lie with the organisation** rather than the individual engineers.

Assessment

6.33   We recommend the **principle of System Safety Assessment Reports** (also called safety cases) described in paragraphs *2.57ff*.

6.34   We recommend the **principle of independent safety assessment**. Four degrees of independence should be considered, involving:

1.   a team from the design group or department;

2.   an independent team from another part of the company;

3.   an independent team (e.g. a firm of consultants);

4.   a national body (with government backing).

Programme of Research

6.35   We recommend a programme of research to deal with the following issues which arose during the course of our study. In general, these relate to systems, to hardware and to software, and to the whole extent of the Safety Lifecycle.

1.   Research into and analysis of previous experience. Means of allowing this experience to be explained must be available, disseminated and used if we are to avoid the repetition of earlier errors.

2.   Determination of how and to what extent different individual factors contribute to safety integrity; how their amalgamation contributes to safety integrity; the development of quantification in relation to individual factors and to their amalgamation; development of understanding of the relevance of individual factors in particular applications and situations.

3.   Refinement of the 'technical framework', including characterisation of different types of systems and appropriate sets of methods for them.

4.   Listing of architectural forms and their appropriateness for particular safety-related systems applications.

5.   Research to establish and if possible quantify the benefits of diversity of systems, software and hardware.

6. Testing and the general subject of statistical inferences drawn from experience.

7. Investigation of complexity, its measurement, and its relationship to other measures.

6.36   We recommend the establishment within SERC of a Safety-Critical Interdisciplinary Research Centre as a means of prioritising funding and administering these programmes of research.

APPENDIX A   BASIC CONCEPTS

Safety, Systems and Uncertainty

A-1   Safety is a concept which is not fixed in either time or space. Attitudes to safety, and tolerance of danger, are subjective and variable over time and circumstance. Industries have attempted to address this problem by identification of more objective aspects of safety, with particular definitions of words such as 'hazard' and 'situation'. Specifications of safety, whether required or claimed as achieved, should be based on these more objectively defined terms.

A-2   It is essential to consider the safety aspects of software in the context of the safety of the systems in which it is embedded, or to which it contributes in some other way. It is the system which is safe or unsafe, not the software. Further, we mean not just the DESIGN of systems on paper or computer disk, but systems as specified and designed for a real world which we may not understand perfectly, which we may not be able to describe in a universally understood manner, and as built and operated in that same uncertainly known and described real world.

A-3   The uncertainty in our knowledge of the real world creates the potential for our specifications to be wrong, including being incomplete. This is apart from any mistakes we may make and uncertainties we may introduce when we come to describe the requirements in specifications.

A-4   This uncertainty of description arises from the need to model the real world, in a specification, in terms of abstractions which are open to subjective interpretation. So even when we think that we understand the requirements of a system, there is inevitably some, even considerable, indefinition in any requirements specification. This is sometimes described pejoratively as 'ambiguity' in the specification, but, although some indefinition may be removed, some will inevitably remain, so that an entirely unambiguous specification is strictly not feasible.

A-5   In the face of all this uncertainty let us now introduce, as a reference, the notion of 'ideal operation'. This is what we would like a system to do, whether or not we know what that is, or are able to describe it, or are able to specify, design, build, and operate the system to do it. It is an entirely notional basis for considering what is required, and what can be achieved.

A-6   One of the differences between safety-related systems and others is that, even though 'safety' is not a fixed concept, whatever it means for a particular application we want it. We want the safety-related aspects of 'ideal operation' satisfied, regardless of the uncertainties in other aspects of the specification and its interpretation.

A-7   It might be argued that the specification is our best understanding of the requirements, and that its errors and ambiguities are not our concern. That may, perhaps, be the contractual position on some bespoke projects. But the engineering challenge is to meet the subset of the requirements concerned with safety, in the real world, regardless of the specification. Many of the engineering practices of safety-related systems are therefore directed to reduce uncertainty and cope with residual uncertainty, while taking account of the needs for timeliness, economy, and contractual constraints.

Design and Definition

A-8   At each stage of design, the specification is, in effect, transformed into a more detailed design specification, or build definition, in terms of software language statements and hardware and software components. Sometimes it is said that such a final specification is in some sense a concrete representation of the specification. However, as long as the design is still that – a design, as yet unrealised physically – then it is composed of abstractions. These may represent realisable functions or objects which are intended to perform functions, but they are not those functions.

A-9   So at each design transformation, the abstractions of the specification are transformed into other abstractions. In terms of the uncertainty in the specification, and its impact on the eventual operation, these abstractions fall into three classes, identified for the purpose of this discussion as realisable, definite, and indefinite.

A-10   Starting with those which represent realisable objects or functions, their uncertainties concern whether they will be correctly realised in construction (will the compiler work?), whether they will perform as expected (what does 'add' mean for a computer representation of real numbers?), or as specified, and whether they will be used as intended.

A-11   Next come those abstractions which represent universally well-understood concepts, such as logical relationships, which are not yet expressed in a realisable form from the first class. They are 'definite' in that there should not be scope for misinterpretation. They nevertheless suffer the uncertainty of accurate retention through design transformations, and accurate transformation into realisable form, followed, of course, by the uncertainties of the first class above.

A-12   Finally, though generally first in the chronology of a system development, there are those abstractions which represent our best effort to describe something over which there is no guarantee of common understanding of the intended meaning, however 'obvious' it may seem to any particular reader. These indefinite aspects of requirements include the important sub-class of things well-understood in the application domain – or in a sub-set of it – but not necessarily by system designers and builder. The uncertainties of this class (in addition to those of the previous two classes) arise from the most difficult question of all – whether there is mutual understanding of these requirement abstractions as they are transformed into realisable form.

A-13   The process of design is, then, one of increasing definition, transforming the abstractions of specification until there is a fully realisable representation. Some indefinite elements are made definite, and definite elements made more definite, until they are realisable. At each transformation there is potential for a variety of types of error, each of which gives rise to a different type of uncertainty about the operation of the eventual system. But the distinction between the different forms of uncertainty is of most value in assessing the contribution of different techniques used in safety-related systems development.

A-14   Beyond design there are potential errors of construction and operation. It is not enough for a designer to design on the basis that they will not happen. They should be taken account of and accommodated by the design. After all, the customer wants a system which performs its ideal operation, at least for the safety-related aspects, regardless – not just on a good day. This is usually achieved by some degree of fault detection, coupled with fault tolerance, often involving an acceptable reduced functionality – perhaps a fall-back capability or fail-safe protection.

A-15   There remains the real world, which may not 'perform as expected'. Though perhaps not strictly within the remit of 'design', there are approaches to system development which address this problem. Many of the engineering techniques of safety-related systems are concerned with recognition that we require safety even with uncertain understanding of the world. For instance, where possible, fail-safe protection of a controlled process will be based not on computation which requires understanding of the process, but on monitoring of unarguable physical parameters. Prototyping is not always easy or even possible, but where it is it can contribute to understanding of the real world as much as of the system under development.

Correctness

A-16   Unfortunately, this seemingly straightforward word has acquired a number of different usages, where the differences can be very significant. To many, engineers as well as the public, it means conformance between actual and ideal operation – between what a system actually does in the real world and what we would have liked it to do had we realised what we really wanted.

A-17   To some it means conformance of design, or build, or perhaps operation, to the specification. For contractual purposes this may avoid some of the uncertainties in our knowledge of the real world. But given the inevitable uncertainties inherent in the use of abstractions in a specification, this is not such a useful distinction as it would appear, since we must then ask – whose interpretation of the specification?

A-18   A third usage is that of mathematicians, who sometimes mean that part of the second usage which may, in principle, be demonstrable as mathematical or logical consistency between system descriptions – such as that between one level of software specification and a more detailed level of design.

A-19   Care must therefore be taken in interpretation of the term 'correctness' in the literature about safety-related systems. In this document, it will be avoided unless it is qualified to indicate the particular sense in which it is used.

Completeness

A-20   This is really about incompleteness, and types of incompleteness, rather than completeness. Incompleteness can be considered to be no more than one form of incorrectness. But a distinction might be drawn between errors of commission and errors of omission. Both are incorrect in the broadest sense, but errors of omission can be considered as incompleteness errors, in which case 'incorrectness' is then sometimes used in a narrower sense, for errors of commission.

A-21   Discussion of incompleteness, especially with regard to the determinability of the 'correctness' of a system, can be clouded by confusion between different types of incompleteness. What follows is not intended to be a definitive categorisation of incompleteness, but an indication of the range of types.

A-22   Firstly, there may have been a failure to identify all the pertinent factors which must be considered in deciding the response of a system in any situation. ('Factor' is an appropriate word since in system design there is a concern to factor- ise the range of all the conditions to which a system must respond into its significant sets of conditions.)

A-23   Secondly, the factors which have been considered may not have been prop- erly characterised. The range of possibilities for these factors may be either not suf- ficiently extensive or not sufficiently finely divided.

A-24   Thirdly, the responses of a system to the considered factors may be wrong. This last sounds like an error of commission rather than omission. However, if it arises because of a lack of realisation that within the responses to a give set of circumstances there should have been further subdivision – recognition of special cases, for example – then it is in some sense an omission, much like the previous case.

A-25   Indeed, whatever the cause of incompleteness, a system will nevertheless, whether by default or deliberate design, usually do something. Certainly for on-line sys- tems even stopping, or failing to respond to an event, counts as 'doing something'. In such cases, it can be said to have been designed to do the wrong thing. Hence a confu- sion between errors of commission and omission. Is the 'something' which the system does an error of commission? Or does the reason that the correct response was not designed – a lack of identification and characterisation of relevant factors – make it an error of omission?

A-26   Finally, there is a rather different type of incompleteness – that of indefini- tion – where a requirement or design is insufficiently definite, so that among the pos- sible interpretations there is scope for some which are incorrect. Purists would argue that errors in this class are in general one or other of the other types.

Certification, Conformance, and Objective Test

A-27   Many safety-related systems are developed in an environment where regulatory and licensing authorities require 'certification' of some kind. But there are limitations, both in practice and in theory, to the assurance that such certification can provide. First, the key concept, which is essential to certification schemes, of conformance assessment based on objective testing, will be discussed.

A-28   We mean, by an 'objective test', one about which all members of the community of interest would have, literally 'in effect', the 'same' interpretation. Harking back to the earlier discussion of design and definition, the specification of an objective test is definite, at least with regard to the purposes of the test. (Note that 'test' is used in here in the widest sense, rather than the usually restricted input-output sense implicit in 'software test'.)

A-29   The word 'conformance' has two distinct uses in the field of systems development. In a broad sense it is a special case of the general English language usage, referring to the consistency between two things, but with the added implication of completeness. So if we consider the conformance of a design with its requirement specification, the design must be not just consistent with the requirements, in that it does not explicitly contradict them, it should also explicitly address all the requirements.

A-30   'Conformance assessment' is the determination that something or someone satisfies, in this sense, the definite element of an objective test. 'Conformance' is often then used in its narrower sense as shorthand for recognition that a number of such tests have been satisfied.

A-31   We must be careful with the term 'certification', since it can be interpreted in very different ways. Though most would agree that it is associated with some kind of pass/fail assessment, there the agreement ends. Firstly, there are those who assume that it is dependent on only objective tests − a formal recognition of conformance. Certainly this is usually an ambition of certification schemes; but existing schemes do not necessarily preclude elements of subjective appraisal. Secondly, there may be requirements for conformance which are not encapsulated in explicit 'certification' requirements, but which have the same type of objective.

A-32   By definition, conformance and certification against objective tests cannot address the uncertainties of either the real world or specifications. In other words, 'complete' conformance to all the real-world safety requirements can never be demonstrated. So the prospect of releasing into service only systems which have been 'completely' certified as safe, against objective tests, is simply, if sadly, not viable.

Verification and Validation

A-33   There are no universally accepted definitions of these terms or of the distinction between them. Nevertheless a distinction is often made between conformance to a specification and correctness of actual operation in the real world with respect to ideal operation, regardless of the specification. Working definitions of verification and validation are therefore that they are concerned with assessment, proof, or providing confidence of conformance and correct actual operation respectively. Colloquially, verification then addresses the question 'Are we building the product right?' and validation 'Are we building the right product?'

A-34   In fact verification is generally considered to be concerned with attempting to establish conformance of a representation of design or requirements with an earlier representation, of which the earliest is the original specification.

A-35   Given the preceding discussion of specification, design, and conformance, then even if conformance is achieved, setting aside the question of ideal operation, a design or a system as built may not be what was intended. It may be one interpretation of a specification, but it may not be a valid interpretation.

A-36   Some verification techniques go beyond strict conformance as discussed previously. They attempt to establish that the later definite or realisable representations satisfactorily interpret the earlier indefinite counterparts from which they were derived. Such techniques require human intervention, since they are attempting to determine mutual understanding of abstractions. The techniques (see chapter 3) are therefore designed to assist human understanding of different representations. They usually provide different 'views' for either analysis or comparison in order to identify differences of interpretation of the requirements. Such differences of interpretation may imply that one or other is incorrect.

A-37   However, in some ways perhaps more importantly for safety-related systems, verification is itself limited, since it starts with the specification rather than the real world. Dealing with our uncertain understanding of the real world is the subject of validation.

A-38   Correctness of actual operation compared with ideal operation is, then, addressed by validation. We try to determine that our understanding of the requirements, as embodied in a system or its design, is right. This cannot be 'proven' in the mathematical sense. We can gain only confidence, and not confirmation, that it has been achieved – and will be in future. This confidence can come only from evidence that the system or its operation is consistent with the real-world requirements, i.e. does not contradict them, so far.

A-39   This is why there are disputes over the role of testing – over whether testing is to demonstrate correctness or to find faults. ('Testing' is used here in the narrow sense of exercising a system or part of it.) Even if testing is to demonstrate correctness, the only way to do that by exercising a system is to fail to find faults.

A-40   In limited cases, such as for some very specific conformance tests, it may be possible to exhaustively exercise a system over all of a limited range of conditions. But in general the problem of testing is that it is impossible to be exhaustive and difficult to be sure of the coverage and usefulness of the tests which are performed. Nevertheless, however crude, system testing – if not low-level 'module' testing – does have the advantage that the accuracy and sufficiency of our understanding of the controlled process and its environment can be tested, albeit perhaps in a rather hit or miss fashion, whereas the other techniques are somewhat introspective.

A-41   Indeed, testing is the most common form of validation. Other techniques include prototyping, animation, analysis, and walkthrough. The objective is the same in each case – to present a different view of the system from its design representations.

A-42   Here we see the similarity with the 'beyond conformance' aspect of verification. The multiple views seek to compare interpretations, not of the specification this time, but of the real-world requirements. But the approach is often similar, and may be the source of the confusion between verification and validation. It is the same confusion that can exist in 'Are we building the right product?'. This can be read as 'Are we building the intended product, given the indefinite nature of the specification?' or 'Are we building the product which will do the right job in the real world?' Here, the former has been considered to be addressed by verification, and the latter by validation.

A-43   To summarise validation there is, in general, no such thing as a correctness proof for the operation of a system – except in the old-fashioned sense of proof as a test. 'The proof of the pudding' is a particularly apposite analogy.

Conclusion

A-44   There are fundamental limitations to the assurance that can be gained about the operation of practical, entire, safety-related systems.

APPENDIX B   OVERSEAS STUDY

A. Introduction

B-1   The study was carried out between 1st January 1989 and 31st August 1989 by The Centre for Software Engineering Ltd (CSE) for the Institution of Electrical Engineers under a DTI contract. A full report (*A study of the computer based systems safety practices of UK, European and USA industry*) will be issued later by the IEE. The recommendations at the end of the Appendix are made by the Overseas Study Team.

Objective
B-2   The principal objective was to collect information on the use and promotion of safety standards for computer-based systems by major companies and regulatory bodies in the UK and other European countries, and in the USA.

Method
B-3   Fifty-six organisations in the following eleven countries were consulted:

UK	USA
France	Holland
Belgium	Germany
Switzerland	Austria
Denmark	Italy
Norway	

The organisations were chosen on the basis of knowledge gained from other CSE activities and were

1. Companies working in safety-related/high integrity systems.

2. Companies active in their home market and concerned about potential competition from imports.

3. Companies currently active in the export market.

4. Regulatory bodies responsible for establishing safety in specific processes and products.

Figure B.1 represents the distribution of respondents by industry sector.

B-4   Summaries of a preliminary version of the main study and of a proposed IEC standard (Ref. 68) were sent to each person concerned to provided a focus for the consultation. Meetings were conducted as personal interviews. Following each meeting, a questionnaire designed to aid the analysis of the information was completed by the interviewer.

B-5   Much of the information obtained was supplied on the understanding that it was non-attributable, and in some cases, that there should be no indication of the participation of the organisation.

B. Results

Awareness and Application of Current Standards

B-6   In general, organisations in all countries visited were found to have considerable awareness of all the major standards and guidelines relating to safety. However, standards concerned specifically with safety are less familiar to the interviewees than general Quality Assurance standards such as ISO 9000. UK organisations are less aware of international standards-making activities than are those in other countries visited.

B-7   Despite this generally widespread awareness, only a relatively small number of industries are applying standards or guidelines of any sort. For example, in the UK only 28% of the industries interviewed are using the Health and Safety Executive (HSE) Guidelines (Refs 53 and 54). This is particularly worrying in the case of the small companies producing systems which are replicated a large number of times.

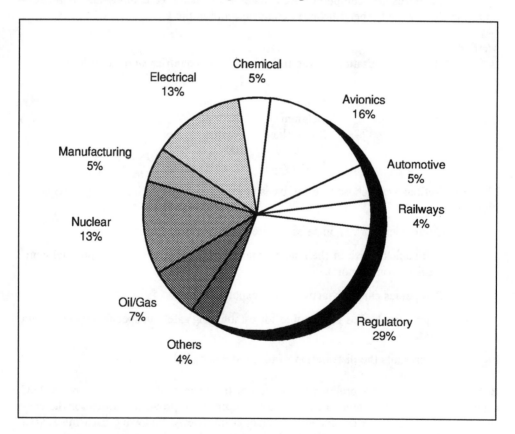

Figure B.1 Industrial Sectors Consulted

B-8   Some UK industries are having problems following and adapting their procedures to the HSE Guidelines. European and USA companies, whilst having an interest in these guidelines, are experiencing difficulty in obtaining copies.

B-9   Some organisations producing safety-related systems do not use standards internally. Confidentiality does not allow identification of an example.

Comparison of Areas of Concern

B-10   Although there is a high level of concern over software, industry is, in general, most concerned with the safety of the system as a whole. Other aspects particularly considered were hardware and system operation (which includes human reliability factors). The relative importance assigned to the different categories is shown in Table B.1.

Table B.1 Industry Concern by Aspect

Extent of Concern Aspect	None(%)	Little(%)	Medium(%)	Great(%)	Extreme(%)
System	0	2	7	86	5
Software	0	11	34	48	7
Hardware	0	20	60	20	0
Operation	10	52	35	3	0

Safety Integrity Levels

B-11   Questions were asked about the usefulness of integrity levels (see paragraph 2.44). The proposed IEC ranking of levels was used as an example. This has levels ranging from 1 (High) to 5 (Normal: for software which is not safety-related). [**Note:** The proposed IEC ranking has since been changed, from 0 (Normal) to 4 (Very High).] Interviewees were asked whether they agreed with the IEC ranking, whether they wanted a more complex or a simpler system, or whether they required that 'No ranking' be used, i.e. that software is categorised only as safety-related or non-safety related. Responses are shown in Figure B.2: they indicate 85% agreement on a five-level system.

Software Tools and Programming Languages

B-12   The majority (90%) of industrial interviewees supported the use of software tools in the specification and design of a safety-related software project. There is no consensus of opinion on the best method. With regard to formal methods, for example VDM and 'Z', only 9% of those interviewed in the UK believed that they should be used for specification and development. Among those in Europe and the USA who felt able to comment, the general feeling was that such methods are insufficiently mature. With reference to structured methods, the Yourdon method was most often referred to both by those employing such methods and by those considering their use.

B-13   The lack of enthusiasm for Formal Methods appears to be due to scepticism about the extent of their applicability, the value of the results which they produce, and their cost-effectiveness. Industry expects that extra resources will be necessary and will eventually result in a higher cost for the product (time, money, manpower etc.), and a lack of trained personnel.

B-14   In general, UK industry takes the view that high level strongly-typed block-structured languages are to be preferred and that C and Basic should not be used. UK interviewees were asked whether they considered that certain languages should or should not be used. The response to this question is shown in Table B.2. The use of assembler languages is considered to be troublesome. Some interviewees believe that its use should be limited to circumstances in which it is unavoidable.

B-15   76% of industry think that their organisation will, as a result of an increased need to comply with existing and developing standards, change its approach to the use of tools and languages in the next two years.

Impact of Standards on Trade

B-16   European organisations generally considered that the introduction of international standards for safety-related systems will result in an increase in the number of firms competing for particular contracts. By contrast, UK organisations take the view that the introduction of standards will (in relation to the UK as a whole) reduce both export potential and competition. The expected impact of new standards on trade is shown in Figure B.3.

B-17   Some European countries, for example France, are developing national standards for safety-related software as a means of protecting markets.

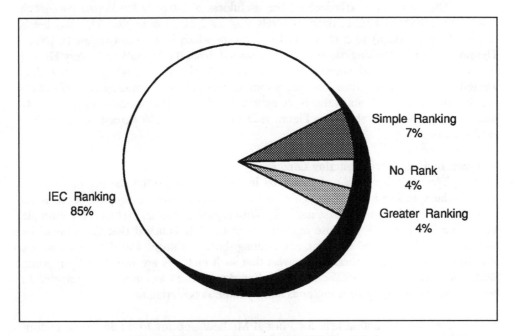

Figure B.2 Safety Integrity Levels (All Countries)

Table B.2 Use of Programming Languages

Language	Number of respondents	Should be used (%)	No view (%)	Should not be used (%)
Ada	8	100	0	0
Modula 2	4	100	0	0
Pascal	11	82	18	0
Coral	3	66	34	0
Fortran	3	34	66	0
C	12	0	25	75
Basic	6	0	34	66
Assembler	4	0	34	66

B-18   Companies in Europe and the USA acknowledge that the UK leads the world in awareness of the broad range of issues in the development and assessment of safe systems: this is exemplified by the HSE guidelines. They consider however that UK companies are not sufficiently aggressive in exploiting the very rich potential market which results from this perception, and are leaving it open to their competitors from other countries.

B-19   There is evidence of reluctance on the part of UK industry to embrace new standards and it may well find that as a consequence European competitors are more able to supply assessed systems. In Europe and the USA there are more positive expectations.

B-20   Nevertheless, UK companies have commented that the lead will be eroded unless more money is spent on research into the contribution made to safety assurance by the various techniques, singly and in combination, and unless there is adequate promotion of techniques already developed.

Impact of Standards on Costs and Prices
B-21   Interviewees in many industries are unable to predict the effect of new standards on cost and price. In the UK there is an expectation that the standards will not affect costs and prices in both the home and export market, while Europe expects a decrease in costs and prices in their home and export markets. The USA view is evenly balanced. However a few interviewees, predominantly in the UK, expect the costs and prices of their products and services to increase. This view is not universally supported. In particular in Switzerland and the Netherlands respondents feel strongly that there will be a reduction in both the home and export markets. The expected impact of new standards on costs and prices in home and export markets is shown in Figure B.4.

Impact of New Standards on Design Philosophy
B-22   Industry feels that the adoption of new international standards will result in a significant change in design philosophies. Although most industries believe that they currently use state-of-the-art design techniques, they feel that in order to comply with those standards they will need to use different techniques.

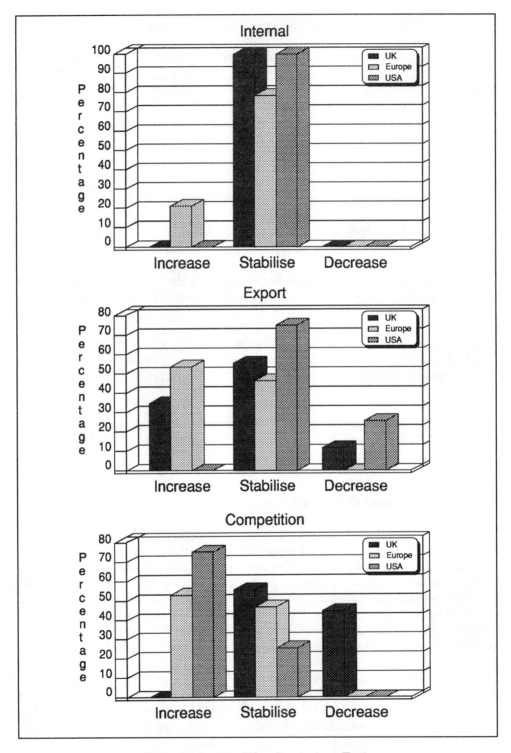

Figure B.3 Impact of New Standards on Trade

Training Requirements

B-23   In all industrial sectors in the UK, it is felt that equal priority should be given to the training of developers and assessors. Experience is believed to be by far the more important source of knowledge for both groups; thereafter approximately equal weighting is given to the development through further education of skills in hazard analysis. Structured design methods, such as Yourdon, and Formal Methods were given the least emphasis. Figure B.5 gives more detailed information. In Europe and the USA there was no consensus on this point. The degree of importance attached to individual skill and experience of developers and assessors implies a requirement for a high degree of professionalism on their part.

Certification

B-24   In Europe, software certification already has an established basis in the CENELEC Memorandum of Understanding M-IT-03 which deals with conformance testing and certification.

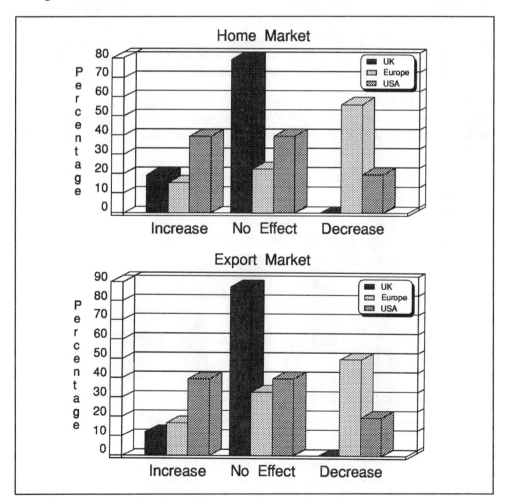

Figure B.4 Impact of New Standards on Costs and Prices in Home and Export Markets

B-25   The Health and Safety Executive (HSE) is the most widely known body believed to be involved in the certification of safety-related systems, with its influence spanning most industry sectors. HSE would not welcome this view (it does not regard itself as a regulatory body), but it is widespread throughout industry in the UK, Europe and the USA, particularly in Germany where the Technische Uberwachungs-Verein (TUV) performs that function. The TUV is a systems assessment and approval organisation, with several specialised branches throughout Germany.

B-26   Other regulatory bodies are industry-specific; they are much less visible and their standards have much less use outside those industries.

B-27   Certification of safety-related systems is a major issue repeatedly raised by UK industry. Questions were asked as to whether certification is necessary, and if so by whom and with respect to what (chapter 5 of this document refers).

B-28   The majority of all interviewees in favour of certification do not foresee insurmountable problems with third party assessment. Those who do anticipate problems are concerned almost equally with confidentiality and cost. The majority of UK industry felt that if the problems can be resolved, certification should be conducted by a third party. The degree of support for third party certification is shown in Figure B.6.

Experience and Qualifications of Person(s) Carrying out Certification
B-29   In the UK, the majority (68%) of interviewees feel that certifiers should have as a minimum a degree in an engineering discipline and 53% of interviewees

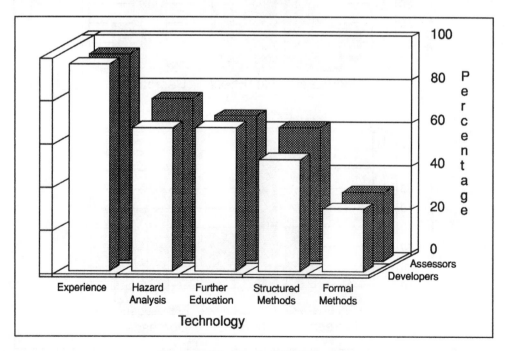

Figure B.5 Training in SCS (UK only)

commented that the certifier should have an additional specialist professional qualification at the level of Chartered Engineer, Professional Engineer or Dipl.Ing.

B-30   The range of length of experience thought to be necessary for a qualification as a certifier varies from one to five years. The average of the views of interviewees in all geographical areas is that a minimum of three years' experience is necessary.

Basis for Certification
B-31   Amongst all those interviewed, there is a marked preference that the basis for certification of a safety-related system should be determined by the needs of the application (i.e. the kind of system in which the computer subsystem/software is to be used), rather than by the personnel involved in its development.

Legal Liability
B-32   Table B.3 shows the percentages of all interviewees who appeared ignorant of the legal position (in both their home and foreign countries). As might be expected, greater ignorance exists in the UK with respect to the legal implications in other countries in Europe and the USA, and vice versa. It should be noted that 38% of UK indus-

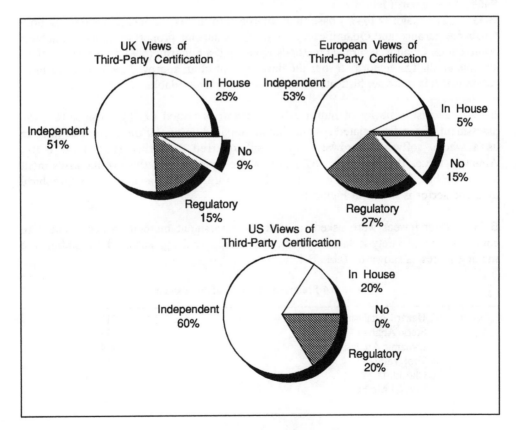

Figure B.6 Certification by Third Party

try is not aware that the concept of strict liability now applies in the UK as a result of the Consumer Protection Act 1987 implementing the EC Directive on Product Liability, and that 62% of UK industry is not aware of the legal position in foreign countries. There is also a lack of appreciation of the potential effects of different legal traditions. For example, it came to light during the study that within different legal systems approaches to interpretation of the law are different; for example whereas in the UK the law is interpreted according to the letter, in France it is interpreted according to the spirit.

Table B.3 Awareness of Legal Position

	Home	Foreign
	(%)	(%)
UK	38	62
Europe*	25	32
US	0	29

* In the case of Europe, 'foreign' refers to other European countries.

Safety Assessment Methods

B-33   The majority (64%) base their approach to the assessment of systems on both Quality Assurance and Quantification methods. A smaller proportion (26%) base their approach on Quality Assurance methods alone, and a minority (5%) do not assess their systems at all. The majority favour the development of an approved method of quantification which is more sophisticated than those currently available.

B-34   A vast majority of industry in all countries visited (95%) consider that the assessment of a safety-related system should be based on one of the categories (system as a whole, software, hardware, operation) referred to earlier (paragraph B-10). Amongst these, the majority (56%) are of the opinion that the overall assessment should be based on the system as a whole. A more detailed analysis by geographical area and sector is shown in Figure B.7.

B-35   Interviewees were asked to rank the assessment methods which would give confidence in a Safety-Related System. An overall ranking, achieved by adding the ranking scores, is shown in Table B.4.

Table B.4 Preferred Methods of Assessment

Hazard Analysis	212
Static Analysis	137
Dynamic Analysis	134
Tool Validation	113
Checklists	99
Formal Methods	98
Others	77

C. Recommendations

Development and Use of Standards

B-36   UK participation in the development of international standards must continue so that the methods and techniques used in UK industry for the development of software are reflected in any new or revised standards. This will help to preserve the present UK advantage in competing for business in Europe and the USA, and will help to ensure that any new or revised standards are of value to and are used by UK industry.

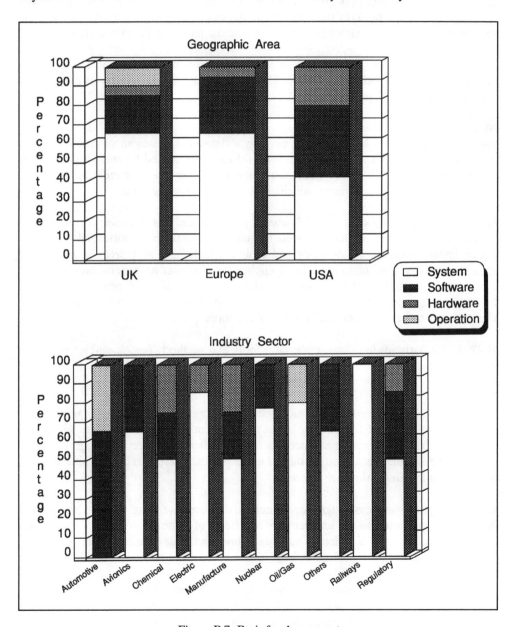

Figure B.7 Basis for Assessment

B-37   The DTI needs to do more to make industry aware of standards and guide-lines, and particularly those concerned with safety as distinct from quality, and to per-suade them of the benefits of compliance with them.

B-38   The development of industry-specific standards, like Def Stan 00-55, should be discouraged unless they are based on generic international standards.

B-39   The DTI should take steps to ensure that common standards apply throughout the EC. In particular the DTI should promote the work of CENELEC with respect to the subject in general and to the Memorandum of Understanding M-IT-03 in particular.

B-40   The UK must make efforts in Europe to promote the ideas in the proposed IEC standard. Their widespread use in Europe will benefit UK industry as they largely reflect established UK practice.

Methodologies and Tools
B-41   There should be a study to develop a detailed assessment of common auto-mated methodologies and configuration control tools being used by and within industry and to compare these with the many requirements of the various standards. The study should also address requirements which are not met by existing tools.

B-42   There is a need to establish coding practices and analysis tools for the C pro-gramming language. C is the preferred language for small-scale embedded micropro-cessor systems because of the skills and tools available, and an increasing number of such systems are used in safety-related applications, so that its general lack of accep-tance causes a problem. It is not however the language itself which poses the problem, but the way in which it is currently used. It would therefore be possible to overcome this problem by providing practices and analysis tools.

B-43   Similarly an initiative to develop tools and methods for Assembler program-ming is indicated.

Liability
B-44   The DTI should mount an awareness programme to make engineers and industry more aware of the liability issues that currently exist. UK industry will other-wise lose orders to European competitors through their ignorance of foreign practices. It is highly desirable that action be taken before the EC Directives on Machinery Safety and General Product Safety are enacted.

B-45   In the awareness programme mentioned above (paragraph B-44) there should be a clear explanation to the engineer of the effects of different systems of legal inter-pretation. The subtlety of different interpretations, and their possible effects, must also be made known to those involved in importing systems from abroad.

B-46   Work should be undertaken jointly by practitioners in law and in safety assess-ment to clarify (as far as may be possible) the position with regard to liability for safety-related systems and to make industry aware of the position.

Assessment

B-47   Interviewees feel that there is need for quantification of software characteristics. Further research should be undertaken on quantification to develop a practical method of measurement which will enable developers and assessors to decide whether software has achieved the acceptable safety integrity level.

Certification

B-48   Adoption of third party certification will place a demand on assessing organisations and on procedures for the accreditation of such organisations. In the initial stages, these accreditation procedures will require support, comparable to that given to BS 5750 at its introduction, to ensure that the facilities are available to industry when they are needed and bottlenecks are avoided.

B-49   Certification cannot be pursued in isolation, since unless system design and development can be carried out using methods which assure success, certification will be a cause of conflict and delay.

Training

B-50   If the requirement for a change in development and assessment practices put forward by UK industry is to be achieved then a significant training programme will be needed.

B-51   To have the greatest impact in the shortest time, training will need to be balanced to the stated requirements of industry and cannot concentrate too heavily on particular specialised topics.

B-52   Effort is needed to make the knowledge and experience of the broad range of aspects of development and assessment of safety-related software which already exists in particular industrial sectors more widely available through the rapid establishment of post-experience courses and other mechanisms for technology transfer.

B-53   Priority should be given to generally applicable areas of Hazard Analysis rather than Formalised or Formal Methods.

B-54   Emphasis should be put on the inclusion of languages such as Modula-2 and Ada in training at all levels, to develop their use in preference to C.

B-55   Assessment of safety at the system level is a multi-disciplined task and implies a body of understanding embracing the effect of the software on the underlying hardware. This must be taken into account in providing training capacity and designing syllabi.

Cost-Benefit Analysis

B-56   Investigations, based on actual cases, of the costs and benefits of adopting safety practices should be carried out in the manner used for quality costs in the past.

APPENDIX C   DTI GRANT SCOPE

C-1   Subject to certain terms and conditions, the Secretary of State for Trade and Industry made a grant to the Institution of Electrical Engineers under Section 5 of the Service and Technology Act 1965 for consideration of Safety Critical Systems at Savoy Place, London, in collaboration with the British Computer Society, the grant to cover two thirds of the net eligible costs up to a stated maximum. The project had to be conducted in accordance with the Department's letter dated 24 November 1987 under the Department's Support for Innovation, and the detailed proposal submitted to the Department on 3 December 1987.

C-2   The Department's letter contained the following statements:-

1. ...Our hope is that such a joint project will help to ensure co-ordination between the many activities in the safety critical systems field and it is essential that the IEE/BCS work is complementary to work being led by the Health and Safety Executive. We would expect the work to cover the aspects described below and I hope these accord with the objectives of the Public Affairs Board Software Engineering Committee and its sub-group as well as with those of the BCS safety critical committee.

2. On regulatory aspects we would expect the study to identify and describe current requirements for systems (standards and codes of practice as well as the formal legislative requirements) in the UK and internationally. This would assist companies and individual systems engineers to prepare for market requirements. Assessment of the overlaps and inconsistencies in standards and codes and identification of the gaps in coverage would help to point the way forward. It will be necessary to address different applications and sectors of industry separately in order to consider whether current requirements cause problems or are adequate. The study would need to consider both commercial and technical trends and their implications for regulations and guidance, including evaluating new methods and approaches which might be appropriate in some market sectors. The aim of the review should be to set out a framework within which practical issues regarding standards development, certification or liability can be addressed.

3. Any review of regulatory aspects must be carried out in close liaison with the Health and Safety Executive.

4. In order to avoid unnecessary divergence of standards between defence and civil sectors it would be important for the IEE/BCS to establish liaison with MoD who are currently drawing up standards in this area.

5. On liability it would be necessary to interact with existing IEE, BCS and Computing Services Association groups who are looking at liability issues. The problems facing the individual systems engineer and companies may be increasing. In some sectors there is likely to be an impact from new product liability legislation while in others the emphasis will remain on proving negligence. Systems in use in medical diagnosis and medical care may deserve special attention and it would also be useful to consider a range of applications such as vehicle control systems as well as process control.

6. Certification issues will need to be covered as part of a study of the regulatory framework for safety critical software. You will need to look at certification for the individual systems engineer, for assessors of systems, for supply organisations and at the certification of systems (as they are developed as well as they go into use) and of products. It might be useful to consider whether certification schemes already in use in one applications field could be applied in other areas.

C-3   The detailed proposals submitted to, and agreed by, the Department included the following statement:

Aspects to be covered

1.   Regulatory

(a) Describe current requirements for systems (standards, codes of practice, formal legislative requirements) in the UK and internationally, covering different application areas and sectors of industry.

(b) Assess overlaps and inconsistencies in standards and codes; identify adequacy of current requirements and gaps in coverage.

(c) Consider commercial and technical trends and their implications for regulations and guidelines. Evaluate new methods and approaches which may be appropriate in some market sectors.

(d) Set out a framework within which practical issues regarding standards development certification or liability can be addressed.

(e) Liaise closely with the Health and Safety Executive, the Ministry of Defence and the NCC (STARTS initiative).

2.   Liability

(a) Interact with existing IEE, British Computer Society and Computing Services Association groups studying liability issues. Consider the impact of new product liability legislation.

(b) Give special attention to systems used in medical diagnosis and medical care.

(c) Consider a range of applications such as vehicle control systems as well as process control.

3.   Certification

(a) Review and compare certification schemes already in use. Consider their applicability to other areas.

(b) Consider certification requirements for: –

- individual systems engineers

- assessors of systems

- supply organisations

- systems in development

- systems in use.

APPENDIX D   **DEFINITIONS**

Introductory Note: Figure D.1 illustrates relationships between certain of the terms.

Availability:
The probability that a system will be able to perform its designated function when required for use.

Compliance:
A synonym for conformance (*q.v.*). Alternatively compliance may be used distinctively from conformance. Where a distinction is made, conformance implies reference to a standard with objectively assessable requirements, and compliance implies reference to documents such as codes of practice in which some or all of the requirements stated in terms such that they are not readily amenable to objective assessment of being met.

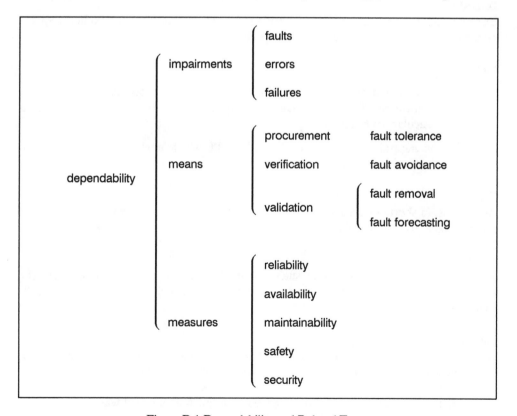

Figure D.1 Dependability and Related Terms

Conformance:
A product or process is said to conform to a standard when it meets the relevant requirements within it. (See also Compliance.)

Dependability:
The property of a PES that allows reliance to be justifiably placed on the service it delivers.

Dependability is a term covering all the principal characteristics used in connection with safety-related software. (See Figure D.1.)

Design Fault:
A design (specification, coding) fault results from a (human) failure occurring during the design of a system. A design fault causes an error, which may reside undetected within a (sub)system until the input values to that (sub)system are such that the produced result does not conform to the specification. This constitutes the failure of that (sub)system. If the same input values appear again, the same erroneous results will be produced.

Diversity:
Existence of different means of performing a required function (e.g. other physical principles, other ways of solving the same problem).

Environment:

1. The situation and conditions within which a system exists and operates. The specification of a safety-related system may refer to the requirements of a particular environment (e.g. submarine).

2. The natural and man-made human world, which might be at risk from the failure of a safety-related system.

Error:
An error is, in short, a detected deviation from the agreed specification of requirements which is liable to lead to failure.

Fail-Safe:
The built-in capability of a system such that predictable (or specified) equipment (or service) failure modes result only in the system reaching and remaining in a safe fall-back state.

Failure:
A system failure occurs when the delivered service deviates from the specified service, where the service specification is an agreed description of the expected service.

A failure, in short, is a manifestation of an error in the system or software.

Fault:
A fault is a defect that gives rise to an error.

Fault Avoidance:
The process carried out prior to the bringing of a system into operation in order to maximise its reliability: these include thorough testing of individual modules, and validation of the design.

Fault Recovery (Re-try Mechanism):
Fault recovery refers to the inclusion in software of elements intended to ensure that, in the event of a failure of a piece of software (a module or part thereof), there will be an automatic attempt to re-try that piece of software.

Fault Tolerance:
The built-in capability of a system to provide continued correct execution, i.e. provision of service as specified, in the presence of a limited number of hardware or software faults.

Formal Methods:
Formal methods are mathematically based techniques whose rigorous application enables the correctness of software to be verified against the specification of that software. For this process to take place, there must also be a formal specification. The creation of this specification is itself part of formal methods.

Graceful Degradation:
When a failure is detected in a system, the system may respond by ceasing to operate completely. Alternatively it may continue to operate partially, thereby providing those of its functions which are not affected by the failure. Further failures may lead to further diminution of functionality. This second alternative (and the provision of appropriate warnings to operators) is referred to as graceful degradation.

Hazard:
A situation in which there is actual or potential hazard to human life or limb, or the environment.

HAZOP:
Hazard and Operability survey technique (paragraph 4.12).

Maintainability:
The ability of an item under given conditions to be retained in or restored to a state, in which it can perform the required function.

Mandatory:
Implies a requirement to conform. This requirement may derive from legislation, governmental or other regulation, or from codes of practice, etc. agreed by a professional or trade association.

Mistake:
A mistake is a human failure. It is a human action that produces an unintended result (in design, programming or operation).

Modularity:
An attribute of software, which refers its being comprised of a structure of highly independent computer program units (modules) that are discrete and identifiable with respect to translating, testing and combining with other units.

Programmable Electronic System (PES):
A system, based on a computer, connected to sensors and/or actuators on a plant for the purpose of control, protection or monitoring.

Physical Fault:
Physical faults are either caused by an ageing effect of a component of the system or by external interference (magnetic, electrostatic, etc.). If a component becomes damaged, then the fault is a permanent fault; otherwise the fault is a transient fault.

Redundancy:
Provision of additional elements or systems so that any one can perform the required function regardless of the state of operation or failure of any other. Redundancy can be implemented by identical elements (identical redundancy) or by diverse elements (diverse redundancy).

Reliability:
The probability that during a certain amount of time a system performs the functions described in the specification of requirements under the stated conditions (environment, costs, inputs and hardware, time constraints).

Requirement:
A statement of a criterion which must be met if a particular product or process, etc., is to be deemed to be acceptable, in relation to a technical or procurement specification.

Risk:
The combination of the frequency, or probability, and the consequence of a specified hazardous event.

Robustness:
The extent to which systems and subsystems, including software, can continue to operate correctly despite the introduction of invalid inputs and/or faults in systems components.

Safe Fall-back State:
A safe state which can be attained by the system at any stage in operation. The attainment of this safe state may mean that the system does not meet its specification of requirements.

Safe State:
A state of a system in which there is no danger to human life, economics or environment.

Safety:
Freedom from unacceptable risk of personal harm (BS 0: Pt 3: 1981, Clause 10.11). The likelihood that a system does not lead to a state in which human life or environment are endangered. (**Note**: Safety relates to all aspects of a system, all its subsystems, to the environment in which it operates, to human factors such as operator error or wrongdoing, and to incorrect data. Some factors related to safety can readily be quantified; others may only be considered qualitatively.)

Safety Integrity:
The likelihood of a safety-related system achieving the required safety functions under all the stated conditions within a stated period of time.

Safety-Related Software:
Software which forms part of a safety-related system.

Safety-Related System:
A system by which the overall safety of a process, machinery or equipment is assured.

Security:
Fault tolerance against deliberate interaction faults (intrusion) from internal or external sources.

Software:
Programs, procedures, rules and associated documentation pertaining to the operation of a computer system.

Software Safety Integrity Level:
An indicator of the extent to which there is assurance that software is safe.

Software Lifecycle:
The period of time that starts when software is conceived and ends when the software is no longer in use. The software lifecycle typically includes a requirements phase, design phases, an implementation phase, test phases, an installation phase, and a maintenance phase.

Standard:
A document which establishes criteria by which the qualities of products or processes may be objectively assessed; each criterion involves a requirement. Standards of this kind are specifically referred to as normative standards.

More generally, 'standards' also refers to guidelines, codes of practice, etc. These may be concerned with advice, with methods by which the requirements of a normative standard can be met, or with standard-like information which is, however, open to interpretation rather than being capable of objective assessment. Some standards contain both requirements and guidelines as to the achievement of those.

System:

A system is a set of components which interact according to a design. A component of a system can be another system (called a subsystem). Such components (subsystems) may be:

- controlling or controlled system;

- hardware, software, human interaction;

- input and output subsystems.

Tolerable Risk:

Because (a) absolute safety can never be guaranteed and (b) there is a point at which increased safety measures cannot be justified because they add to the cost of a product to an extent which cannot be justified in relation to the added protection they provide, it is necessary to accept that a certain level of risk has to be regarded as acceptable. (**Note**: in this respect, cost refers not only to economic costs, but to operational and functional requirements, convenience, etc.) [Based on BS 0: Pt 3: 1981, Clause 10.2]

Validation:

The test and evaluation of the integrated software conformance/system to ensure with a statement of the user's requirements (see also note under Verification).

Verification:

The process of determining whether or not the product of each phase of the software life cycle development process fulfils all the requirements specified in the previous phase.

Validation is generally used to refer to a larger process than verification. In particular, whereas verification tests software against the specification for that software, validation of a system is concerned with whether the operation of the system provides the results needed by the user. Validation therefore involves consideration of whether the specification of a system sufficiently and accurately represents the needs of the intending user.

APPENDIX E — ACRONYMS

ACARD	Advisory Council for Applied Research and Development (UK)
ACOPS	Approved Codes of Practice [used by Health and Safety Commission (UK) see paragraph 3.5]
API	American Petroleum Institute
AQAP	Allied Quality Assurance Publications (NATO)
ASIC	Application Specific Integrated Circuit
ASME	American Society of Mechanical Engineers
BCS	British Computer Society
BS	British Standard
BSI	British Standards Institution
CAA	Civil Aviation Authority (UK)
CASE	Computer-Assisted Software Engineering
CEGB	Central Electricity Generating Board
CEN	European Committee for Standardisation (Comité Européen de Normalisation, see paragraph 3.7)
CENELEC	European Committee for Electrotechnical Standardisation (Comité Européen de Normalisation Electrotechnique)
CIMAH	Control of Industrial Major Accident Hazards Regulations (UK, 1984)
CPA	Consumer Protection Act (1987, UK)
Def Stan	Defence Standard (issued by MoD)
DoD	Department of Defense (USA)
DoE	Department of the Environment (UK)
DoH	Department of Health (UK)
DTI	Department of Trade and Industry (UK)
DTp	Department of Transport (UK)
EC	European Community
EEMUA	Engineering Equipment and Material Users Association

EPA	Environmental Protection Agency (USA)
EPROM	Erasable Programmable Read-Only Memory
EUROCAE	European Organisation for Civil Aviation Electronics
EWICS	European Workshop on Industrial Computer Systems
FAA	Federal Aviation Authority (USA)
FAR	Federal Airworthiness Regulations (USA)
FCC	Federal Communications Commission (USA) (medical)
FDA	Food and Drug Administration (USA)
FMEA	Failure Modes and Effect Analysis
FMECA	Failure Modes, Effects and Criticality Analysis
HAZOP	HAZard and OPerability survey technique
HSE	Health and Safety Executive (UK)
HSWA	Health and Safety at Work [etc.] Act (1974, UK)
IAEA	International Atomic Energy Agency
ICAO	International Civil Aviation Organization
IEC	International Electrotechnical Commission
IEE	Institution of Electrical Engineers
IFAC	International Conference on Automatic Control (Düsseldorf)
IRC	Interdisciplinary Research Council
Mil Std	Military Standard (US)
MoD	Ministry of Defence (UK)
MMI	Man–Machine Interface
NALM	National Association of Lift Manufacturers
NAMAS	National Measurement and Accreditation Service
NES	Non-Erasable Storage
NESC	National Energy Software Center
NIHHS	National Institutes of Health and Human Services
NPL	National Physical Laboratory
PES	Programmable Electronic System (see Appendix D, Definitions)
QRA	Quantified Risk Assessment
RSRE	Royal Signals and Radar Establishment
RTCA	Radio Technical Commission for Aeronautics (USA)

SAFECOMP	Safety in computer systems. Series of conferences organised by IFAC (see Ref. 95)
SERC	Science and Engineering Research Council
STARTS	Software Tools for Application to large Real Time Systems (DTI) (Refs 100*ff*)
TRA	Technical Requirements Analysis
UKAEA	UK Atomic Energy Authority
VDE	Verein Deutscher Ingenieure

APPENDIX F

BIBLIOGRAPHY AND REFERENCES

The bibliography contains items documented during the study. However, the inclusion or otherwise of any item should not be taken as indicating that it was or was not considered, and inclusion of an item does not imply that the views expressed in it are supported by the Project Team. Some references are to work not yet completed and to unpublished items.

1 [Anon]
   Product liability – Commission begins proceedings against Member States. *EEC FOCUS* March 1989. p 15.

2 Advisory Council for Applied Research and Development
   Software: a vital key to UK competitiveness. HMSO, 1986.

3 Alvey Software Reliability Modelling Project
   Guidelines for the reliability and safety assessment of software (GRASS). [Under development.]

4 Anderson, T
   Safe and secure computing systems. Blackwell Scientific, 1989.

5 Backhouse, R
   Program construction and verification. Prentice-Hall, 1986.

6 Barnes, M
   Seeking a standard framework for dependable computing. *Nuclear Engineering International.* May 1989. 30-32.

7 Bennett, P
   Safety critical control software. *Control & Instrumentation* 20(9) September 1988. 75, 77.

8 Bloomfield, R E and Froome, P K D
   Aspects of the licensing and assessment of computer safety systems. In Anderson, T. *Safe and secure computing systems,* Chapter 1. Blackwell, 1989.

9 Bramson, B E
   Design recommendations for the production of safety critical software. (Unpublished paper from RSRE, September 1986).

10 British Computer Society
    IT standards policy for the BCS. BCS, November 1988.

11 British Computer Society. Safety Critical Systems Group
    Report of the Education Working Party. Revised report appears as part III of this book.

12   British Standards Institution. BS 0: Part 1: 1974
     A standard for standards: introduction to standardization. BSI, 1974.

13   British Standards Institution. BS 4778: 1979
     Glossary of terms used in quality assurance (including reliability and maintainability terms). BSI, 1979.

14   British Standards Institution. BS 5655: Part 1: 1986.
     Lifts and service lifts: safety rules for the construction and installation of electronic lifts. BSI, 1986 (EN 81: Part 1: 1985).

15   British Standards Institution. BS 5750: Part 0: Section 0.1: 1987
     Quality systems: guide to selection and use. BSI, 1987 (ISO 9000 – 1987).

16   British Standards Institution. BS 5750: Part 0: Section 0.2: 1987
     Quality systems: guide to quality management and quality system elements. BSI, 1987 (ISO 9004 – 1987).

17   British Standards Institution. BS 5750: Part 1: 1987
     Specification for design/development, production, installation and servicing. BSI, 1987 (ISO 9001 – 1987).

18   British Standards Institution. BS 5750: Part 2: 1987
     Quality systems: specification for production and installation. BSI, 1987 (ISO 9002 – 1987).

19   British Standards Institution. BS 5750: Part 3: 1987
     Quality systems: specification for final inspection and test. BSI, 1987 (ISO 9003 – 1987).

20   Carre, B A *et al.*
     SPADE: Southampton program analysis and development environments. In Sommerville, I. (Ed.) *Software engineering environments,* Ch 9. Peregrinus, 1986.

21   CENELEC
     Guide to certification of products not fully covered by safety standards because of technical progress. CENELEC, 1980 (Memorandum no. 7).

22   Central Electricity Generating Board
     Guidelines for the use of programmable electronic systems for reactor protection, by M E Jolly and S W Johnson. CEGB, November 1987.

23   Civil Aviation Authority
     Report of the System Integrity Working Party. CAA, 1986.

24   Civil Aviation Authority
     Software management and certification guidelines. CAA, July 1986. (Airworthiness Notice, no 45A).

25   Commission on Technical Specifications, Testing and Certification
     Policy statement of the Commission . . . a global approach. DTI, November 1988.

26   Crouch, E A C and Wilson, R
     Risk assessment and comparisons: an introduction. *Science* 236 1987. 267.

27   Cullyer, W J and Pygott, C H
      Application of formal methods to the VIPER microprocessor. *IEE Proceedings E*
      134(3) May 1987. 133-141.

28   Curritt, P A *et al.*
      Certifying the reliability of software. *IEEE Transactions on Software Engineering*
      SE-12(1) January 1986. 3-11.

29   Daniels, B K (Ed.)
      Achieving safety and reliability with computer systems. [Proceedings of a confer-
      ence held at Altrincham, November 1987] Elsevier Applied Science, 1987.

30   Daniels, B K and Hughes, M
      Literature survey of computer software reliability. UKAEA, 1979.

31   Department of Defense. Mil Std 882B
      System safety program requirements. Department of Defense.

32   Department of Defense. Mil Std 1629A
      Procedures for performing a failure mode, effect and criticality analysis. Department
      of Defense.

33   Department of Defense. Mil Std 2167A
      Defense system software development. Department of Defense [1988].

34   Department of Defense. Computer Security Center.
      Trusted computer system evaluation criteria. Department of Defense, August 1983.
      (CSC-STD-001-83).

35   Dorling, A *et al.*
      Software standards strategy: a special study for the DTI. [Unpublished] Jan. 1989.

36   Duke, E L
      V & V of flight and mission-critical software. *IEEE Software* May 1989. 39-45.

37   Electronic Engineering Association
      *Assessment criteria for reviewing emerging standards, guidelines and codes of prac-
      tice in the field of safety critical systems.* EEA, April 1989.

38   Engineering Employers Federation
      *Management of software projects: a guide for senior managers in the engineering
      industry.* EEF, April 1988.

39   Eurenberger, W D *et al.*
      Licensing issues associated with the use of computers in the nuclear industry. Cen-
      tral Electricity Council, no date (Contract no EC1-1415-B7221-85-D (CEC)).

40   EWICS TC 7
      *Guidelines for the maintenance and modification of safety-related computer sys-
      tems.* EWICS, November 1987.

41   EWICS TC 7
      Safety assessment and design of industrial computer systems: techniques directory.
      Editor P G Bishop. EWICS, November 1987.

42   Fetzer, J H
     Program verification: the very idea. *Communications of the ACM* 31(9) September
     1988. 1048-1063.

43   [Finniston Report]
     *Engineering our future: report of the Committee of Enquiry into the Engineering Pro-
     fession.* HMSO, 1980 (Cmnd 7794).

44   Food and Drug Administration (US)
     Draft guidelines for reviewers of computer-controlled medical devices.

45   Froome, P and Monahan, B
     The role of mathematically formal methods in the development and assessment of
     safety critical systems. *Microprocessors and Microsystems* 12(10) December 1988.
     539-546.

46   Gardner, A
     Human factors guidelines for the design of computer-based systems. MoD/DTI,
     1989.

47   Gruman, G
     Software safety focus of new British standard [Def Stan 0055]. *IEEE Software*
     May 1989. 95-96.

48   Gütegemeinschaft Software e V
     Software with a quality seal. Gütegemeinschaft Software, 1988.

49   Hatchard, L
     Applying the principles of the HSE guidelines to programmable electronic sys-
     tems in safety-related applications. *Safety & Reliability* 8(1) Spring 1988. 30-36.

50   Health and Safety Commission
     *The protection of persons against ionising radiation arising from any work activity:
     the Ionising Radiations Regulations 1985.* HMSO, 1985.

51   Health and Safety Executive
     Essentials of health and safety at work. HMSO, 1988.

52   Health and Safety Executive
     Industrial robot safety. HMSO, 1988.

53   Health and Safety Executive
     *Programmable electronic systems in safety-related applications. 1 – an introductory
     guide.* HMSO, 1987.

54   Health and Safety Executive
     *Programmable electronic systems in safety-related applications. 2 – general techni-
     cal guidelines.* HMSO, 1987.

55   Health and Safety Executive
     Safety-related software study [ongoing project]

56   Health and Safety Executive
     Safety-related software study: news release. HSE, October 1988.

57 Health and Safety Executive
Tolerability of risk from nuclear power stations. HMSO, 1988.

58 Helps, K A
Some verification tools and methods for airborne safety critical software. *Software Engineering Journal* 1(6) November 1986. 248-253.

59 Henderson, P
Functional programming, formal specification and rapid prototyping. *IEEE Transactions on Software Engineering* SE12(2) February 1986. 241-250.

60 Holloway, N
The significance of human actions for plant safety. *Atom (379)* May 1988. 2-7.

61 Imperial Chemical Industries plc
Safety engineers workbench (techniques and tools for computer safety and reliability). (Unpublished project proposal, accepted June 1988).

62 Institution of Electrical Engineers
Software requirements for high-integrity systems: proceedings of a colloquium, London 1988. IEE, 1988.

63 Institution of Electrical Engineers
Programmable electronic systems and safety – HSE guidelines: proceedings of a colloquium, June, 1987. IEE, 1987 (Digest no 74).

64 Institution of Electrical Engineers
Health and safety legislation, and consumer legislation: guidance for the engineer: professional brief. IEE, 1988.

65 Institution of Gas Engineers
The use of programmable electronic systems in safety-related applications in the gas industry [draft for comment]. Institution of Gas Engineers, July 1988.

66 International Civil Aviation Organisation. All-Weather Operations Panel *The assessment of the integrity of systems containing safety critical software.* ICAO, October 1987.

67 International Electrotechnical Commission
Functional safety of programmable electronic systems: generic aspects (proposal for a standard): Part 1: General requirements. IEC (not yet issued; reference is SC65A/WG10).

68 International Electrotechnical Commission
Software for computers in the application of industrial safety-related systems (proposal for a standard). IEC, June 1989 (Document number SC65A/WG9/45).

69 Jones, C B
Systematic software development using VDM. Prentice-Hall, 1986.

70 Leveson, N G
Software safety: why, what and how. *ACM Computing Surveys* 18(2) June 1986 125-163.

71 Leveson, N G and Harvey, P R
Analysing software safety. *IEEE Transactions on Software Engineering* SE-9(5)
September 1983. 569-579.

72 McDermid, J A
The role for formal methods in software development. *Journal of Information
Technology*2(3) September 1987. 124-134.

73 McDermid, J A
Principles of an assurance algebra for dependable software. University of York,
Dept of Computer Science, September 1989. (YCS 123).

74 McDermid, J A
Towards assurance measures for high integrity software.
In *Proceedings of Reliability 89.* Institute of Quality Assurance, 1989.

75 McDermid, J A and Ripken, K
Lifecycle support in the Ada environment. Cambridge University Press, 1984.

76 Ministry of Defence. Def Stan 00-31.
Development of safety critical software for airborne systems. MoD, 1987.

77 Ministry of Defence. Def Stan 00-55
Requirements for the procurement of safety critical software in defence equipment
(draft for discussion). MoD, May 1989

78 Ministry of Defence. Def Stan 00-56
Requirements for the analysis of safety critical hazards (draft for discussion). MoD,
May 1989.

79 Ministry of Defence
Standards for Defence, Section 4: Defence Standards Index, issue 5. MoD, January
1989.

80 Mitchell, I H
The design and testing of applications databases for a railway signalling system. In
*International Conference on Software Engineering for Real Time Systems, Cirences-
ter, September 1987.* IERE, 1988. 159-164.

81 Munro, D
Spotting software errors sooner [MALPAS static analysis system]. *Nuclear Engineering International* May 1989 33-34.

82 National Association of Lift Makers
Programmable electronic systems in safety-related applications. National Association of Lift Makers, August 1988.

83 NATO. AQAP 13
NATO software quality control system requirements. August 1981. [available from
Directorate of Standardization, Ministry of Defence, Glasgow].

84 NCSR(UK)
Guidelines for the reliability and safety assessment. (in preparation; being developed under the Alvey Software Reliability Modelling Project).

85   Neely, R B and Freeman J W
Structuring systems for formal verification.
In *Proceedings of the IEEE Symposium for Security and Privacy, 1985.* IEEE Computing Society Press, 1985. 2-13.

86   Neilan, P
The assessment of safety-related systems containing software. In *Proceedings of the CSR Conference on Certification, 1988.*

87   Nuclear Regulatory Commission (US). NUREG-0492
Fault tree handbook. NRC, January 1981.

88   Nuclear Regulatory Commission (US). NUREG-2300
PRA procedures guide. NRC, 1988-89 (EPI Report NP5613).

89   Nuclear Regulatory Commission (US). CR-4780
Procedures in safety and reliability studies (2 Vols). NRC, January 1983.

90   Nunns, S R and Kilby, M A
Introduction to software hazard and operability procedures. [Unpublished ICI paper.]

91   Nunns, S R *et al.*
Programmable electronic systems safety: standards and principles: an industrial viewpoint. In *SAFECOMP '86. Proceedings of the 5th IFAC Workshop, Sarlat.* Pergamon, 1986. 17-20.

92   O'Neill, G and Wichmann, B A
A contribution to the debate on safety critical software. NPL, September 1988. (NPL Report DITC 126/88).

93   Ould, M
Safe software: the state of the art. *Information Technology and Public Policy.* 6(3) Summer 1988. 215-218.

94   Radio Technical Commission for Aeronautics (US)
Software considerations in airborne systems and equipment certification. CAE, March 1985 (RTCA/D0-178A; EUROCAE-ED12A).

95   SAFECOMP '86
Trends in safe real time computer systems. Proceedings of the 5th IFAC Workshop, Sarlat, France, 1986. Pergamon, 1986.

96   Sennett, C T
High integrity software. Pitman, 1989.

97   Shore, J
Why I never met a programmer I could trust. *Communications of the ACM* 31(4) April 1988. 372-375.

98   Slovic, P
Informing and educating the public about risk. *Risk Analysis* 6(4) 1986. 403-415.

99 Starr, C
Risk management, assessment and acceptability. *Risk Analysis* 5(2) 1985. 57-102.

100 STARTS Purchasers' Group
IT-STARTS developers' guide. STARTS Secretariat, National Computing Centre, March 1989.

101 STARTS Purchasers' Group
Successful procurement strategies for large real time systems. STARTS Secretariat, National Computing Centre, 1988.

102 STARTS Purchasers' Group
STARTS purchasers' handbook: software tools for application to large real time systems. National Computing Centre, 2nd ed 1989. (Chapter 7: Software in safety-related systems.)

103 Thomas, M
Should we trust computers?
Fraud & Security Bulletin 10(12) October 1988. 6-11 (part 1); and 1(1) November 1988. 15-21 (part 2). [Also in *Information Technology and Public Policy* 7(3) Summer 1989. 174-186.]

104 *Workshop on Software Testing, Analysis and Verification, 2nd, Banff, July 1988. Proceedings.* IEEE Computer Society Press, 1988.

UK Statutes

105 Civil jurisdiction and judgements act. 1982.

106 Civil liability (contribution) act. 1978.

107 Consumer protection act. 1987.

108 Health and safety at work (etc.) act. 1974.

109 Sale of goods act. 1979.

110 Supply of goods and services act. 1982.

APPENDIX G IEE/BCS OPEN CONSULTATIVE MEETING ON SAFETY-RELATED SYSTEMS

held at the IEE on 26 September 1988

Excerpts from the summing-up speech by the afternoon Chairman, **Dr Brian W Oakley**:

It seems to me that we have been tackling today a problem which seems in a sense new to us: though I suppose that in our different ways we have all been conscious of it looming over us whenever we suddenly realise that we have got too complex. I think there must be many people in this hall who had this reaction when that point was raised today. Presumably somewhere in Birdcage Walk the professional society tended to get rather worried after the Tay Bridge disaster led on to certification of one sort or another, and there must have been a very similar sort of exercise at the IEE after the early Ferranti power station disasters. I think we are agreed that there are a lot of precedents that we can learn from, and we must do so.

We have really concentrated today on harmonisation to try to get the best, not the lowest common denominator, out of the various approaches that are being taken. I think that the professional societies are perhaps best equipped to strike this balance, and that must be their aim. I think we have to face a fact which is sometimes unwelcome: safety is always a matter of what you're prepared to pay. There is no absolute level of safety, in that there is some price which society, or individuals, are prepared to pay but no more. Maybe one of the great lessons from today is that safety does cost, and perhaps as an industry we are not really ready at the moment to pay what we know we will be forced to pay after the first serious disasters.

If I pick out some of the highlights from today, I think that the Health and Safety Executive is giving us a lead, as they have produced a guide primarily to help other bodies produce regulations for their specific sectors. We heard the rather depressing thought that only hardware can be given a measure of fault tolerance with any hope of it being correct. Perhaps some of us will argue with that but it is a sobering thought.

MoD tell us that the Defence Standard 00-55 will be out for comment early in 1989. We heard quite a firm statement that all personnel involved should have suitable training, though it wasn't yet defined just what that meant, and possibly should be required to acquire chartered software or chartered system safety standard. (Incidentally we have really been talking about systems all day, even though perhaps more often than not we were thinking of the software part of it.) I think MoD also said that they will possibly require the listing of key chartered personnel in contract documents and that Def Stan 00-55 will include formal methods as a requirement; they also pointed out that something like half of the safety problems found by them have been in the understanding of the specification, the area perhaps where formal methods can give most help.

I have to say that I feel that we are right at the beginning of our understanding of what we can do with formal methods and there really is a light in the tunnel there. A great deal more research is going to be required before we can pull them through to their full utility, but we shouldn't trample on what does look to me to be a very hopeful line even though, as we have so often said today, it is never going to cope with the whole problem, particularly when it comes to specification.

I think the presentations today raised the question of the relationship between MoD and the IEC activities and clearly we must be concerned about this. My feeling is that on the panel there is great goodwill to try to harmonise and the very fact that we are all here, which perhaps we would not have been a year or so ago, does suggest that we are working towards that.

There was an interesting discussion about just how far one had to take the safety critical area. Can one really keep it to a very limited area as MoD said? Maybe that's really back to the economics. IEC/TC65A Working Group 9 aim to complete a draft by, I think, 1989. Whether there will be four years of revision likely to follow that draft, or whether one can hope to have a complete specification by the end of 1989 is open to question: both points were made, and I suspect both are true. IEC/TC65A Working Group 9 believe strongly in third party assessors, and so I think do MoD. We look forward to the secretariat paper in June.

We have to ask what the differences will be between the TC65A/Working Group 9 draft and the Defence Standard. We were assured there would be 70–80% overlap but no doubt it is an area where continuing work will help to minimise the differences. There are different fields, and I think we have all accepted that each sector is going to have its own areas to some extent, but, without going to the lowest common denominator, we must try to ensure that the area of commonality is left as large as can sensibly be done. As I understand it, Working Group 9 will not require the certification of individuals, which is interesting.

The legal liability side I think can be easily summarised, and that is that unless you are careful you will find yourself in the law courts and subject to real liability. Certification may give a good defence against the claim of negligence but it certainly doesn't give absolute protection. It is fair to say that there have not been all that many cases, though there undoubtedly have been some.

Our prime aim must be harmonisation: the definition of the area in which we can work together, but accepting that there will be industry-special standards outside the harmonised area. It was emphasised by one speaker that a calamity in this field was really an absolute inevitability, it was only a question of when. This reminds me of the true story about Bernal, who, during the war was asked before the first thousand-bomber raid what was the probability of an accident between the bombers. He said 'Well, with the numbers that you're talking about and the sort of packing density, there will be one collision in 100 years of bombing'. The first night over Cologne two of the bombers collided and when they turned on him and said that 'you said ...', he replied 'Yes, that's quite right, it's occurred'.

Well, we must try to get a system established before the disaster occurs. Our attention was quite rightly turned to the other ACARD report point which perhaps we haven't yet dealt with, which is what we will do when that disaster occurs – we need to be prepared. The concept of certification of the product is one which gets too little attention. It will be covered in the draft report: it certainly deserves full attention. The draft report will go out to everybody who has been registered for this meeting. We do ask you for your comments; that is very important.

I myself feel very strongly that the IEE and the BCS have a responsibility as the professional bodies to give a lead. We also understand something of this problem, and thus owe it to society and to our members to give a lead here. I do believe that this Working Party is one of the most important activities that the two professional bodies are tackling at this time and I think that you feel that too.

APPENDIX H

FULL ANALYSIS OF RESPONSES TO QUESTIONNAIRE

PAGE

Question 4: **Legal Framework**   110

Question 5: **Classification of Hazards**   113

Question 6: **Current Practice**   120

Question 7: **Certification**   128

Question 8: **Quantified Risk Assessment**   130

Question 9: **Insurance Position**   132

Question 11: **Techniques in Use**   133

Question 12: **Particular Concerns in the Industry**   136

Question 13: **Future Developments**   139

Question 14: **Overseas Activities**   140

Note: This appendix is arranged in Question order. Within each question, the numbers in parentheses refer to categories of respondent, namely:

1. Avionics	10. Steel Industry
2. Nuclear	11. Chemical Industry
3. Medical	12. Automotive Industry
4. Railways	13. MoD
5. Road Transport	14. Industrial Control Systems
6. Petroleum Offshore	15. Automation and Robots
7. Mines and Quarries	16. Software Houses and Consultants
8. Coal Industry	17. General/Technical
9. Gas Industry	

Legal Framework (Question 4)

Legal framework and application; supervisory agencies.

(1) Avionics

The Civil Aviation Authority demands CAA 690. System Integrity Working Party report issued Dec 1986. Within the MoD reference is made to the Flight Navigation Act, and A&AEE operates as a self-regulatory agent. Def Stan 0016 NES 620, 08/5, AQAP 13 and 14 are called and Interim Standard 0031 – *Development of Safety Critical Software for Airborne Systems* is now available. RTCA/D0-178A – *Software considerations in a/b systems and equipment certification* which has also been coordinated with EUROCAE WG 12. Company directors handling either civil or military contracts must sign Form 100D.

Very project specific, but normal product liability law applies.
The Air Navigation Order (1985) and Regulations.
Currently USA and France have similar documents to CAA 690.
UK Defence and US Military Standards.
British Civil and US Federal Airworthiness Requirements.
(American). No legal requirements. Agencies FAA and DoD.

Federal Aviation Administration (FAA) – is responsible for granting certification to civil aircraft in the USA, using a set of safety requirements enshrined in US law; the Federal Air Regulations (FARs).

The FAA differs from the UK CAA by the use of Designated Engineering Representatives (DERs), who are accredited persons who may be company (rather than FAA) employees, tasked with the assessment of (and the responsibility for signing off) the safety impact of engineering details on behalf of the FAA. Overall compliance with all applicable requirements, procedures and documentation is assessed by the applicant's local regional FAA office. Task forces are sometimes appointed to make special studies of unique certification concerns and such efforts may be centered in a regional office rather than the applicant's local office.

RLD – responsible for the certification of civil aircraft in the Netherlands.

RLD and most European countries use Joint Airworthiness Requirements (JAR), with a small number of National Variants and Special Conditions.

The airworthiness of the design of aircraft built in one country but registered in another is usually accepted by the certification agency of the importing country, based on recognition of the expertise and integrity of the manufacturing country's authority. In many cases there is a reciprocal agreement between the countries' authorities, although some review, and frequently the imposition of 'special conditions', by the importing country's authority, is common.

(2) Nuclear Industry

The Nuclear Installations Inspectorate does not issue standards or codes of practice for nuclear plant. They expect each applicant for a licence to develop their own design safety criteria. For MoD the UKAEA make the following standards mandatory: NES 620, AQAP-1, AQAP-13, Def Stan 00-16, BS 5750, BS 5882, and Def Stan 00-55 when complete. General advice is given from IEC Standard 880 (BSI 88/71049) and EWICS TC7 documents. The CEGB have issued some guidelines which are currently for comment and trial use.

The construction of Nuclear Power Stations is in general governed by the Nuclear Installations Act 1965. The Act also refers to the role of the Nuclear Installations Inspectorate, defines the progressive procedure for licensing and the procedure in the event of occurrences. Clause 19 deals with the cover required for licensees liability. Many other acts and regulations are relevant. The Health and Safety at Work Act 1974 and the Ionising Radiation Regulations 1985 are examples.

The main supervisory body is the Nuclear Installations Inspectorate of the Health and Safety Executive, although more than a dozen other national and international bodies exercise supervisory functions over the total nuclear fuel cycle.

(3) Medical Equipment

There are many specialist codes of practice but there are no requirements or tests specific to software controlled equipment which have legal or mandatory status. BS 5750 and BS 5724 or other relevant standards are often made a condition of contract. For general quality assurance requirements Department of Health operates a voluntary 'Manufacturers Registration Scheme'.

FDA in the USA has a policy covering medical computer products taking authority from 1976 Medical Devices Amendments to the Federal Food, Drugs and Cosmetics Act.

IEC TC 62 'Electrical Equipment in Medical Practice' has set up a new working group WG2 – Safety of computer systems used in medical electrical equipment.

In FRG, compliance is mandatory to 'Verordnung über die Sicherheit Medizinisch – Technische Geräte (Medizingeräteverordung – Med GV)'. Published 14 January 1985 effective 1 January 1986, and it is known that software safety validation is under active consideration.

(4) Railways

DoT Railways Inspectorate operate by means of monitored commercial development. They employ UK AEA to carry out safety audits under contract. Safety-related software must be given validation by a separate group of engineers but whether second or third party, or software specialists is unspecified.

The overseas picture is unspecified and widely diverse, often involving consultant specified requirements. The European Railway Authority have advisory standards and codes of practice.

Supervision is by the Railway Inspectorate.

(5) Road Transport Vehicles

UK regulatory requirements exist and are added to as needed, setting performance criteria for certain aspects of vehicle construction to achieve acceptable (road) safety and environmental standards. For many years in Europe and internationally there has been harmonisation of national requirements regarding vehicle construction. This harmonisation is well advanced and manifests itself in EC directives and in ECE model regulations (which are used widely both inside and outside the European Community). Both systems require a formal type approval by a government, or government recognised agency, of vehicle or component as appropriate. UK performance standards are framed around these international specifications unless there is a special reason for having a separate national requirement. These standards are expressed in terms of a performance standard relating to the end result required. The manufacturer is free to choose the most appropriate methods of achieving the desired performance level.

At present there are no vehicle regulations, either national or international that deal specifically with computer techniques. There are requirements that will apply if computer techniques are used as part of a system to achieve the desired performance. These relate to anti-lock braking systems, there are two requirements that will be important when microprocessors are used as part of the system to achieve the desired overall braking performance. In the event of a failure of the anti-lock, the residual braking performance must be that prescribed for the normal service brake. In other words failure or malfunction of the anti-lock or its control system must have a benign effect on the overall braking performance required for the vehicle. Also anti-lock devices must not be affected adversely by magnetic fields. The interpretation of these requirements is left to the type approval authority, which may be national or foreign depending on the country in which approval is granted.

Near to completion is an EC directive concerning electromagnetic compatibility which will apply to electrical and electronic equipment, including that used in motor vehicles.

(6) Petroleum Offshore

Health and Safety At Work Act 1974.
Mineral Workings (Offshore Installations) Act 1971.
Oil and Gas Enterprise Act.
Other Statutory Instruments brought in under the above acts.

(9) Gas Industry

The Gas Act of 1986.

(11) Chemical Industry

Long list of supervisory agencies but none in this field bar HSE. Health and Safety at Work etc. Act 1964 as modified by Control of Substances Hazardous to Health Regulations (1988) with effect from 1st October 1989. BS 5750 and/or ISO 9001 may be made conditions of contract.

Pharmaceutical and agrochemical products subject to product registration schemes of each national market. For the UK the DOH and DOE administer such schemes. For the USA the F&DA and EPA administer such schemes. Compliance is a legal requirement and includes regulation of the data collection, storage and analysis techniques to be used to collect evidence for registration.

Pharmaceuticals for sale in USA subject to F&DA guidelines for Good Manufacturing Practice which regulate manufacturing control systems and records.

Carriage, Packaging and Labelling (CPL) regulations, US DOT and IATA air transport regulations cover the transport of chemical products. Manufacturing control systems must ensure that goods are packed and labelled in accordance with CPL regulations.

(12) Automotive Industry
Laws, Directives and Regulations are legion, as are the Standards and Regulatory Authorities. There is no indication that any of these are alive to or have a grip of SRS problems.

(13) MoD
Supervisory Agent – Ordnance Board.

(14) Industrial Control Systems
The Health and Safety at Work Act 1974 and other statutory amendments and codes of practice, e.g. Control of Industrial Major Accident Hazards Regulations 1984 (CIMAH).

(15) Automation and Robots
HSE has codes of practice for specific industries. Factory inspectors and insurance assessors are used as supervisory agents.

Covered by associated Building Regulations and National Standards General requirements of BS 5750 and associated product liability implications (lifts).

Classification of Hazards (Question 5)

(1) Avionics
MoD –

Safety critical: an item is safety critical if a single or multiple failure effect within the item could cause a hazardous situation.

Safety-involved: an item is safety involved if a single or multiple failure effect within an item can cause a hazardous situation when operating in combination with the same failure effect within a different item.

Definition of hazard
A hazardous situation is one in which conditions arise which threaten the safety of the crew and/or aircraft but from which the aircrew may be able to return the aircraft to safe flight.

Military Aircraft System Safety Assessment

Categorisation of Hazard Severity is indicated in Table H.1 for Catastrophic, Critical, Marginal and Negligible categories.

Table H.1 Hazard Severity Categorisation

Catastrophic	An event, or combination of events, which **make it impossible** for the aircraft to continue safe flight and landing. Death and/or aircraft loss will result.
Critical	An event, or combination of events, which **reduce the capability of the aircraft to continue safe flight and landing**, i.e. there is a high probability that the event(s) would become catastrophic. Events which could cause severe injury, occupational illness, or major aircraft damage should also be given this severity classification.
Marginal	An event, or combination of events, which **has some potential for adverse effects on aircraft or personnel safety**. Events which could cause minor injury, minor occupational illness, or minor aircraft damage should also be given this severity classification.
Negligible	Events have no effect on safety.

Civil Airworthiness

European requirements – JAR 25.1309
USA requirements – FAR 25.1309
RTCA/EUROCAE doc – DO-178A/ED12A (software)

Comparison of these three systems is given in Table H.2.

MoD Weapons Systems

Categories:

- Mission critical

- Life critical

CAA cite JAR 25.1309

   Catastrophic Effect (Software Level 1)
   Hazardous Effect   (Software Level 2)
   Major Effect   (Software Level 2)
   Minor Effect   (Software Level 3)

CAA (NATS) Navigation Aids approved in relation to purpose and environment, e.g. ILS has three categories depending on operational use (Category 3 covers zero-visibility operation).

Table H.2 Relationship between probability and severity of effects

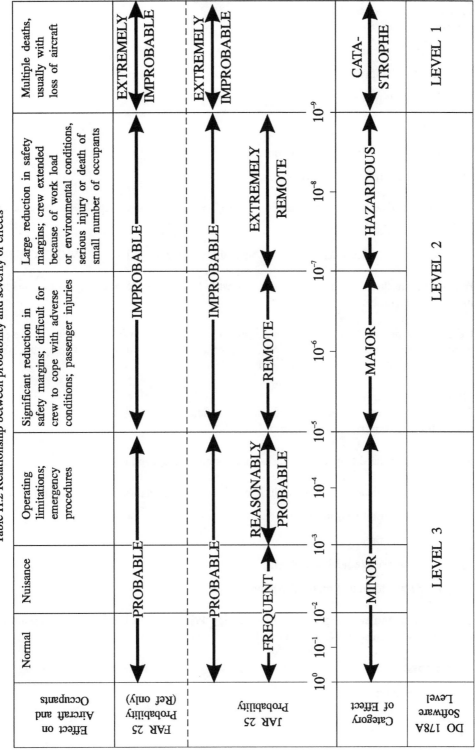

(2) Nuclear Industry

Rolls-Royce use:

1. Safety critical;

2. Availability critical;

3. Safety-related.

HSE (Civil) use:

1. Top level (high risk to population;

2. Safety-related (plant controls etc.).

[HSE has a risk criteria document out for discussion, covering levels of risk to society.]

Other hazard classifications are said to be available from UKAEA or EWICS TC7.

EC document 'licensing issues' associated with the use of computers in the nuclear industry gives Tables H.3 and H.4.

CEGB does not use a classification system. Faults and hazards are studied to determine possible consequences and frequency of occurrence estimated. From this, the required integrity of the protection system is derived.

(3) Medical Equipment

Department of Health operate no formal classification but note CENELEC proposed to develop a system of classification of hazards.

Suppliers use 'hazard to patient or user under single fault condition'.

FRG specific application categories in Med GV (Regulations for medical equipment):

1. Life support equipment;

2. Implantable devices;

3. Powered medical equipment;

4. Other technical medical equipment.

USA operate similar categories to FRG under 1976 Medical Devices amendments to Federal Food, Drugs and Cosmetics Act.

(4) Railways

1. Failsafe;

2. Non-failsafe.

Table H.3 Proposed classification of computer systems in nuclear power stations in the FRG

Class	Functional requirements	Systems involved
I	Highest requirements of nuclear safety	Systems that release automatic actions for protection of human life and environment
II	High requirements of nuclear safety	Systems that act for the protection of human life and environment by • guiding safety variables under abnormal conditions; • causing operator actions deterministically
III	Normal requirements of nuclear safety	Systems that • limit plant variables to specific values; • avoid scrams; • report disturbances in systems of class I and II
IV	High requirements of plant safety	Systems that • release actions automatically for protection of persons in the plant; • protect important parts of the plant
V	High requirements of plant availability	Systems that • increase plant availability; • protect normal parts of the plant
VI	High functional requirements	Systems that serve for optimal plant operation, e.g. with respect to efficiency or manoeuvrability
VII	Component-related control	Systems for simple requirements

Table H.4 Proposed reliability demands for computers in nuclear power plants in the FRG

Class according to Table H.3	I	II	III	IV	V	VI	VII
Value for the unavailability	10^{-5}	10^{-4}	10^{-2}	10^{-4}	10^{-2}	10^{-1}	10^{-1}
Value for the safety-related unavailability	10^{-7}	10^{-5}	10^{-4}	10^{-5}	—	—	—
Failure probability per year	10^{-4}	10^{-2}	—	10^{-2}	—	—	—
Probability for dangerous failure per year	10^{-7}	10^{-5}	10^{-4}	10^{-5}	—	—	—
Failure probability during an accident	10^{-6}	10^{-4}	10^{-3}	10^{-4}	10^{-2}	—	—

(a) Collision or derailment of trains, potentially leading to multiple deaths and injuries of railway passengers and staff.

(b) Collision of trains with road vehicles or pedestrians at level crossings potentially leading to multiple deaths and injuries.

(c) Collision of trains with track workers, potentially leading to multiple deaths and injuries of railway staff.

[**Note**: For low-cost areas (e.g. very low traffic lines) some reliance on operating staff allowed to provide safe working, e.g. radio-based signalling.]

(8) Coal Industry
Fail safety defined by engineers in accordance with British and Industry Standards – relating to likely danger to personnel.

(9) Gas Industry
Explosion, fire and toxic hazards associated with Natural Gas (gaseous and LNG), LPG, SNG and hydrocarbon condensates.

(11) Chemical Industry
There are recognised industry norms for hazard classification. The most comprehensive are contained in American legislation. Key components are:

- Sections 307 and 311 of Clean Water Act.

- Resource Conservation Recovery Act.

- Comprehensive Environmental and Liability Act.

- Hazardous Materials Transportation Act.

- Occupational Health and Safety Act.

- Substances considered hazardous by National Institute of Occupational Safety and Health, the National Toxicology Program, or the International Agency for Research on Cancer.

The CPL regulations provide comprehensive criteria for hazard classification together with a scheme of coded 'risk phrases'. The CPL classifications are:

Hazard Type:	Very Toxic
	Toxic
	Harmful
	Corrosive
	Irritant
	Unclassified
Flammability Classification:	Explosive
	Oxidising
	Extremely Flammable
	Highly Flammable
	Flammable
	Dust Explosive

Carcinogen:	Proven
	Suspect
	Possible
Mutagen:	Proven
	Suspect
	Possible
Teratogen:	Proven
	Suspect
	Possible
Skin irritation:	Yes
	No
Sensitiser:	Respiratory
	Skin

The above classifications can be used to identify those substances whose intrinsic properties make their control and handling safety critical. Risk phrases expand upon the nature of risks associated with handling the materials.

(12) Automotive Industry
Safety of driver, passengers, pedestrians and other road users.
Safety of dealership servicing personnel.
Safety of our own Company personnel.
Protection of the vehicle components from permanent damage.

(14) Industrial Control Systems
Manufacturers use HSE Codes of Practice for specific industry as guidance.

Lift manufacturers classify hazards into:

- Environmental;

- Electrical;

- EMI.

Hazards are classified as part of the process, e.g. Methane Gas. Software itself is not a hazard, only in its relationship to the process can it affect the degree of hazard.

(15) Automation and Robots
CEC document compares HSE PES guidelines with BIA (W Germany) and INRS (France) treatment of hazard levels and related requirements (see Tables H.5 and H.6).

HSE publication *Industrial Robot Safety*, 27 June 1988.

Table H.5 Safety Integrity Criteria (BIA proposals)
(Note: It is assumed that the process has a safe state)

Architectures	Hazard level	Requirements
System 1 → PES [SW | HW] →	• Very low level. Small injuries (no longer than three days absent from work)	Designed and constructed in accordance with the state of techniques. No special safety requirements for the software. Hardware requirements also concern the electrical safety. For instance: one should not be able to touch dangerous voltages.

System 2
 	
→ PES [SW | HW] →
	• Medium (reversible) injuries (14 days absent from work) and low risk.
	Cases without broken bones or high hazards but extremely low probability of occurrence because of the circumstances of the dangerous situations.
	For instance:
	• slow development of the danger
	• slow movement
	• Possibility to prevent the accident (Industrial Robot at reduced speed)
		Very advanced selfchecking methods:
		  watchdog timer
		  plausibility checks
		  'pre-flight' test etc.
		Extremely carefully designed and tested software.

Current Practice (Question 6)

Current practices – regulations, codes of practice, standards (national, European, international and de facto), guidance notes and common practice. (State mandatory levels, scope of application, possibilities for conformity assurance.)

(1) Avionics

Reliability based on MIL HDBK 217E. Failure modes and effects analysis (FMEA) standard practice. Software design and test to DoD-STD-2167.

Regulations

Federal Airworthiness Regulations (FARs). This set of regulations sets down the safety requirements in as generic a form as possible. Ancillary documents provide interpretive material, including acceptable means of compliance.

Table H.5 (*continued*)

Architectures	Hazard level	Requirements

System 3
 	
PES
SW | HW
 	
NON-PES
	• death
	• severe injuries (loss of hand, foot, arm, leg, etc.)
	
	and
	no possibility to prevent the accident.
		The non-PES system has to be an independent means, for instance, a safety interlocking system. The PES is not safety-critical in the sense that it may fail if the safety function is not requested, but the non-PES system must not fail.
		Therefore there are no special safety requirements for the PES. The non-PES system has to fulfil the following requirements:
		1. Approved components, for instance:
		   • safety limit switches
		   • transformers according to VDE etc.
		2. In the case of failure in the non-PES system this failure has to be detected by the system itself.

System 4 PES1 SW1 | HW1 FSC PES2 SW2 | HW2 FSC = Fail-Safe Converter	• death • severe injuries (loss of hand, foot, arm, leg, etc.) *and* no possibility to prevent the accident.	The *diversity of the HW* is on the component level. They have to be of different types and – if possible – of different technologies (TTL, CMOS). *Not* the same type from different manufacturers. The development team for both HW_1 and HW_2 may be the same. The *diversity of software* development has to start at least before the coding of the software begins. There have to be different software teams. The software development steps have to be checked very carefully by external reviewers until development splits. *Systematic failures* must not be caused by environmental factors (humidity, temperature, vibration, EMC, etc.). This has to be carefully examined by the auditor.

Table H.5 (*continued*)

Architectures	Hazard level	Requirements
System 5 PES1 SW1 | HW1 FSC PES2 SW1 | HW1 FSC = Fail-Safe Converter	• death • severe injuries (loss of hand, foot, arm, leg, etc.) *and* no possibility to prevent the accident.	Failures of certain elements or components must lead to a dangerous situation. Any single failure has to stop the machine at once if it would lead to a dangerous situation. If the failure would not lead to a dangerous situation, than it has to be detected within a predefined short time. The *homogeneous redundancy* is applicable only if the following requirements are fulfilled: 1. Simple PES's for instance: Programmable Controllers 2. Very small instruction set 3. Long experience of use (in not safety-critical applications) of both hardware and firmware. 4. Extremely careful examination of the software. *Systematic failures* must not be caused by environmental factors (humidity, temperature, vibration, EMC, etc.). This has to be carefully examined by the auditor.

One of the key requirements for the certification of systems is FAR 25-1309. This contains the requirement to limit probability of occurrence of a particular system fault effect to a level associated with the severity of the hazard that the effect would produce.

Other FAR paragraphs in effect expand and interpret the high level requirement by setting test conditions and/or numerical limits which define boundaries between hazard severities. Much of this material is contained in appendices called Advisory Circulars (ACs). ACs are informal documents except where referenced by FARs, which in effect gives them the equivalent legal status.

As an example of the way this structure operates one might consider one part of the autopilot requirements. FAR 25-1329 makes very generic statements about autopilot design, but AC 25-1329 deals in detail with flight path excursions potentially resulting from autopilot faults and sets out not-to-exceed specified limits, together with specified assumptions about flight crew recognition of, and recovery from, the fault effect. Similar detailed interpretive ACs exist for automatic landing, etc.

Digital system safety is dealt with in AC 20-115A, which calls attention to the Guidance Note: Radio Technical Commission for Aeronautics (RTCA) DO-178A, *Software Considerations in Airborne Systems Equipment Certification*.

The nature of DO 178A has been misunderstood by some observers: it is not a specific software methodology whose rigorous application would provide a recipe for safe software. It is a guidance document, giving a review of methodologies from which a judicious selection enables a supplier to assemble his own set of specific procedures and standards with which to assure the quality of his software output. It recognises that different applications require different levels of assurance, dependent upon the safety sensitivity of the task performed, and provides guidance on appropriate levels of documentation to be available or supplied to the certifying authority.

UK and US Defence Standards
Codes of Practice Mil STD 2167, DO 178A, JSP 188. Much of the work of NATS is directed towards meeting the requirements of the International Civil Aviation Organisation, ICAO. ICAO, which has 157 member states, develops the Standards and Recommended Practices (SARPS) for systems performance and also provides guidance to the aviation community. A number of other standards and guidance documents are also called up in system specifications as required. They include a range of British Standards, Ministry of Defence standards and NATO standards. NATS places mandatory requirements on its suppliers to meet some of these standards, for example BS 3192 (safety requirements for radio transmitting apparatus). Suppliers may have to be approved to BS 5750 on Def Stan 05-21 for Quality Systems. RTCA DO 178A and AQAP 13 are currently used for software development and more recently the requirements of the STARTS Guide and the HSE guidelines on PES have become relevant.

Civil: CAA AN-45A
           RTCA DO/178A
           IEEE 1012 Software Verification and Validation Plans

Military: Def Stan 00-31
           Def Stan 00-55
           AQAP 1/13
           RCTA DO/178A
           DoD-STD-2167

For a large, multi-national project such as the European Fighter Aircraft, the project organisation (Eurofighter) draws up and proposes to the customer organisation (NEFMA) a System Safety Programme Plan (SSPP) covering all aspects of System Safety Assessment and certification (including numerical 'loss rate' customer safety requirements). A prime reference for this approach is MIL-STD-882(B). Software safety is but one aspect of the integrated systems approach. Mandatory procedures, techniques and reviews are incorporated to ensure that hazard categorisation is correctly translated into software classification (there is a distinct lack of public domain standards in this area). Project Software Development Standards are established based upon international standards such as RTCA-DO-178A, DoD-STD-2167,...and available national and corporate standards. Software Quality Plans, Configuration Management Plans, etc. are also established.

Table H.6 Safety Integrity Criteria (INRS)

Type of Systems	Guidelines	PES Characteristics	
		Architectures	Qualitative and Quantitative Specifications
Materials Processing Machines	French Regulations Act 233-97 of July 15, 1980 (General requirements for all machines)	All types of architectures are accepted as long as they meet specifications shown at right.	One failure, one breakdown or one deterioration of the energy supply system or of *machines* and devices must not: <ul><li>cause unexpected start-up of a moving element of the machine;</li><li>prevent automatic or normal stopping of moving elements, whatever they may be;</li><li>neutralise the protective devices for moving elements.</li></ul>
High Risk Machines (specifically Metal Presses)	French Regulation: Acts 80.543 and 81.938 October 13, 1981	Operating I.S. (eventually D.S.) Future Concept	General requirements: the relevant specifications of Act 80.543 are strictly applied. Preliminary design certification is required for high-risk machines. Particular requirement for testing fail-safe criteria for common-mode failures and EMC interference.

High Risk Machines (specifically Metal Presses) (*continued*)			
Industrial Robots	Draft NFE 61.110	All types of architectures, safeguarding, and other safety measures which satisfy fail-safe criteria.	Fail-safe criteria for roboticised systems in normal production.
		All types of architectures which satisfy fail-safe criteria.	Fail-safe criteria for roboticised systems in other conditions (for example, set-up, teaching, maintenance).
Presence sensing devices such as photo-electric safety systems.	French Regulations Act 81.938 October 13, 1981, for example.	All types of architecture which satisfy fail-safe criteria and testing. • ESD; • fail-safe single system; • hardware and software redundancy (similar or dissimilar) with fail-safe comparator.	Fail-safe criteria These devices must satisfy testing for: • EMC; • fail-safe for single failure and common-mode failure. Dynamic systems, full function monitoring.

Direct safety (D.S.) concerns functions for which there is a correlation between the occurrence of a failure and the risk of injury.
Indirect Safety (I.S.) concerns monitoring devices for which the degradation of performance has no direct impact on the risk.

When established and agreed, adherence to standards is mandatory and is ensured by the Quality Assurance function. The scope of application is project dependent and can include test equipment software, development environment software and system firmware.

(2) Nuclear Industry

Mandatory   NES 620 AQAP-1 AQAP-13 Def Stan 00-16 (soon 00-55)
General advice   EWICS TC7: IEC Standard 880 BSI88/71049
                   AQAP 1 & 13. BS 5750. BS 5882. ASME standards.

The lead document is the Safety Assessment Principles for Nuclear Power Stations (HSE 1979). CEGB uses its own Design Safety Guidelines and its own Design Safety Guidelines for the use of PES in Protection Systems is in trial use.

(3) Medical Equipment

Various, but none having requirements specific to software.

UK   Voluntary compliance to   BS 5724 (IEC 601) BS 800, BS 5750
FGR   Mandatory compliance to   VDE 0750 (IEC 601) and VDE 0875
USA   Voluntary compliance to   UL 544 FCC Regs 47CFR Pt15

(4) Railways
Codes of Practice
Various by Office for Res & Exps (ORE) of International Union of Railways.
Some specs, including software standards issued by Railway Industry Assoc.
GEC-General Signal maintains its own CoP.

For classical railway signalling based on relay technology there exists in British Rail a very extensive range of regulations, specifications, and codes of practice.

For processor-based safety systems there exist:

- A draft specification for software standards.

- A set of guidelines for software validation.

The above are generally applicable. For a specific system, the British Rail Solid State Interlocking (SSI), there are codes of practice for design, data preparation, installation, and testing. All are British Rail documents, and were produced before documents such as the HSE guidelines were available. The currently proliferating guidelines and standards for safety systems are being studied with interest.

(6) Petroleum Offshore
All International Standards
API/IP Codes
Guidance Notes published by DoE.

(9) Gas Industry
British Gas, I Gas E, British & ASME Standards
Statutory Requirements (NIHHS, CIMAH)

(11) Chemical Industry

Contracted compliance to BS 5750 and/or ISO 9001. Pharmaceutical manufacturing and process control systems required to meet US F&DA. Good Manufacturing Practice Regulations and Guidelines. Determines nature and integrity of manufacturing control systems.

Food, agrochemical and pharmaceutical research and development systems required to meet US F&DA. and EPA Good Laboratory Practice Regulations and Guidelines. Specific recommendations on software quality assurance made by F&DA/industry consensus 'Red Apple' book and DOH document *The Application of GLP Principles to Computer Systems*.

(12) Automotive Industry

Documented Departmental computer programming standards.
Documented Departmental testing and sign for procedures.

Responsibility divided as follows:-
    Control strategy design.
    Software design implementation & simulation testing.
    Vehicle based commissioning.
    Calibration to meet safety, emissions and driveability standards.

(13) MoD

Ordnance Board Procedures and Defence Standards.

(14) Industrial Control Systems

Pharmaceutical and Agrochemical – American Food and Drug Administration GLP and GMP. Some Home Office Regs on R & D Practice.
BS 5750   ISO 9001
Gas: British Gas, I Gas E and ASME Standards.
NIHHS and CIMAH statutory requirements.
There is evidence that current practice varies from company to company and even within companies.

(15) Automation and Robots

BS 6491 (1984). Set of HSE Guidance Notes (PM 41).
Few possibilities of conformity assurance at systems level.

With regard to regulations and code of practice, these comply with CEN Code 81 which is equivalent to BS 5655 from a UK point of view. Some other individual European codes present problems in compliance. Others have local deviations from the general European code. From the lift industry code of practice point of view, software systems will have regulations defined by the responsible engineering source. From a purely internal Otis point of view the Engineering centres based in North America, Germany and Japan will define regulations in reference to software systems. In addition individual design centres will also define codes of practice. Overriding these internal codes will be Worldwide Otis Quality Standards for software systems which have been prepared after agreement by the various engineering responsible centres.

(16) Software Houses and Consultants
Def Stan 05-21. NES620. BS 5887. Mil Std 1815.
LIFESPAN package often used.
In comms area RS 232. RS 422. HDLC.
AQAP 13. Extra rigour for safety critical.

Certification (Question 7)

Certification – method, application and coverage; accountability, signing off responsibilities.

(1) Avionics
Military: A&AEE make recommendations based on theoretical and experimental results for which it is fully accountable.

In USA the FAA reviews all test and analysis data and provides certification of the electronic engine control.

Certification plan developed and approved early in project. Pride taken in self regulation. Cost considerations are present but spectre of potential product liability litigation also comes into play.

DO 178A used for all software in civil systems. DoD-STD-2167 used for most military applications. Otherwise 'in house' standards.

Equipment performance and design standards to be declared by applicant and certified by means of a Declaration of Design and Performance. Applications accepted only from CAA approved organisations (UK) or overseas organisations via their national certifying authority. Design signatories are vetted by CAA and authority given to certify DDP's. Similarly, installed systems certified by issue of a Type Certificate for prototype aircraft, or Airworthiness Approval Note for modified aircraft, subject to receipt by CAA of reports showing compliance with requirements. CAA may witness tests or perform their own tests as deemed necessary.

Generally speaking, systems are approved following an extensive series of factory and field tests, analysis and acceptance testing against the requirements specification. They are accepted into service following successful commissioning which for ground-based navigational aids includes flight inspection and analysis also. The permitted category of operation however, may depend upon further evidence gained over time. With ILS for example, a new system would not be permitted into full category 3 service until it had demonstrated appropriate reliability, typically an MTBF of 4000 hours to 95% confidence. A certificate is issued to the aerodrome operator for the category of operation for which the system qualifies. Issue of the certificate is a NATS HQ function.

The CAA Safety and Regulation Group, SRG, is responsible for the certification of all UK registered aircraft; avionic/electrical equipment and systems and their installation in aircraft. (SRG is making a separate response to this questionnaire.) Chief Software Engineer signs off for software aspects of each equipment.

Certification activities are project dependent, but primarily comprise

- the demonstration of compliance (principally by testing) that the system fulfills the requirement defined in the system specification

- from the contractor to the certifying agency that software aspects of the System Safety Programme have been fulfilled.

(2) Nuclear Industry

No specific certification of persons in CEGB. Designs and equipment are assessed by the Inspecting Authorities on their merits. For on-site modification a Safety Committee may call for an independent assessment.

(3) Medical Equipment

Department of Health – Declaration of conformity to relevant standard called up in the purchase contract. Third party certification not mandatory but BSI Testing Services for testing to BS 5724 is recognised. (See *Consultants*.)

Institute of Physical Sciences in Medicine – Worried by proliferation of use with no formalised safety standards.

Self certification but may require independent certification by May 1992.

FRG: Good certification to type testing and GMP inspections.

USA: FDA GMP inspections and UL type test only.

(4) Railways

All Systems are finally signed off by the operating railway authority who then assume responsibility for the continued safe operation of the system.

Overseas practices vary.

The generic design of safety systems is certified by the Director of Signal and Telecommunications Engineering on completion of the type approval procedures implemented by this Department's Development Section.

Each individual installation must be signed off by the Regional or Project Engineer concerned.

(6) Petroleum Offshore

Certification of every installation by survey.
Certification undertaken by appointed Certifying authorities.

(9) Gas Industry

Certification is 'in house' but accountability is to HSE based on case law.

(11) Chemical Industry
No known certification procedures for safety-critical manufacturing control software except GMP inspections for pharmaceuticals and voluntary BS 5750 certification.

Data collection and data analysis software for handling pharmaceutical and agrochemical product registration data is subject to DOH and F&DA or EPA inspection. Standards expected are those described in *The Application of GLP Principles to Computer Systems* (UK DOH) and the 'Red Apple' book (US F&DA).

(12) Automotive Industry
Formal 'Software Design Verification' (SWDV) is undertaken using mainframe simulation.

(14) Industrial Control Systems
LC Automation – Certification to appropriate BS standard by independent test house, covering the design of the hardware. On installation certificate given to user that appropriate codes of practice followed.

In the process industry it is necessary to assess the process, its control system and its operations as a total entity. Such assessment will normally be carried out by in-company personnel. (**Note:** the normal method is assessment rather than certification).

(15) Automation and Robots
NALM – To BS 5655, Part 10 with an associated certificate (Lifts).

The accountability for signing-off a lift over to the client is usually accepted by the client's authorised agent. In the UK, for example, the certification used to approve the lifts performance would be in line with BS 5655, Part 10. In other parts of the world appropriate codes such as TRA200 and the CENELEC would be used. Code Inspectors and authorised Test Agencies would over-view the performance in the area of handover.

(16) Software Houses and Consultants
Miscellaneous company standards are closely followed. Design documentation reviewed by superior, then by an in-house independent reviewer, and then by the client. If safety a secondary effect only a proportion of the programme may be reviewed.

Cambridge Consultants Ltd – varies with project – on medical electrical equipment BSI Testing Services to BS 5724.

Quantified Risk Assessment (Question 8)

Quantified Risk Assessment (QRA) – methods used and application.

(1) Avionics
Military – 'Standard risk analysis techniques'.

Civil – FMEA or similar techniques.

- Hazard Analysis;
- FMEA;
- Fault Tree Analysis;
- Integrity Analysis;
- State Diagrams.

Standard techniques for hardware only. DO-178A guidelines used for software. Quantified attributes are not associated with software.

(2) Nuclear Industry
RR (MoD work) and CEGB use:

- Analysis;
- Sequence Diagrams;
- FMEA;
- Fault Tree Analysis;
- Event Tree Analysis;
- Probability Risk Assessment.

(3) Medical Equipment
Department of Health – QRA not applied (BS 5724 based on qualitative single fault).

Suppliers – no obligatory or advisory practices. FMECA or reliability based techniques used in many cases.

(4) Railways
Models for safety quantification.
Fault tree analysis.
FMEA
(Some customers specify 'mean time between unsafe failures'.)

BR – 'not applied in railway signalling'.

(8) Coal Industry
Assessment implemented by Senior Engineers.

(9) Gas Industry
Fault Tree Analysis
Consequence Analysis by Modelling
System Modelling by Simulation
Failure Mode and Effects Analysis
Cause Consequence Methods

(12) Automotive Industry
Design verification Plan & Report (DVPR) includes FMEA.

(14) Industrial Control Systems
Hazard assessment carried out to BS 5304 or HSE PM41.
QRA not formally carried out for machine guarding. Custom, practice and experience used.
PES guidelines being introduced into internal procedures.

ICI Hazard and Operability Study (HAZOP) system widely used in chemical manufacturing and offshore petroleum industry.

[HSE survey showed that 40% of dangerous chemical processes investigated had not been subjected to hazard assessment.] Process design used QRA at instigation of insurance companies.

Risk assessment to lift manufacturer's internal manual. Features would be:

- Reliability modelling;

- Reliability allocation;

- Reliability prediction;

- Assessment.

Process Industries – Individual companies' responsibility and most use some form of Quantified Assessment for hazards, e.g. HAZOP.

(15) Automation and Robots
CEC document on Robotics gives much information on UK, German and French situation.

Insurance Position (Question 9)

(1) Avionics
US companies do not carry out liability insurance for engine control failures – difficult to prove negligence.

CAA certification activities are covered by a public liability insurance. CAA has made provision for insurance against all risks appropriate to its function.
Covered by general Aviation Product Indemnity Insurance.

(2) Nuclear Industry
NEI/C&I Systems – partly client covered, partly NEI plc.

The position regarding cover for licensee's liability is defined in the Nuclear Installations Act 1965 Clause 19.

(3) Medical Equipment

Manufacturers might be expected to provide additional information on SCS but this has not yet been the case.

(4) Railways

GEC – General Signal Ltd has normal product liability insurance.

BR makes no specific provision.

(6) Petroleum Offshore

Owner's of installations responsibility.

(9) Gas Industry

British Gas insure through an external company.

(14) Industrial Control Systems

Varies among individual companies, but must conform to Employers' Liability (Compulsory Insurance) Act 1969.

(15) Automation and Robots

NALM – Insurers have a close involvement with BS work and often carry out the statutory six-month inspection on lifts.
Minimum required by Third Party Liability (lifts).

(16) Software Houses and Consultants

CAP – has public and employee liability insurance. Product Liability insurance under review. No special treatment for safety-critical software.

Techniques in Use (Question 11)

Techniques in use for hardware and software development, such as risk containment systems, formal methods, animation and simulation, tools, languages.

(1) Avionics

(MoD) Formal methods (MALPAS) for software verification.

(USA) Formal procedures to MIL-STD-2167
Design reviews; qualifications test.

Design for certification. Parallel redundant system architecture (redundancy management; common mode fault analysis). Formal methods being developed, not yet applied to flight control system specification. Simulation is key feature of software verification and validation. Tools used are mainly developed in-house. Ada adopted for future systems. Criticality partitioning to restrict Level 1 code (RCTA DO-178A guidelines).

MoD Weapons Systems: VDM, High Order Logic (HOL), Predicate Calculus, ELLA, SPADE, MALPAS.

Design Techniques in use:

- Failure survival;

- Diverse or dissimilar redundancy;

- Back up system;

- Standby channels;

- Fault tolerant architecture;

- Graceful degradation;

- On-line and off-line monitoring;

- Defensive programming;

- Formal specifications;

- Requirements analysis;

- Risk containment;

- Animation and simulation.

Software Methods: VDM, Core, Jackson, Yourdon, Mascot.

CAA (NATS) – evaluating new techniques.

(2) Nuclear Industry
Hardware redundancy diversity and majority logic testing.
Formal specifications (VDM).
Animation.
SPADE – PASCAL.
Static analysis (SPADE, MALPAS).
Dynamic analysis (providing diverse implementation).
TYPHOON & KONTRON testing.
LIFESPAN configuration control.
Fault tolerance and defensive programming features.
Self-test fail safe design.

(3) Medical Equipment
Poor level of awareness of special techniques (S/W & QA).
In some cases untrained staff developing patient equipment.

Formal techniques in infancy (training required).
Sophisticated tools too costly for very small companies involved.

(4) Railways
Single channel: securely-coded information, extensive self testing.
Multiple channel: identical H/W and S/W. Validation of Software.
(No formal methods or proprietary validation tools used).

MULTISAT (BR) for triple channel redundancy.
Diversity and on-line testing.
Similar systems in Japan. Siemens uses two channel.

BR use quasi-formal methods of validation, plus in-house tools for structural and informational flow analysis. SPADE to be used in future.

(7) Mines and Quarries
Design techniques in use:

> Duplication;

> Fail safety;

> Diversity;

> Hardwired (where applicable);

> Error detection;

> Extensive testing;

> Controlled trial installations.

(9) Gas Industry
Static Analysis.
Research into applicability of formal methods.
Software Quality methods.

(11) Chemical Industry
Third Generation Languages.
Plant and process simulation.
Formal structured methods such as SSADM, LBMS, Yourdon, CASE tools.

(12) Automotive Industry
Simulation.
Development tools.

(14) Industrial Control Systems
Duplicate channel with diversity.
Formal structured software techniques, each channel S/W written independently.

Lift manufacturer uses real-time simulation and in-circuit emulation features.

(16) Software Houses and Consultants
SPADE PASCAL program validation.
VDM Requirements Spec (not all that useful).

Simulator used for test vector generation.

Use formal methods where appropriate.
Separate test team.

Formal methods (Z and VDM) used for appropriate safety-critical systems. Quality System approved to AQAP 13. Company policy on software tools and methods for all types of system development.

Formal methods of specification for in-house software, with rigorous development techniques. Proprietary tools used in many cases.

Particular Concerns in the Industry (Question 12)

(1) Avionics
Thoroughness of FMEAs.
Neglect of generic faults in redundant systems.
Thoroughness of testing software.
Establishing the correctness of requirements.

Particular concerns in the industry;

- Generic failure possibilities in systems with long exposure times.

- Dissimilarity; understanding of the benefits and the requirements for ensuring sufficient dissimilarity.

- Demand for increased levels of integration; wherein many previously separate systems share a common computing and data transfer complex; leading to possibly more severe consequences of failure, insidious interactions, greater problems of complexity management, etc.

- Deferred maintenance, whereby masked failures of redundant resources may be carried until a 'convenient' maintenance opportunity arises; leading to the possibility of erosion of safety levels and requiring adequate redundancy management techniques.

Certification concerns include the acceptance of software controlled systems used for full time critical systems e.g. primary flight and engine controls without mechanical reversionary controls. Such systems are investigated thoroughly by the certifying authorities on an individual basis. The CAA involvement in these projects is, therefore, considerable.

There is concern that software is included in systems design for the right reasons and with due regard for the consequences in verification and validation of the system to the required level. Quality and reliability should be included as a matter of course. Concern over rapidly changing certification requirements and lack of skilled manpower.

A spectrum of concerns exists within the industry. Customer concerns are easily inferred from the MoD draft Policy Statement on Safety Critical Software. Supplier concerns lean more towards timescale, cost and liability implications of adopting formal techniques.

(2) Nuclear Industry
Producing suitable methods to deal with new technology (e.g. VLSI).
Producing suitable methods for large, complex, multifunctional systems.
Lack of continuity of demand.
Lack of support for development compared to overseas manufacturers.

The concerns in the Nuclear Industry relating to the use of PES in safety-related applications are common, no doubt, to most other industries. It should be clear that in this industry it is generally mandatory for control and protection to be separated which generally puts the systems we use into a different context to those in use in many life critical systems where a single channel of continuous control is used, failure of which will lead almost immediately to accident or death. By contrast it is extremely rare for a Nuclear Reactor Protection System to be invoked though when it is, it must respond highly reliably. This leads to rather different design methods than are commonly found elsewhere. Techniques of redundancy, diversity, failure-to-safety and self test etc. etc. are extensively used to ensure that the reliance placed on any component or system is not unreasonably high. Nevertheless concerns remain, some of which can be listed:

1. It is not presently possible to quantify the reliability of software.

2. It is not presently possible to quantify the benefits of using diverse software.

3. It is often not possible to carry out FMEA of complex microprocessor hardware in a PES to the level previously done for 'conventional' designs.

4. It is not normally possible to test a PES in all its possible modes. What constitutes a 'sufficient' degree of testing is not clear.

5. Control of versions of hardware and software and the control of modifications is difficult. The life cycle of particular microprocessor based equipment is likely to be much shorter than the life of a power station. Obsolescence will be a major problem.

In general it is much easier to design a reliable system, than it is to demonstrate that a particular specified reliability has been achieved in a way which will be sufficiently convincing to present to a Licensing Authority.

(3) Medical Equipment
Require rough guidelines to indicate right kind and extent of effort to minimise hazards. Resources severely limited because of small numbers manufactured.

Growing concern but only FGR has regulations. In UK Department of Health doing study on evaluation of software-based products.

(4) Railways
Preclusion of validated software by arbitrary regulations would be major setback. Magnitude of work content of safety analysis and software validation present serious limitations. Current validation tools of doubtful use. Concern for correctness of computer programs for design calculations.

To maintain existing levels of safety with new generations of equipment.

(6) Petroleum Offshore
The reliability/integrity of software systems when used for emergency shut down and fire and gas detection systems.

(14) Industrial Control Systems
Increasing systems complexity with blurring of boundary between hardware and software makes 'testing' of final product impossible. Independent certification of product becomes certification of the design process and there are no accepted methods for doing this.

Most companies are very aware of the needs for safety but are very concerned that arbitrary regulations and pseudo legislation may be generated with no regard for specific industries and that such measures may unnecessarily reduce the competitiveness of UK companies in the world markets.

(15) Automation and Robots
The major concerns of our industry, with particular reference to electronic components, is the reliability of the components, particularly the EPROMS and the correct testing of the software including a fully de-bugging process.

(16) Software Houses and Consultants
The tools used for checking programs often have bugs themselves and are very slow.

The design development and manufacture of specially designed VLSI components. There are techniques, still not mature, which provide high confidence but not a guarantee of safe operation. They are expensive and time consuming. Many industrial sectors are unaware of the fallibility of most software and are reluctant to invest in the necessary degree of rigour.

Proof of compliance with specification is no guarantee of meeting user's need.
Lack of software metrics including reliability.
Lack of guidelines on methods.
Without consensus, standards and prescriptive regulations will be counter productive.

(Agro chemical and pharmaceutical.)
Introduction of BS 5750 and ISO 9001.
Lack of regulated hardware and software standards.
Cost of safety-related systems, and interpretation of 'reasonably practicable'.
Variety of small systems being introduced haphazardly to meet different pieces and aspects of legislation.
Speed of technology advance causing discontinuities.
Industry conservatism and inertia.

The range of safety-related systems is widening at a tremendous rate. The greater penetration of the cost effective use of computers and microprocessors into all walks of life is turning up many new safety-related applications which may not be recognised at first.

Future Developments (Question 13)

Future developments in the use of safety-related systems.

(1) Avionics
Engine control with no mechanical back-up.
Integration of engine controls and flight controls.

Trend towards increased levels of integration using a shared redundant computing and data transfer system to handle diverse and previously separate avionics and airframe functions.

Most critical applications already software implemented in flight control and weapon release. Future development in more integrated and more sophisticated applications.

These include collision avoidance, global navigation, precision area navigation, on-board software loading, micro-wave landing systems and flat panel displays together with extensive system integration.

The next generation of systems to support the air traffic control function will have an increasingly safety-related role and these systems will use software. Evolving standards such as Def Stan 00-55 will have some influence on future systems development.

Fully integrated tool-set covering the whole of the systems life cycle.

(2) Nuclear Industry
Greater use of computers as diagnostic aids.

More important to consolidate. Current technology meets requirements but validation and testing needs development.

(3) Medical Equipment
Unlimited applications even if only handling interfaces.

Increasing use of software during the design process.
Increasing use of custom logic devices which have a narrow boundary from programmable systems.

(4) Railways
Continuing applications in all signalling safety functions.

Further development of on-train signalling systems.

(5) Road Transport Vehicles
If in the future more specific requirements are needed concerning the safety features for computer techniques used in motor vehicles, these are most likely to be developed as international requirements in the European Community and the United Nations fora. If this happens then the likely result will be an extension of the present type approval system to take account of these techniques.

(9) Gas Industry
Use of PLC and other PES facilities for all forms of gas flow and pressure control.

(11) Chemical Industry
BS 5750 compliance will create pressure for software quality assurance. Systems will be needed to meet COSHH regulations. Anticipate greater use of automatic environmental monitoring. Expect Expert Systems Techniques to be utilised for hazard prediction and for closed loop process control.

(14) Industrial Control Systems
There is evidence that the publication of the HSE Guidance has caused a move away from programmable systems in safety-related applications.

(15) Automation and Robots
Investigating benefits of use of artificial intelligence.

(16) Software Houses and Consultants
MASCOT 3 with Ada seems likely to replace MASCOT 2 with Coral 66, particularly for large systems.

Consumer Protection Act threat will provide impetus to industry to advance research and instil real engineering discipline.

(17) General/Technical
The increasing complexity of units undergoing ATE inspection will lead to greater difficulty in assessing fault coverage of ATE software, and how that affects the safety-critical functions of the unit.

Improved man/machine interface and condition monitoring. Use of expert systems.

A project at Edinburgh University is to cover Mathematically Proven Safety Software. Eureka Project EU 263 is for the development of a Safety Engineers Workbench.

Overseas Activities (Question 14)

Comparative activities, regulations and methods overseas; overseas contacts for further information.

(1) Avionics
Europe and USA: Very much in common with UK.

(2) Nuclear Industry
Much information is exchanged with overseas utilities and contractors though on an informal basis. The overseeing body is the IAEA. There is as yet no uniformity of standards and practices though this may be considered. There are a few IAEA Standards, also IEC Standard 880 is relevant. The work of EWICS TC7 is important.

(3) Medical Equipment

IEC TC62 Electrical Equipment in Medical Practice has set up new Working Group WG2 Safety in Computer Systems used in Medical Electrical Equipment. Food and Drug Administration (FDA) in the USA devoting substantial effort in this area. New FDA guidelines expected shortly.

France: Often applies additional technical requirements above published standards.

Rest of Europe – Generally looks for compliance of IEC 601.

Canada and Australia: Legislation requires conformance with standards.

Japan: Lengthy assessment period but general compliance to international standards is sufficient.

Rest of world: IEC 601 accepted. Certain countries may insist on compliance as a condition of import.

(4) Railways

In the USA, France and Sweden single-processor systems seem to be favoured.

Germans, Japanese, Italians and others favour multi-channel systems with identical software in each channel.

(11) Chemical Industry

In USA testing of products FDA Good Laboratory Practice Regulations and Guidelines (GLP).

FDA and Environmental Protection Agency, Rules for Product Registration and Hazard Evaluation.

(16) Software Houses and Consultants

Foreign companies much more willing to spend capital on software tools, giving greater productivity.

Use of international computer tools and languages, with a much larger user base than UK ones, seems to mean fewer bugs.

Guidelines on medical electrical equipment containing software due from USA FDA shortly.

(17) General/Technical

IEEE Computer Society is dealing with software standards and techniques for the test and diagnosis of digital systems.

APPENDIX I

LIST OF CONTRIBUTORS

The following individuals contributed to the preparation of the Report. The inclusion of their names should not however be assumed to imply that they, or the organisations with which they are affiliated, agree with all the views expressed in it; nor should it be assumed that they acted as representatives of the organisations with which they are affiliated. Some others, while not disagreeing with the content, have asked that their names should not appear on the list.

Chairman of the Project Team:

Mr R E Malcolm	Malcolm Associates Ltd
Mr R E B Barnard	GEC-General Signal Ltd
Mr G Belcher	GEC Avionics
Mr R Bell	Health and Safety Executive
Dr P A Bennett	The Centre for Software Engineering Ltd
Mr J W Bibby	Ministry of Defence
Mr P Brown	The Centre for Software Engineering Ltd
Mrs A A Canning	ERA Technology Ltd
Mr M Chudleigh	Cambridge Consultants
Dr D E Clark	
Mr B Davison	British Coal
Dr B W Finnie	The Centre for Software Engineering Ltd
Mr P J B Fergus	Consultant
Mr P J Giles	Safety and Reliability Consultants Ltd
Mr D Grocock	British Steel plc
Mr D J Hawkes	Civil Aviation Authority
Mr M E Jolly	CEGB
Professor J A McDermid	University of York
Dr R G Mellish	Department of Health
Mr P Neilan	Civil Aviation Authority

Mr S R Nunns	ICI plc
Mr M A Ould	Praxis plc
Mr P Robinson	Rolls-Royce and Associates Ltd
Mr B Sefton	The Engineering Equipment and Material Users Association
Mr R C Short	British Railways Board
Mr D J Smith	British Gas plc
Mr M Thomas	Praxis plc
Mr P R Wyman	GEConsult Ltd

DRIVE REPORT

Review of Current Tools and Techniques for the Development of Safety-Critical Software

D L Clutterbuck
Program Validation Ltd

1. Preface

As the demand for computerised control systems grows, to improve the efficiency of our road usage for example, so does our reliance upon their safe operation. In addition, the importance of computers as a means of improving safety, through their ability to monitor many signals and to respond at great speed, must not be underestimated. Whatever the justification for its use, we need to establish the fitness for purpose of any safety-critical computer-based system before it is used operationally.

This report is the deliverable of activity SG3 of DRIVE project V1051 'Procedure for Safety Submissions for Road Transport Informatic (RTI) Systems'. It is a review of software engineering tools and methods currently in use for the development of safety-critical computer-based systems. For more detailed information on the subjects considered, the reader is encouraged to follow up the references.

The work on DRIVE project V1051 is being carried out by a consortium comprising TÜV Rhineland, TNO Netherlands, Leeds University and Program Validation Ltd. Little, if any, of this report is specific to the automotive industry.

2. Introduction

In developing any safety-critical system there is a trade-off between the risk perceived in the use of the system and the cost involved in overcoming or reducing the risk. To help with this, recent draft safety standards [IEC WG9, WG10] have identified integrity levels for systems based on the severity of the hazard(s) resulting from a system failure and on the estimated frequency of occurrence of each such failure. For a given level of integrity an appropriate package of measures (not defined) is to be used for the design, production and assessment of the system.

This approach assumes that we are able to identify the hazards, to quantify their severity and frequency of occurrence, and to select an appropriate package of measures. Unfortunately, each of these tasks is fraught with uncertainty. Clearly, every effort must be made to identify, examine and document all possible hazards. If incident data is available for similar systems, this must be used. However, there can never be a guarantee that all potential hazards have been considered. This is a fundamental problem in the development of any safety-critical system.

Also, we need to assess the severity of each hazard and to determine its probability of occurrence. This is extremely difficult. We must recognise that the assessment of hazard severity is application-dependent and, even within a particular industry, complications can arise. Clearly, in the automotive industry the situation of a failure could dramatically affect the severity of it (windscreen wiper failure at speed in torrential rain, temporary loss of brakes in a crowded area). Also, when attempting to judge the frequency of occurrence of an accident, one often finds there is insufficient evidence on which to base a judgement. For an interesting discussion of this the reader is referred to [HSE 1989].

The final problem, and the one which concerns us here, is to select an appropriate set of design and development procedures once the system hazards, their severity and their frequency of occurrence have been established. Ideally the selection is based on quantitative measures of the effectiveness of the different design and development methods. However, no reliable measures exist. Although we can assess physical failure rates of hardware-based systems, based on the 'mean time between failure' of components, we cannot assess the probability of the introduction of systematic (specification and design) hardware and software errors. This is an extremely complex function of system complexity, staff competency, suitability of proposed approach, familiarity with approach, work environment, project control etc [McDermid 1989]. We can only seek to eliminate these errors by employing 'best practice' during development. Needless to say, what constitutes best practice is often a matter of expert debate and may in fact be dependent upon the application.

Software is of particular concern. Because of the complexity of most computer programs, their sensitivity to error (there is no accepted notion of 'tolerance' of minor errors: each may be catastrophic [Parnas, van Schouwen & Kwan 1990]), and the difficulty in testing software (which results from the myriad of possible states), great care and skill will always be required for the implementation of safety-critical software. Consequently, we must ensure that evaluation activities are not confined to 'black box' testing of the end product, but are carried out during the entire system development, and that the development techniques we employ are suited to rigorous (internal and external) review at all stages. In addition, suppliers must provide full visibility of their development procedures as well as all the supporting documentation.

In this report we examine the different procedures used for the development of software used in computer-based safety-critical systems. We do not attempt to assign merit points to these techniques, instead arguing for a reasoned approach to software development which provides for traceability from requirements to object code. Tools to support these techniques are also discussed where this is felt to be appropriate, although no attempt has been made to reference all applicable tools. Addresses of the vendors of tools referenced in the report, but not given in the STARTS guide [STARTS 1987], are listed in Appendix A.

We have assumed that an ISO 9000 or equivalent quality system is already in use. A more detailed study of standards for safety-critical systems is presented in the report SG1 of V1051 [Buckley, Jesty, Hobley & West 1990].

3. A System Development Lifecycle

System development is often described in terms of a lifecycle, defining a progression from the original statement of requirements through to implementation (and beyond to delivery, installation, maintenance). Although this model is not perfect, suffering from many variants and being too static in many respects, it is intuitively attractive and provides a basis for the definition of development standards (as required by ISO 9000 for example). We have therefore chosen to structure our report around the key phases of a lifecycle development. We do not describe the basic properties of these stages in great detail, this being adequately covered in [STARTS 1987] for example, but instead concentrate on those aspects which relate specifically to safety-critical software-based systems. Management of the development process is discussed in section 8. Comprehensive documentation guidelines can be found in [IEE 1989].

3.1. The Safety Lifecycle

The safety of a system must be considered throughout its development, from project inception to delivery, and beyond to in-service use and maintenance. To ensure that this is done effectively a safety lifecycle should be identified at the start of each project as an extension to the standard project lifecycle. This safety lifecycle will define project deliverables, milestones, review stages etc., but it will additionally emphasise the safety aspects of the system, for example by defining the process of continual safety assessment and by identifying the documentation required to record those decisions relating to safety, together with the manner of their implementation.

A safety lifecycle has been defined in [IEC WG9, WG10] which readers are encouraged to adapt for their own use. We do not discuss it here.

3.2. Insecurities within the Development Lifecycle

Consider a (simple) lifecycle model which involves the creation of the following objects,

- a Statement of Requirements
- a Specification
- a Design
- a Program Implementation
- a binary code representation of the program.

In satisfying ourselves that the system is 'fit for purpose' we need to demonstrate that each of the these objects is *well-formed* (i.e. in accordance with the rules of construction defined to support system evaluation), and that each object is *functionally consistent* with its parent object.

This will support our ultimate goal of establishing the correctness of a software-based system by showing, through logical analysis, that the (final) system requirements are clear, consistent, unambiguous and (as far as can be ascertained) complete, and that the binary code implementation meets the requirements. (We assume here that the system's safety properties are defined as a part of the system requirements, and hence become a 'correctness' goal.)

However, we must accept that in practice our development methodologies are not as systematic as we would wish. In particular,

1. the initial statement of requirements (which may not be stable) is necessarily based on intuition and is often incomplete;

2. the specification may not be formal (in the mathematical sense) and even if it is, any lack of precision in the requirements may have resulted in an incorrect interpretation in the specification;

3. the transformation of a specification (describing *what* is required) into the design (describing *how* the requirement is to be met) and the transformation of the design into the program code is informal and error prone;

4. the programming language may suffer from ambiguities and insecurities and may not therefore be amenable to analysis by logical reasoning;

5. the compiler or assembler used to generate object code from the source program may be defective;

6. the processor specification may be imprecise, and the device may fail to meet it in various ways.

These potential insecurities must be addressed when we are choosing our development methods, and indeed the justification of the choice of tools and techniques will form a part of the safety case for the system.

4. Statement of Requirements

A statement of requirements is a broad outline description of the required system and is produced pre-development, during project initiation. It is sometimes referred to as a User Requirement Specification, and serves to identify the functions required of the proposed equipment. More importantly for us, it also defines any *safety-invariants* (precise statements of the required safety properties) for the system. This may force the early introduction of design constraints (see section 6) identified as essential to a demonstration that the safety-invariants are not violated. Safety should be considered according to the basic function required of the system *and* to what the current state of the art for hardware and software will safely allow.

The safety-invariants for the system are identified by a Preliminary Hazard Analysis [Def Stan 00-56] or similar. This phase is essential, as it underpins all safety-related aspects of the system development. A subset of the system safety-invariants will relate to the software (depending on the partitioning of the system function between the hardware and the software) and will drive the software verification process (section 8). We shall see in section 6 how this information could be used as the specification for a safety monitor – a processor separate from the main control processor.

The Preliminary Hazard Analysis is a high-level appraisal of the system ideally undertaken by a multidisciplinary team, containing at least two members with in-depth knowledge of the application area. Initially, the team must establish the boundaries between the proposed system, the systems with which it may interact and the environment beyond that. Following this, and based on a description of the system structure and function, potential system hazards must be identified, together with any accident sequences which can be envisaged at this early stage.

The team undertaking the analysis should be allowed relatively free rein, the ability to think laterally being a distinct advantage! However, all relevant aspects must be systematically addressed: a checklist should be used to assist with this. If incident data is available for similar systems, it must be used. In Def Stan 00-56, produced by the UK's Ministry of Defence, ten views of the system are suggested, and guidelines for considering each viewpoint are presented. HAZOP [Knowlton 1981] is another approach to hazard analysis, widely used in the chemical industry.

Assessment of system safety continues throughout the system development, extending and refining the safety-invariants in step with the implementation. As the system design proceeds other techniques, such as fault tree analysis (FTA) and failure mode and effect analysis (FMEA), may be used. These are discussed in section 8.

5. Specification

The Specification is produced by the supplier in response to a Statement of Requirements. The specification must be developed in close collaboration with the system procurer and is formally agreed by both parties. It is usually a contractually binding document.

The main purpose of the specification is to define precisely the intended operation of the system. It will comprise a functional description, performance targets, a description of any interfaces with other systems (including human operators), the safety-invariants and any unavoidable (for reasons of safety) design constraints.

The specification provides the basis for a demonstration of the fitness for purpose of the system, and must therefore support an objective assessment of whether the system meets the specification (and hence the requirements). Ideally therefore it will be complete, correct, unambiguous and consistent, at least to the satisfaction of a body of reviewers with appropriate expertise. (A formal demonstration that the specification has all these qualities may not be possible.)

Beyond any design constraints felt necessary for reasons of safety, the specification should allow maximum design freedom. However, some consideration of design issues is inevitable, to ensure that the system is efficiently implementable for example, and to define its interfaces.

Most commonly a natural language is used for the specification, interspersed with any relevant control laws or similar. This is not the ideal: it can be ambiguous and it is difficult to check for consistency. There are a number of possible ways of overcoming these problems, partially at least, ranging from the use of structured English and diagrammatic notations, through to formal notations such as state machines, decision tables, Petri nets and formal methods such as Z and VDM.

5.1. Structured/Semi-formal Techniques

Techniques which reduce the potential for ambiguity and support some degree of consistency checking, but which are not supported by a rigorous mathematical semantic definition are often called structured or semi-formal techniques. They may use textual or graphical notations, or both.

Advanced tools providing support for requirements analysis and specification, and favoured in the UK and Germany respectively are CORE and EPOS, both of which are described in the STARTS guide.

In the CORE method eleven steps are defined to help gather relevant information, to propose data and process relationships, and to check the consistency of these relationships. An abstract requirement is subdivided into more manageable viewpoints (displayed graphically or textually), which are in turn subdivided, resulting in a structured hierarchical definition. This process can be continued down to the level of detailed design (section 6) although other design-specific tools and methods may be more appropriate for this. CORE can help trace each requirement through to the design, and it includes a data dictionary which supports consistency checking. EPOS is similar, supporting a wide range of lifecycle activities.

Another method, now a widely used UK government standard is SSADM. This was designed primarily for commercial application but it is believed by some to be of wider relevance. SSADM is based on entity-relation modelling techniques and data flow diagrams.

Other methods, such as Jackson structure charts, Yourdon data flow diagrams and structured languages (which aim to restrict the power of expression provided by a natural language) are also used. However, we believe that these methods are more appropriate for lower levels of 'specification', i.e. once a system has been decomposed into smaller subsystems and other design work has been carried out.

These semi-formal techniques are clearly applicable to the description of functional requirements, but are not well suited to the definition of non-functional requirements. Also, whilst diagrams may appear easier to understand, diagrammatic methods can produce very bulky specifications, and must be well structured to support any assessment of their completeness. An underlying database which allows one to trace the requirements through into the lower-level specification and design documentation, will help significantly both development and assessment.

To associate a semantics with a specification produced in this manner, additional, more precise notation is required, for example to specify the safety-invariants of the system or the control laws in use.

5.2. Formal Methods

Computer systems can in general be satisfactorily modelled with discrete mathematics – set theory, propositional and predicate logic [Woodcock & Loomes 1988]. This mathematical base means that software engineers can, in line with other engineering disciplines, construct formal system models whose consistency can be demonstrated [Cohen, Harwood & Jackson 1986], and from which implementations can be rigorously derived.

Two formal specification languages favoured in the UK are Z and VDM. Both support a model-based approach to specification, in which a system model is constructed from abstract primitives. VDM [Jones 1986] encourages a layered top-down development of systems. At the top level a specification is an abstract model which identifies the system states, and defines the system operations. Data objects are specified as abstract mathematical data types, such as sets and mappings, and the operations on these data objects may be functions, specified with pre- and post-conditions. Z [Spivey 1988, 1989] is based on set theory and predicate logic, but has an additional abstraction mechanism, called a schema, to help structure a specification. Z is the subject of a great deal of research, particularly at the Programming Research Group in the University of Oxford, although VDM, being particularly well suited to 'low-level' (concrete) specification, is perhaps more widely used in industry for embedded system specification. There is also progress towards a British and International VDM standard.

An alternative style of specification is property-based, in which a specification comprises axioms which define the relationships between the operations of the system. Algebraic specification languages such as OBJ [Goguen 1984] fall into this category. A strength of the model-based approach is that the resulting specification can be more clearly related to the proposed system, and is therefore better suited to 'what if?' analyses and comparison back to the original statement of requirements. Checking the consistency of the rules in an algebraic language is difficult, and the problem of determining whether an arbitrary set of rewrite rules is convergent, i.e. that they will terminate and the result will be independent of their order of application, is known to be algorithmically undecidable [Musser 1979]. Other formal languages are in use, many of which are under evaluation in various applied research projects. A good overview of formal methods can be found in [Cohen *et al.* 1986].

Formal specification can be carried out at varying levels of abstraction, as appropriate to the complexity of the system being implemented. As the system is decomposed, further details will emerge and the formal specification may be extended. Indeed, both VDM and Z have an associated set of rules and procedures which support refinement (or reification) of specifications towards implementations. Each such refinement can (in theory) be proved correct. This is done in VDM by showing retrospectively that the derived implementation satisfies necessary conditions, defined by domain, result and adequacy rules. An approach proposed for Z is a 'refinement calculus' where correctness of refinements is assured by their method of construction [Morgan 1990]. Either way the work involved in formally verifying the correctness of the refinement steps is very substantial and is still a research topic. A less formal approach, sometimes called the rigorous approach – an intuitive argument which could (one assumes) be backed up by formal proof, is more usual. In fact it has been argued [Hall 1990] that formal methods are most cost-effective when used for abstract specification without proof of refinement.

A good formal specification comprises a natural-language description with embedded mathematics. It should read clearly with the mathematics omitted. The procurer of the system can then easily read the document and may also review the mathematics. In addition, this 'redundancy' provides a source of reference against which an external reviewer can assess the formal description.

Tool support for formal methods is developing and a number of syntax editors and type checkers now exist for VDM (e.g. SPECBOX, GENESIS) and Z (e.g. FUZZ, CADIZ). In addition theorem provers and proof assistants are being developed (e.g. MURAL) to discharge the proof obligations resulting from the specification and refinement work. Prototyping as a means of checking the specification is considered in section 8.

Formal methods are no panacea: it is possible to construct a 'poor' formal specification – which is difficult to check for well-formedness and functional consistency. Also, the completeness of any specification (formal or otherwise) can never be fully established. However, formal methods offer many advantages. Their underlying mathematics helps to ensure that a specification is unambiguous, and can support well-formedness and functional consistency checks. Perhaps most importantly, a formal specification will encourage early consideration of relevant issues, and provide a sound basis for review.

As more engineers are trained in this discipline, the tool support will inevitably improve, broadening the application of formal methods still further and increasing our confidence in the techniques. The use of formal methods to clarify requirements, and to perform refinement and verification of designs produced by structured methods, seems a practical way forward.

6. Design

Design is the creative process by which a specification is further refined towards its ultimate implementation. Design involves *abstraction* – to identify the essential system components; *decomposition* – to modularise a system into smaller subsystems; and *elaboration* – to refine the specification of these components until the system is implementable. The process of design may cause interactive revision of the requirements and the specification.

Software engineers often view design as a two-stage process: *architectural design* – which results in a definition of the hardware-software architecture, and of the data structures, interfaces, and main components of the software; and *detailed software design* – which results in a detailed description of the software components, their interface, algorithms, and any constraints (with respect to size, timing and function).

Of course, in practice the design process is more complex, comprising repeated decomposition and 'specification' until the complexity of each subsystem is reduced to manageable proportions. However, a distinction between design stages is useful, encouraging a design review before further work is carried out.

6.1. Architectural Design

Architectural design provides the technical and managerial foundation for the rest of the project. It is a highly creative process which results in a description of the system structure in terms of the hardware and software components, interconnected in a defined manner. The function of each component must be defined and must be related back to the specification. All information expected to be of relevance to the subsequent development stages must be defined. The architectural design therefore identifies subsystems and the tests required to integrate these subsystems.

The range of notations currently used for design description is immense, and includes natural language as well as the formal and semi-formal notations discussed earlier. Different notations may be better suited to different types of subsystem. However, before we consider this further, let us examine design techniques for safety-critical systems.

6.1.1. *Designing for Safety*

A safety-critical system is designed to protect against any potentially unsafe failures of its subsystems. The final design will inevitably take into account the cost of further reducing the likelihood of an unsafe system state arising. Unfortunately, it is not possible to predict the likelihood of a failure caused by a systematic or design error, and all software errors are of this type. One may therefore choose to protect against software errors by employing extra hardware. However, the more protective measures there are in hardware the greater is the potential for their (physical) failure, perhaps requiring backup – in hardware and so on.

There are two basic approaches to protection against failures: *fault avoidance* and *fault tolerance*. Fault avoidance seeks to prevent systematic failure through the use of rigorous development procedures, such as those considered in this report for software. This is a minimum strategy for any critical system. Fault tolerance seeks to provide an acceptable response to failures of whatever type. The IEC standard for safety-related software [IEC WG9] recognises three types of fault tolerance: fail safe; fault compensating; and fault masking.

A fail-safe system aims to ensure that on the detection of a failure of a part of the system, the system is set into a safe state, for example by setting all traffic signals to red. Such a state may not of course be achievable.

A fault-compensating system attempts to maintain a safe level of functionality ('limp home') on detection of a failure. This may be because there is no fail-safe state, or it may be that a latent state ('breakdown') is not acceptable. (In the automotive industry a breakdown through poor system design is likely to result in very significant loss of sales as well as recall costs.) Of course, defining a 'limp home' mode that is safe enough to continue, but sufficiently degraded to ensure rapid repair, may not be easy.

A fault-masking system attempts to continue the operation of the system in the event of a fault occurring. When faults are properly masked there will be little (or no) effect on the functioning of the system. Examples include Hamming codes for data corruption, and two out of three voting systems. A detailed examination of error-detection techniques for microcomputers can be found in [Holscher & Rader 1984]. Regardless of any fault tolerance in the system design, rigorous fault-avoidance procedures should be used throughout the software development.

6.1.2. *Safety Monitors*

A fault-tolerant system often uses redundant hardware and software channels to detect a failure. Redundancy clearly provides protection against random failure of components. Some argue that diversity of implementation between the channels also provides protection against systematic failure. As far as the hardware is concerned this can be accepted to some degree, since different microprocessors will have been developed to different specifications and are therefore unlikely (unquantifiable!) to contain common-mode errors. Different microprocessors will also employ different assemblers or compilers, and probably a different programming language.

The argument for diversity as a means of protection against software failure is much weaker. Common failure modes are likely, for the specification is of course the same and implementation errors usually arise from the same complex aspects of the specification. Diverse systems also need voting mechanisms, and their implementations may themselves be erroneous. Studies under Nancy Leveson (for example [Leveson 1989]) have shown that in practice little or no extra protection is gained from the use of diverse software, and the extra expenditure can be substantial.

One proposed solution to this problem is based on an alternative system architecture. In this approach (for example [Millward 1990]) a two-channel system is replaced by a single channel implementing the control function and a safety monitor. The safety monitor reads the inputs to the control device and monitors the outputs. As soon as the safety monitor identifies a violation of the safety-invariants (defined during the safety assessment activities), it would reset the system to a fail-safe (or alternative) state. To replace a three-channel system, two control-plus-monitor devices could be combined via a fail-safe voter, and for a 'limp home' system the safety monitor could switch to a limited-function backup device.

In this approach it could be argued that the control device is no longer safety-critical, although the much simpler safety monitor would be. This may allow us to use a special-purpose high-integrity microprocessor as the safety monitor, running formally proven software developed with purpose-built high-integrity support tools. The specification for the safety monitor could be formally described.

Such an approach should reduce the complexity of the safety-critical part of the system and would therefore assist both the development and the evaluation activities.

6.1.3. *Designing for Assessment*

A safety-critical system should undergo independent assessment, whether by a separate company or by a managerially separate (to board level) group within the same organisation. Certification of the software within a system must be undertaken by assessment of the whole development lifecycle and should not be based solely on a 'black box' test. Many system procurers now demand far greater visibility of the development process and documentation. System (and software) assessment rarely concludes satisfactorily if the system (and software) has not been developed with assessment in mind.

Clearly an assessment will be easier for the less complex systems. Unnecessary complexity should be avoided in a a safety-critical system. To help control the complexity, it may be possible to design a system which separates critical and non-critical functions (as with the earlier safety monitor). However, care must be taken. For example, if critical and 'non-critical' functions implemented in software access common memory, then all the software should be regarded as safety-critical.

Certain design techniques can conflict with the need to perform rigorous analysis of the system and its software. For example, the choice between an interrupt-based system and one in which input and output ports are polled will depend upon which of these produces the simpler system, where the term 'simpler' is to be viewed in the context of system design *and* system assessment. The analysis of systems based on asynchronous interrupts is extremely difficult.

Similarly, multi-tasking systems (including operating systems) pose difficult analysis problems, particularly of access conflict over shared data items and deadlock between communicating processes. Analysis of such systems is still a research topic. However, it is also the case that a sequential design could result in an extensive use of global variables. This increases connectivity between the program's procedures or subroutines, making analysis more difficult. Nevertheless, currently these are more tractable analysis problems than those posed by multi-tasking systems.

Dynamic memory-allocation strategies can also introduce uncertainty: will a run-time failure arise from excessive use of memory? Memory requirements should be statically determinable.

Further detailed guidelines on necessary and unacceptable practices can be found in [Holscher & Rader 1984] and should be studied.

Clearly there is no single answer, the optimal solution depends upon considerations of timing and complexity, the maturity of the proposed techniques, the development support for the hardware and the software, and the support for analysis. Nevertheless, should any design technique be used which may conflict with published guidelines or with otherwise accepted practice for safety-critical systems, its use must be justified to the satisfaction of the independent assessment team and the procurer of the system.

6.2. Detailed Software Design

Detailed design is the process by which the software components identified during architectural design are refined to the point of implementation, so that the functional and non-functional (e.g. performance-related) requirements are met. In presenting the additional detailed information, it is essential that the need for eventual analysis of the software is reflected in the documentation. It should also be recognised that the expansion of detail will require stringent management and control of documentation, as discussed in section 9.

Once a software component has been identified, together with its data flows and ideally a formal statement of its intended operation, the process of functional decomposition can be continued until implementable data types and procedures or subroutines are identified. For any such subcomponent the following information is required:

- identification of the parent component (to support traceability);
- the data imported and exported by the subcomponent;
- the relationship between the imported and exported data items (i.e. the function of the subcomponent);
- the constraints on the imported data necessary for the correct operation of the subcomponent;
- a description of the algorithm to be used for the implementation, or should further structural decomposition be required, a definition of its structure identifying subcomponents.

For formal verification (section 8) we require that the intended operation of the subcomponent, including any constraints on initial values, is specified in an appropriate formal notation. The use of formal methods during specification and design will assist in this.

The imported and exported variables of a subcomponent are identified during data-flow design, and these can be carried through into the program as annotations (section 7) which are checked for consistency by information-flow analysis (section 8).

As for architectural design, the way in which the detailed design may affect the safety of the system must be re-assessed, and more detailed safety-invariants may result.

6.3. Tools and Methods

In practice, there is often little distinction between the specification, architectural design and detailed software design activities. Consequently, the formal and semi-formal methods and tools already discussed apply also to the design stages, with the same advantages and disadvantages. Other design tools and methods, such as Yourdon [Yourdon & Constantine 1979], Jackson [Jackson 1983], Mascot and HOOD are also available. The plethora of these methods only adds to the difficulty of choosing an appropriate set of techniques for safety-critical or safety-related system development. Should we use data flow diagrams, structure charts, or process diagrams?

What is perhaps more important than the relative merits of the various techniques is the need to examine a system from a number of differing viewpoints, such as its data flow and its functional composition, both diagrammatically and textually, formally and semi-formally.

The need for flexibility is reflected in the STARTS Guide's [STARTS 1987] consideration of various possible extensions to a single-user design tool supporting just one design representation with little checking and no method guidance. These are:

- *Better Method Support.* To provide support for many design representations with thorough checking in and between representations, and to allow transformation between representations. Also training in the use of the method, preferably within the application domain, is required.

- *Team Support.* To allow teams of people working together to share a common database, ideally with built-in configuration and version control.

- *Tool Integration.* To allow interaction between the design stages (and the specification stage), for example to ensure that detailed design decisions do not violate the architectural design, and possibly to generate templates for the detailed design. Also, to interface to project management and verification/test tools.

Recent developments such as the Software Backplane which provides a link between different tools, and the Virtual Software Factory (VSF) (a configurable CASE tool which supports method definition and integration based on a common database) are of interest here, providing mixed viewpoints and tool integration, and supporting traceability of requirements. When coupled to formal notation(s) for the actual specification of function, significant progress will have been made.

Another approach is that of object-oriented design. This is essentially an extension of the abstract data type approach (in which a data type is defined together with the operations supported for that type) to include classes of objects and the notion of object inheritance. It supports the 'separation of concerns' required to reduce system complexity, although experience of its application in real-time control applications is currently limited, as it is most widely used for graphical interfaces.

Whatever combination of techniques is ultimately chosen, the validity of the safety-invariants must be continually re-established as the system design (and hence the safety-invariants) become increasingly detailed, revealing further ways in which the basic safety rules may be transgressed.

7. Program Implementation

In a safety-critical system we must carefully consider the choice of programming language. It is not possible to analyse rigorously a program which uses language constructs whose definitions are ambiguous. In some languages, violations of the definition can only be detected at run-time. Also, what confidence can we have in the compilers of the various languages? Should optimising compilers be used?

In this section we examine the requirements for high-integrity languages and their compilers. We also briefly consider the choice of microprocessor.

7.1. Programming Languages

According to Carré [Carré, Jennings, Maclennan & Farrow 1989] there are six essential considerations for a high-integrity programming language:

- *Logical Soundness:* For formal reasoning to be possible, the programming language needs to be logically coherent and unambiguous, with a formally defined semantics.

- *Simplicity of Definition:* If the formal definition is large (Ada's runs to eight volumes) the coherence of the language is hard to establish, precluding the social process essential to its justification [DeMillo, Lipton & Perlis 1979], reasoning about programs becomes uncertain, and formal tool development impractical.

- *Expressive Power:* The ease with which a specification can be systematically 'refined' into an implementation depends upon the expressive power of the language. Also, with the introduction of structured statements, strong typing, and procedural and data abstraction, much of the burden of program correctness checking has shifted from the programmer to the language and its compiler.

- *Security:* An insecurity is a feature of a programming language whose implementation makes it very difficult (or impossible) to detect violation of the language rules other than by execution. All standard programming languages suffer from insecurities. If any insecurities in a program pass undetected, analysis of the program, formal or otherwise, will be invalidated.

- *Verifiability:* We should ideally be able to show through logical argument that a program is an implementation of its specification. This requires a relatively simple formal definition of the language. In addition, to limit the complexity of the task, we need to be able to reason about fragments of code out of context of the entire program. This requires support for procedural and data abstraction, as well as suitable scope and visibility rules.

- *Bounded Space and Time Requirements:* In real-time control applications we must ensure that adequate memory is available for the running program. Dynamic storage allocation is therefore to be avoided where possible. Strict timing requirements demand explicit, finite bounds on the number of loop iterations.

As might be expected, no standard languages score highly in all of the above. Examples of common difficulties, which can arise in using many programming languages, are:

- *subprogram side-effects* whereby variables in the calling environment may be unexpectedly changed, even causing ambiguities when they occur in function evaluations within an expression;

- *aliasing* whereby two or more distinct names refer (possibly inadvertently) to the same storage location, so that a change to one variable may also modify a seemingly different variable;

- *failures to initialise* resulting in the use or potential use of a variable before it has been assigned a value;

- *expression evaluation errors* which might result for instance from an array subscript being outside the permitted index range, from the use of a partial function with invalid arguments (e.g. division by zero) or from arithmetic overflow.

Ada is extremely complex and contains many insecurities [Wichmann 1989]; Pascal's support for abstraction is limited; C is poorly defined, with many insecurities, and is generally regarded as unsuitable for use in high-integrity applications; Modula-2 (perhaps the most suitable language) suffers from a lack of tool support (and users!); assembly languages are very informally defined, have limited expressive power and are too permissive (this prompted an early draft of Def Stan 00-55 to ban the use of assembly languages, although it is now accepted that this is unrealistic). Informal comparative studies can be found in [Cullyer, Goodenough & Wichmann 1991].

An approach might be to define a new language, which satisfies the requirements. In fact, a few languages have been developed with this aim, including Euclid [Lampson *et al.* 1977], NewSpeak [Currie 1989] and m-Verdi [Craigen 1987], although none have become established (and some of which in any case do not meet all the requirements). The reluctance of the industrial computing community to adopt a new language is largely because of the enormous investment required to develop reliable compilers and other support tools, and to train and establish a community of users sufficient for its use in critical systems. (The political and financial support behind Ada for example was very great.)

An alternative approach followed in the UK has resulted in the definition of subsets of the more suitable standard languages. Examples include SPARK (an Ada subset) [Carré *et al.* 1989], SPADE-Pascal [Carré & Debney 1985], and a M68020 assembly language subset [Clutterbuck 1989]. Each 'high-integrity' subset is developed from the parent language by disallowing any construct which is in some sense unverifiable (see above), and by adding annotations (formal comments) to help eliminate insecurities from those constructs which remain, for example by defining the import-export relations for the module (as given in its detailed design description). This allows us to build on existing technology, by providing more rigorous definitions of commonly used languages, by training users in programming techniques which assist in the analysis process and by providing analysis tools.

7.2. Compilers

Programming languages cannot be considered in isolation from the compilation support provided for them. Compilers are complex programs which may themselves introduce errors. Some argue for the use of assembly code in small, very high-integrity systems simply to avoid this problem (assemblers are much simpler and are therefore less error prone). Clearly, compilers of the highest integrity are needed.

Currently, no formally developed compilers are commercially available ([Polak 1981] documents the verification of a Pascal-like compiler). The construction of such a tool is extremely difficult, and for standard languages such as Ada and Pascal, it is perhaps beyond the state of the art to produce a formally verified, efficient compiler. However, academic interest in this subject remains, most notably through projects at Oxford University [Hoare 1990], at Computational Logic Inc. in the USA [Good 1989], and at Kiel University [Karger 1990], and progress can be expected. In the meantime we must rely on less rigorous development techniques, and certification of compilers by recognised authorities, such as, in the UK, the British Standards Institution (e.g. Pascal), and the National Computing Centre (e.g. Ada). Some work on the verification of compiler-generated code has also been carried out [PVL 1990].

Although the suite of tests used by the compiler validation centres cannot be relied upon to establish the 'correctness' of the object code generated in all circumstances, it does at least help to demonstrate that the compiler conforms to the language standard – a minimum requirement. It should also be noted that compiler 'evaluation' centres also exist (BSI for Ada). Evaluation provides further assessment of the compiler, more generally relating to its fitness for purpose. The evaluation software or reports on evaluated compilers can be purchased.

It is often argued that the optimisations performed by a compiler are complex and hence should not be used for high-integrity software. However, work into the verification of compiler-generated object code (from Ada to M68020) [PVL 1990] has shown that the situation is not clear cut. It was found that for the analysis to proceed with the minimum of difficulty it was often necessary to use the compiler with optimisation enabled. As the compiler generates intermediate code assuming optimisation is enabled, very often the unoptimised code contained a significant number of additional program paths and redundant statements. Optimisations which reduced this redundancy were helpful. However, optimisations which cause 'code motion' (hoisting loop invariants, reduction of loops to common form) or which 'in-line' subprograms were unhelpful. In the former case the correspondence between an execution state in the source and in the target program had not been clearly preserved (making it difficult to re-use proof information from the source program), and in the latter case because the optimisation increased the complexity of the code fragment to be verified. Clearly, greater control over the optimisations performed by existing compilers would be helpful.

7.3. Microprocessors
There are numerous microprocessors in use throughout the world and a comparison of their relative merits would be an enormous task. However, the work carried out in the UK and in the USA on the development of high-integrity microprocessors is worthy of a mention.

In the UK, the Royal Signals and Radar Establishment formally specified and subsequently developed a 32-bit microprocessor called VIPER [Kershaw 1985]. This is a simple device, which does not support interrupts and which will stop on detecting an error condition (such as an illegal opcode). VIPERs can be combined in dual master–slave fault-tolerant configurations. However, VIPER's relatively slow speed limits its application in real time control. In the USA, a 32-bit microprocessor has been formally developed down to gate level [Hunt 1986]. The aim is to formally develop all the necessary support software also [Good 1989].

The work on formally developed microprocessors was prompted by concerns about 'undocumented' opcodes, second-source masking discrepancies and informal functional descriptions. It was believed that higher assurance would be gained through the use of a formally developed microprocessor. However, industry has yet to be convinced, preferring instead to rely upon those microprocessors with a large body of generally satisfied users. There is clearly a parallel here with the attempts to introduce new programming languages. Nevertheless, further significant advancements in this area can be expected.

8. Software Evaluation

Assurance in the fitness for purpose of the software within a system is very largely gained by checking (insofar as it is possible) that the statement of requirements for the software is 'adequate' and that the implementation meets these requirements. This is often referred to as validation (is it the right product?) and verification (is the product right?). Verification proceeds by comparing the specification to the requirements; the architectural design to the specification; the detailed design to the architectural design; the code to the detailed design. This requires unambiguous, clear and precise documentation at each of these lifecycle stages, where each document is clearly derived from the previous stage. Without this 'logical thread', documentation produced to satisfy quality assurance requirements is often aimless, making verification (formal or otherwise) impossible, and preventing meaningful validation of the system.

In fact, some argue that the level of rigour one wishes to apply to the software verification and validation activities should relate to the levels of integrity proposed within the IEC software safety standard [IEC WG9]. In other words, for the highest level of integrity we would expect to be able to perform formal code verification, for the lowest perhaps only a limited dynamic test would suffice. This in turn affects the choice of specification technique, programming language etc. needed to support the verification.

Validation is initially performed prior to the production of the statement of requirements, and encompasses the Preliminary Hazard Analysis. Validation continues throughout the development and verification stages.

In this section we briefly address safety assessment techniques (already a well established subject area) before considering software specific validation and verification activities such as the prototyping of specifications, program walkthrough, dynamic test, static analysis and program proof.

8.1. Safety Assessment

In order that the safety-invariants of the system are not violated as the system is refined through the various stages of specification and design, it is important to assess the safety implications of all design decisions, by reference to the Preliminary Hazard Analysis work. This not only supports the system development but also provides 'integrity targets' for any third-party assessment of the system, allowing detailed considerations of the unsafe failure modes. There are two commonly used techniques for this: fault tree analysis and failure mode and effect analysis.

In fault tree analysis (FTA) the system is examined to determine how each potential hazard identified by the Preliminary Hazard Analysis may arise. A graphical approach based on a set of logical combinators (AND, OR etc.) is most often used. Any potential route to a hazard must then be either eliminated or protected against.

Failure mode and effect (and criticality, a variant) analysis (FMEA) operates from a different viewpoint. Here the task is to identify a failure mode for each component of the system and to determine the impact of that failure on the total system. This can lead to a very comprehensive examination of the system, but consequently it can also be an unwieldy and very lengthy process for a system of any complexity. It also assumes that the component failures are known (or predictable) and does not consider coincident failures. The criticality analysis (FMECA) includes an assessment of the criticality of a given component to the system failure and aims to identify those components deserving special attention, although ranking criticality is not a trivial exercise!

FMEA techniques can be employed to feed the fault tree analysis and can be used with varying degrees of abstraction. For more information the reader is referred to [IEC C0138] for example. The application of these techniques to software (other than at a 'black box' level) is less advanced, as a failure mode for software is often difficult to determine. However, some detailed studies have been carried out [Leveson & Harvey 1983].

8.2. Prototyping

A particularly difficult task in any system development is to ensure that the statement of requirements is adequate and that it has been correctly represented by the specification. Very often discrepancies only appear late on in the development, when some (or all) of the implementation has been completed. Peer review is clearly essential for the assessment of the statement of requirements, and for the Preliminary Hazard Analysis. To help with the examination of the specification, it may be beneficial to animate it. This is a technique known as *prototyping*.

A prototyped specification helps the procurer and the supplier to assess the adequacy and correctness of the specification. It can also be used to help with safety assessment, by experimentation with various input conditions. A prototype may be maintained throughout the development to evaluate proposed changes for example [Bromell & Sadler 1987].

Prototyped software is often implemented in functional or logic programming languages, such as Prolog, which allow for very rapid development. These languages are not in general efficient enough in execution to be used in the final implementation (and do not satisfy bounded memory constraints for safety-critical systems). This must be regarded as a good thing, for continued iteration of a prototype to a final solution is very difficult to control. If a more traditional programming language is used for the prototyping, there should be no attempt to modify the prototype for actual service.

A prototype is difficult to construct without first undertaking significant system design work. This may undermine its viability.

8.3. Design and Code Analysis

Following on from the specification there will be the architectural and detailed design activities. Prototyping may be used to assess the effectiveness of different design approaches, as well as their conformance to requirements. If the specification is formally stated it is in theory possible to show by logical reasoning that system requirements have been maintained by the design. However, we have already stated that this is a difficult task, and a formal approach which instead concentrates on the safety-invariants may be more practical. The existence of a data dictionary at the design stage will assist the code-verification activity.

Designs should be formally reviewed. Guides for this are available, for example from the IEC TC56 working group. To undertake a review a comprehensive rationale of the design must be produced. In our experience as third-party assessors this is rarely done, and one is forced to attempt to relate the code directly to the specification. Very little assurance in the fitness for purpose of the system can be gained in this manner.

Code verification comprises three complementary techniques (program walkthrough, dynamic analysis and static analysis) all of which should be used for the assessment of safety-critical software.

8.3.1. *Program Walkthrough*

It is often very revealing to try to read another person's software. One should be able to relate the code to the design and hence to the specification with little or no difficulty. More often than not this is impossible due to poor documentation, an inadequately defined programming language, poor programming style, or all three.

In a code review [Fagan 1976], the code reader should not have to refer to the programmer for clarification. If clarification is required, then this should be made through additional program comments (or perhaps recoding in severe circumstances) and *not* verbally. The code reviewer can also check that the mandated programming standards are adhered to.

At the end of the review, the reviewer's comments should be recorded and the resulting actions followed through and documented under full change control. The value of this approach should not be underestimated. However, because important omissions or errors may be overlooked in a complex system, it must not be totally relied upon.

8.3.2. *Dynamic Test*

Dynamic test is the conventional method of checking programs. The developer's test strategy for a system should be defined during the specification and design phases, and must include module (i.e. procedure, program, subsystem) functional tests (for normal and error conditions) and module integration tests.

A program under test is executed with differing combinations of input data and the results are analysed to see if they are as expected. This requires the creation of tests, an environment (test harness) to apply the tests to the software being tested, the definition of expected results, a comparison of the actual results to the expected results, a procedure for correcting discrepancies (section 10), and a demonstration of test data adequacy.

Although each of the above is a subject in its own right, the most difficult areas are the generation of test data and the demonstration of the adequacy of the test data set. Ideally one would like to say that all possible inputs have been applied to the system. For even a relatively simple program this is obviously impractical; so when do you stop testing?

Unfortunately there is no accepted answer to this. A number of commercially available test systems do attempt to provide metrics for 'test coverage'. These metrics relate to code coverage (statements, branches or paths), system coverage (procedures analysed) and interface coverage (input/output operations). Determining an acceptable coverage for a given risk is difficult. It has been argued [Hennell 1989] that the achievement of adequate levels of testing for safety-critical software is beyond current technology. Parnas argues that assurance in a system rests upon dynamic testing, mathematical review of all development stages, and certification of personnel and process. He also points out that the distribution of the test data must be representative of the operating environment if the testing is to be statistically valid. Indeed, systems whose 'trajectory' of input data is long (i.e. where system behaviour can depend upon events arbitrarily far in the past) cannot be satisfactorily tested [Parnas, van Schouwen & Kwan 1990].

Unless a test strategy is well planned and documented, showing an intelligently selected test data set complete with justifications for the test, then little confidence can be placed in the test procedures.

Commercially available dynamic test tools include TESTBED, which also performs complexity analysis and provides test effectiveness measurement, and SOFTEST and VAX TESTMANAGER, which are primarily test harnesses also providing for the checking of results. The actual choice of tool may be driven as much by supported languages and host machine, as by differences in the functionality of these tools. An emulator may be used to provide a high-level symbolic debug facility, which provides visibility of the software under test. However, with many of these approaches one must be wary of any intrusive effect upon the analysis. Since the integrity of a compiler cannot usually be guaranteed, it is essential that the compiled code is tested in its final executable form.

8.3.3. *Static Analysis*
Static analysis does not require the execution of the program being analysed. It can be used to determine properties of the program which are universally true for all possible execution conditions. Static analysis methods range in sophistication from code-of-practice audit and structural complexity analysis, to flow and semantic analysis, and formal verification.

Code-of-practice audit usually only addresses conformance to naming and layout conventions. It may however also encompass more sophisticated well-formation checks such as language restrictions, control structure, data usage etc. For reliable application of these checks, tool support is required (discussed below).

Attempts have been made [McCabe 1976, Halstead 1977] to define metrics for the measurement of code complexity. However, code complexity depends upon many factors and is difficult to define precisely. Consequently, such metrics are considered to be of little use in assessing the fitness for purpose of high-integrity software.

A more effective application for static analysis is the demonstration of a program's well-formedness with respect to its control, data and information flow, and of its functional consistency with its specification. Such analyses are performed for all paths through the program and for all input data over a defined range.

An example of a static analysis system is SPADE. It comprises flow analysers (the control, data and information flow analysers) and semantic analysis tools (the verification condition generator, proof checker and symbolic interpreter).

Before analysis the program must be modelled in SPADE's Functional Description Language (FDL). This model may be produced by an automatic translator, such as the SPADE-Pascal translator, or manually. The FDL reader then checks the syntactic legality of the FDL text and also performs all possible static semantic checks such as determining the accessibility and converse-accessibility of statements from the start and finish statements respectively; checking type compatibility and the use of labels and variables; checking that exported variables are defined and that imported variables are referenced. (For a valid FDL model, the language of the source program must be well defined and free from ambiguity. A subset of a standard language is therefore a requirement, as discussed in section 7.) If no errors are found, the tools are applied to perform program flow analysis and then (if the results are satisfactory) program verification.

The flow analysers check that a program is well formed with respect to its control structure, data usage and information flow. If a program is found to be defective in any of these respects, the errors or anomalies are described in a flow analysis report. Each flow analyser also produces tabular output.

Typical problems detected by these tools are unstructured code; reference to undefined variables or non-use of variable definitions; incorrect import – export specifications (dependency relations) for a module; stable loop-exit conditions and redundant statements. Ideally flow analysis is done as the code is being developed.

After checking the integrity of a program's control, data and information flow, one can then verify that the program performs the function required of it. This is achieved through the use of the semantic analysis tools, in particular the Verification Condition Generator (VCG) and the Proof Checker. The VCG can generate both path functions and verification conditions.

A path function comprises a traversal condition and an action. The traversal condition for a path states the conditions under which that path is executed; the action expresses the final values of all variables in terms of their values at the initial endpoint of the path. A path function is generated for each path through the program. This information is most often used for direct comparison with the specification document. For example, if the specification states that the windows must automatically close if the electronic key of the driver door is inserted, then we would expect at least one path condition of the program to contain a traversal condition of the form *DoorkeyInserted*, and we would then check that the action for each such path contained the assignment *CloseWindows*. We would also check that no other untoward actions took place under this condition, and that the windows were not closed under any other unspecified condition.

Path-function information can also be used to guide the generation of structural test data. By supplying the traversal conditions of each path through the program the VCG has effectively identified all the input test values required for full path coverage of the program.

Verification conditions are generated if a program proof is to be attempted: our next subject.

Other static analysis tools include LOGISCOPE, for complexity analysis, MALPAS, for flow and semantic analysis, and TESTBED, for code of practice audit, control flow and data usage.

8.3.4. *Program Verification*
The most rigorous technique for showing conformance between implementation and specification is that of formal program verification. Although labour intensive and often requiring considerable skill, such analyses are justified for safety-critical software, where dynamic test cannot by itself be relied upon to show that the software will operate correctly in all circumstances. However, program verification is not a substitute for dynamic test: timing constraints for example cannot easily be verified in this way, hardware and compiler errors may be revealed under dynamic test, and the man–machine interface can of course only be assessed by execution.

To perform a proof of a module (program or procedure), the detailed design description for the module must define the function of the module in an appropriate logical notation. The module specification may in turn be derived from a more abstract formal specification or it may be derived (with more difficulty) from a precise, unambiguous English specification. These 'assertions' (pre-conditions, post-conditions and loop-invariants), are then embedded in the program as formal comments (annotations). From these assertions, theorems (verification conditions) are generated which if proven to be true, verify conformance of the code to the specification. To assist with these proofs, a proof tool should be used.

As already mentioned the SPADE toolset can generate verification conditions from suitable code. SPADE also provides an interactive Proof Checker to assist in the proof of these theorems. The Proof Checker generates a proof script, providing valuable quality assurance support.

Other proof tools being developed for specification languages may also be of use for code verification [Gordon 1987, Jones, Jones, Lindsay & Moore 1991, Abrial 1990].

Formal program proof is not easy. It is currently undertaken for only the most critical systems and by highly trained personnel [O'Neill *et al.* 1988]. However, tool support is gradually improving, and the use of such a technique can be expected to become a requirement for critical systems in the future. Its scope can be deliberately limited, for example to prove only that the safety-invariants hold.

9. The Management of Change

One of the attractions of software is the apparent ease with which it can be changed, as compared to a similar mechanical system. Within the automotive industry, where variations in a system can result from different vehicle models, different vehicle types within a model range, differences between yearly releases, and international differences in emission and other regulations, this flexibility is particularly welcome. However, these changes must be controlled, and the cost of this can be significant, although the cost of failing to do so will be higher.

Considerable re-analysis work is often required for apparently quite simple changes to software, depending of course upon the impact the change has on other program modules. The detailed design documentation can be used to help assess the amount of re-analysis required. This should clearly describe the flow of information into and out of the procedure as well as the function of the module. Changes in the value ranges of variables must be very carefully examined. The exact configuration of each delivered system must be recorded and the various configuration items must remain available for reconstruction (for maintenance and support).

Configuration management is of course only one aspect of project management, and is already well established within manufacturing industries. Standards such as ISO 9000 require configuration management, and standards such as BS 6488 exist to support it. However, its importance to software development cannot be overstated. Documentation must also be controlled in this manner, as it must evolve with the software revisions.

Configuration management comprises three control functions: *version control, configuration control* and *change control*.

Version control is essentially the process of unique identification (by version number) of systems, subsystems, and modules of code, supported by documentation to describe the nature, date and author of variants to the version (including upgrades to the next version). This allows for retrospective examination of the development history of the software, and consequently for restoration of previous systems (provided their configurations are known).

A system is constructed from a collection of subsystems. Each subsystem should have associated with it a version number. The configuration of the system is then defined by the version numbers of the subsystems. Similarly, the configuration of a subsystem may be defined by the version numbers of lower-level units. Clearly, to ensure that the released system comprises the desired subunits etc., some form of *configuration control* is required. This requires knowledge of the interdependencies between the various system units as well as their current status i.e. under development, under analysis, approved etc. Note that for software, individual procedures and functions may be under version control, particularly where these form a part of a 'software library'.

Requests for changes may be generated internally to the organisation or by the organisation's clients. These change requests must be logged, and the procedure defined for the implementation of the change must be followed. A *change control* procedure must encompass the communication of the change request (to gain authorisation for the change), the notification of authorisation, the implementation of the change, assessment of the change, and communication of the change when made. The progress of the change must be rigorously controlled and recorded. A change (or a set of changes) will result in a new version number and hence in a new system configuration.

There are a relatively large number of configuration management tools available. In the UK LIFESPAN is widely used for real-time, defence-related, systems. Other tools frequently used are CHANGEMAN and PAPICS.

In choosing a configuration management tool, the STARTS Guide [STARTS 1987] suggests consideration of the following:

- the overall scope of the tool, with respect to the type of units controllable, i.e. hardware, software, documentation etc.;

- its support for version, configuration and change control;

- the form, maintenance and reliability of historical information produced by the tool;

- the distribution scheme for controlled delivery and acceptance of items;

- the security of the controlled data, to ensure that change control procedures are not circumvented;

- the integrity of the tool (incorrect operation could be very costly);

- the flexibility of the system, for the selection of storage efficient representations and for cross-project control;

- the interfaces to project management, analysis and other tools, perhaps via a commercially available database, or a standard development platform such as CAIS or PCTE.

Careful consideration of each is recommended. It is often quite difficult to tailor a configuration management tool to an existing set of procedures. A re-definition of procedures may be required.

10. Summary

10.1. Systems

- A 'safe' system cannot enter a state which is hazardous to the environment in which it is employed. Safety must be addressed early in the procurement process, before the system requirements are finalised. The safety of the basic function required of the system must be considered together with a judgement of what the current state-of-the-art for hardware and software will safely allow. This is particularly important for the more technically advanced projects, and wherever new techniques are being proposed for critical functions.

- The safety implications of the system must be assessed before any development work is carried out, by undertaking a Preliminary Hazard Analysis. This will identify safety-properties (or safety-invariants) which must be maintained (and continually checked) throughout the development work. A subset of these will become requirements of the software.

- A safety lifecycle should be explicitly defined and followed, together with supporting management procedures. The lifecycle must address the development and maintenance of the system.

- The system should protect against failures through the application of fault avoidance *and* fault tolerance techniques. Novel architectures, such as the safety monitor and control processor combination, appear to offer simplicity of safety-critical function. Software diversity is not regarded as a cost effective technique.

10.2. Software

- The choice of development methods is dictated very largely by the rigour required of the validation and verification activities. This is the way in which the levels of integrity identified by safety standards such as [IEC WG9] should be interpreted.

- Formal specification languages provide the mathematical foundation essential to the process of assessing the fitness for purpose of a specification and should be used. Techniques for refinement of a formal specification towards an implementation, with proof of each refinement step, have been described, but their practical use is still being researched.

- Structured design tools can be used in conjunction with formal methods, although the correctness of any refinement carried out in this way must be demonstrated. Maintaining traceability between refinements will require strict documentation control. A database will assist in this.

- The analysis activities should be based on a combination of design and code review, dynamic test and static analysis. The most rigorous approach to analysis is that of mathematical proof. Although proof can be difficult, it should be carried out on the more critical software modules.

- The choice of programming language and compiler can significantly affect the tractability of the evaluation. For safety-critical software, special-purpose verifiable subsets of standard languages should be used, supported by validated compilers or assemblers. Although work on high-integrity microprocessors is progressing, these devices do not yet provide a viable alternative to commercial microprocessors.

- Many software engineering tools are available. They must not be regarded as a solution in themselves, but the better of them can provide valuable assistance. Careful consideration of the actual requirement of any tool, as well as its integrity of operation, is necessary. Formal methods tool support is not yet as well advanced, although useful tools are available.

10.3. Project Control and Assessment

- The ease with which software can be changed is often a cause of problems. Careful application of configuration, change and version control procedures is required, to ensure that the exact configuration of a released system can be established, and that 'unapproved' systems are not accidentally released. Automated support may prove to be essential.

- Clear documentation of each of the lifecycle phases (specification; architectural design; detailed design; implementation) is required, and must be delivered for evaluation purposes. End-product testing is not sufficient for the assessment of safety-critical software: the procurer (or an independent assessor) must be allowed to audit the work of the supplier throughout the development process.

- In assessing the fitness for purpose of a software-based system there are many factors to consider. These include project management procedures, staff experience, development methods, system complexity, system architecture, and the ease and extent of the evaluation activities. There is no accepted method of quantifying software quality: value-judgements are required, based on evidence of 'best practice'. The essential requirement is that we are able to review the development at all stages.

- An ISO 9000 or similar quality system is a minimum requirement.

11. References

Abrial, J.R. 1990; 'A Refinement Case Study (Using the Abstract Machine Notation)', *Proc. 4th Refinement Workshop*, Springer-Verlag.

Bromell, J.Y. & Sadler, S.J. 1987; 'A Strategy for the Development of Safety-Critical software', in *Achieving Safety and Reliability with Computer Systems*, edited by B.K. Daniels, Elsevier Applied Science.

Buckley, T.F., Jesty, P.H., Hobley, K.M. & West, M. 1990; *SG1: Review of Current Standards for Safety Critical Software*, DRIVE Project Number V1051.

Carré, B.A. 1989; in *Reliable Programming in Standard Languages in High Integrity Software*, edited by C. Sennett, Pitman Publishing.

Carré, B.A. & Debney, C. 1985; *SPADE-Pascal*, Program Validation Ltd, Southampton, UK.

Carré, B.A., Jennings, T.J., Maclennan, F.J. & Farrow, P.F. 1989; *SPARK – The SPADE Ada Kernel*, Program Validation Ltd, Southampton, UK.

Clutterbuck, D.L. 1989; *SPADE-68020: translation strategy document*, Program Validation Ltd, Southampton, UK.

Cohen, B., Harwood, W.T. & Jackson, M.I. 1986; *The Specification of Complex Systems*, Addison-Wesley Publishing Company.

Craigen, D. 1987; *A Description of m-Verdi*, I.P. Sharp Technical Report TR-87-5420-02.

Cullyer, W.J., Goodenough, S.J. & Wichmann, B.A. 1991; 'The Choice of Computer Languages for Use in Safety-Critical Systems', *Software Engineering Journal*, Vol. 6, No. 2, pp. 51-58.

Currie, I.F. 1989; 'NewSpeak: a reliable programming language', in *High Integrity Software*, edited by C.Sennett, Pitman Publishing.

Def Stan 00-55; *Requirements for the Procurement of Safety Critical Software in Defence Equipment*, Interim Defence Standard 00-55, MoD Directorate of Standardization, Glasgow, UK. [Reproduced as part of this book.]

Def Stan 00-56; *Requirements for the Analysis of Safety Critical Hazards*, Interim Defence Standard 00-56, MoD Directorate of Standardization, Glasgow, UK.

DeMillo, R. A., Lipton, R.J. & Perlis, A.J. 1979; 'Social Processes and Proofs of Theorems and Programs', *Communications of the ACM*, Vol. 12, No. 5.

Fagan, M. 1976; 'Design and Code Inspections to Reduce Errors in Code Development', *IBM Systems Journal*, Vol. 15, No. 3.

Goguen, J.A. 1984; 'Parameterized programming', *IEEE Transactions on Software Engineering*, Vol. SE-10, pp. 528-544.

Good, D.I. 1989; *Mathematical Forecasting*, Computational Logic Incorporated, Technical Report No. 47.

Gordon, M. 1987; *A Proof Generating System for Higher-Order Logic*, University of Cambridge, Computer Laboratory, Technical Report 103.

Hall, A. 1990; 'Seven Myths of Formal Methods', *IEEE Transactions on Software Engineering*, September 1990.

Halstead, M.H. 1977; *Elements of software science*, Elsevier North-Holland, New York.

Hennell, M.A. 1989; 'Program analysis and systematic testing', in *High Integrity Software*, edited by C.Sennett, Pitman Publishing.

Hoare, C.A.R. 1990; 'ProCoS: Esprit Project BRA 3104', Keynote Address, Z Refinement Workshop, IBM Hursley, UK.

Holscher, H. & Rader, J. 1984; *Microcomputers in safety technique*, TÜV Study Group on Computer Safety, Verlag TÜV, Bayern/Rheinland.

HSE 1989; *Quantified Risk Assessment: Its Input To Decision Making*, UK Health and Safety Executive, HMSO, 1989.

Hunt, W.A. 1986; *FM8502: A Verified Microprocessor*, Institute for Computer Science, Univ. of Texas, Austin, USA, Technical Report 47.

IEC C0138; *General Considerations for Reliability/Availability Methodology*, International Electrotechnical Commission approved standard, being edited for publication.

IEC WG9; *Software for Computers in the Application of Industrial Safety-Related Systems* (DRAFT), International Electrotechnical Commission SC65A (Secretariat) 94 Working Group 9.

IEC WG10; *Functional Safety of Programmable Electronic Systems* (DRAFT), International Electrotechnical Commission SC65A (Secretariat) 96 Working Group 10.

IEE 1989; *Guidelines for the Documentation of Computer Software for Real-Time and Interactive Systems*, Institution of Electrical Engineers, London, 1989.

Jackson, M. 1983; *System Design*, Prentice Hall International.

Jones, C.B. 1986; *Systematic Software Development using VDM*, Prentice Hall International.

Jones, C.B., Jones, K.D., Lindsay, P.A. & Moore, R. 1991; *MURAL A Formal Development Support System*, Springer-Verlag.

Karger, B. 1990; 'Aspects of Proving Compiler Correctness', SAFECOMP'90, Gatwick, UK, 30 October 1990.

Kershaw, J. 1985; *Safe Control Systems and the VIPER Microprocessor*, RSRE Memorandum No.3805, Malvern, Worcs.

Knowlton, R.E. 1981; *Hazard and Operability Studies*, Chemetics International Ltd, Vancouver, Canada .

Lampson, B.W., Horning, J.J., London, R.L., Mitchell, J.G. & Popek, G.L. 1977; 'Report on the Programming Language Euclid', *ACM SIGPLAN Notices*, Vol. 12, No.2.

Leveson, N.G. 1989; 'Safety as a Software Quality', *IEEE Software*, Vol. 6 No. 3.

Leveson, N.G. & Harvey, P.R. 1983; 'Analyzing Software Safety', *IEEE Transactions on Software Engineering*, Vol. SE-9 No. 9.

McCabe, T.J. 1976; 'A Complexity Measure', *IEEE Transactions on Software Engineering*, Vol. SE-2, No 4.

McDermid, J. 1989; 'Assurance in High-Integrity Software', in *High Integrity Software*, edited by C.Sennett, Pitman Publishing.

Millward, J. 1990; 'System Architectures for Safety Critical Automotive Applications', IEE Colloquium on *Safety Critical Software in Vehicle and Traffic Control*, London, Digest No. 1990/031.

Morgan, C. 1990; *Programming from specifications*, Prentice Hall International.

Musser, D.R. 1979; 'Abstract Data Type Specifications in the AFFIRM System', *Proceedings of the Specification of Reliable Systems Conference*, Cambridge, Mass., USA.

O'Neill, I.M., Clutterbuck, D.L., Farrow, P.F., Summers, P.G. & Dolman, W.C.; 'The Formal Verification of Safety-Critical Assembly Code', *SAFECOMP'88*, Proceedings published by Permagon Press.

Parnas, D.L., van Schouwen, J. & Kwan, S.P. 1990; 'Evaluation of Safety-critical Software', *Communications of the ACM*, Vol. 3, June 1990.

Polak, W. 1981; *Compiler Specification and Verification*, Lecture Notes in Computer Science 124, Springer Verlag.

PVL 1990; *Proving the Correctness of Compiler Generated Object Code*, Program Validation Ltd, Technical Report 1990.

Spivey, J.M. 1988; *Understanding Z*, Cambridge University Press, Computer Science Tract 3.

Spivey, J.M. 1989; *The Z Notation*, Prentice Hall International.

STARTS 1987; *A Guide to the Methods and Software Tools for the Construction of Large Real Time Systems*, STARTS Guide, 2nd edition, Vols 1-2, UK National Computing Centre, Manchester.

Wichmann, B.A. 1989; *Insecurities in the Ada language*, National Physical Laboratory, Teddington UK, report DITC 137/89.

Woodcock, J. & Loomes, M. 1988; *Software Engineering Mathematics*, Pitman Publishing.

Yourdon, E. & Constantine, L. 1979; *Structured Design: Fundamentals of a Discipline of Computer Program and Systems Design*, Prentice Hall International.

Appendix A – Tools Index

This appendix provides addresses of suppliers of those tools referenced in the report but *not* listed in the STARTS Guide [STARTS 1987].

CADIZ: York Software Engineering Ltd, University of York, York YO1 5DD.

FUZZ: J. M. Spivey, Computing Science Consultancy, 2 Willow Close, Garsington, Oxford, UK.

SPECBOX: Adelard, Coborn House Business Centre, Coborn Road, London, UK.

GENESIS: Imperial Software Technology, Cambridge, UK.

MURAL: C. B. Jones, Dept. of Computer Science, University of Manchester, UK.

EDUCATION AND TRAINING FOR SAFETY-CRITICAL SYSTEMS PRACTITIONERS

Edited by John McDermid

1. Introduction

The BCS Safety Critical Systems Group (which pre-dated the current Task Force) set up an Education Working Party to report on the establishment of post-experience education and training courses in software development for safety-critical systems. The working party considered existing reports on education and training for the developers of safety-critical systems and relevant standards, including those currently in force and under development. This report summarises the conclusions of the group, and presents an <u>outline syllabus</u> for a set of related courses on software engineering for safety-critical systems. The course descriptions have been modified to relate to the BCS Industry Structure Model (ISM) following discussions on the syllabus at a public meeting held in September 1990.

The report is organised as follows. Section 2 records the terms of reference for the group. Section 3 gives an overview of the proposed set of courses and, in particular, explains the ethos for these courses. Section 4 addresses the specific questions set out in the terms of reference. Section 5 draws some conclusions about the establishment of suitable courses and discusses future actions by the Society.

This material is based on the initial report produced by the working party but it has been updated to take into account feedback from the public meeting and subsequent discussions at working party meetings.

Annex A sets out the detail of the proposed syllabus and relates the syllabus to the ISM, and Annex B identifies the members of the working party. Annex C gives a report on the public meeting.

2. Terms of Reference

The terms of reference as set out for the working party were: 'The SCS Education working party should produce a report for the SCS Group on the establishment of post-experience education and training in software development for safety-critical systems. The report should cover, but not be restricted to:

1. The course syllabus, identifying the principles, tools and techniques which should be taught, together with guidelines on assessment.

2. Advice on whether or not there should be a formal qualification, e.g. MSc, or Diploma, granted as a result of the course and who would make the award, if any.

3. The method of "delivery" of the material, e.g. residential or distance learning; continuous or periodic attendance.

4. Whether or not the course can, and should, contain modules targeted specifically to the needs of a particular industry.

5. What formal qualifications and experience would be necessary as prerequisites to course attendance.

6. For what roles *vis-à-vis* a safety-critical systems project would the course qualify attendees.

7. Which organisation or organisations can and should put on the course. How should the course material be developed, particularly if there are multiple organisations involved in presenting the course.

8. Should passing the course be regarded as a necessary (or even sufficient) condition to a BCS register. Should there be a register and a relation between passing the course and being on the register.

In producing this report the working party should take account of the training initiative associated with the forthcoming Defence Standard 00-55, and the need for updating after completion of the course.'

Following the public meeting and subsequent discussions it became clear that it was better to think of a set of related courses, not a single course. Section 3 reflects this change in aim, although we still address the above points directly in section 4.

3. Overview of the Courses: Aims and Structure

3.1. Aims and Scope

The intention is that the courses should be provided at a postgraduate, post-experience level. It is anticipated that typical entrants to the courses should have the necessary qualifications and experience to receive Chartered Engineer status, but would not necessarily have been registered as a Chartered Engineer. In terms of the ISM this means staff at level 3 or above. The working party believes that one of the important issues to be covered in the courses is when it is *not* appropriate to use computers and software in a safety-critical system, or steps need to be taken to reduce the criticality of the software. The working party believe that it is necessary for those attending the courses to have a certain degree of maturity and industrial experience in order that they will be receptive to, and can appropriately interpret, guidance on difficult judgemental issues such as when it is appropriate to use software in control of critical systems.

The courses should aim to serve several different 'markets'. First they should seek to provide basic background information for people who will be in managerial positions of responsibility associated with safety-critical systems. Second they should aim to provide a thorough technical grounding for those who should be involved in the development or certification of software-controlled safety-critical systems. This latter group can be subdivided in terms of their role in an SCS project or level in terms of the ISM. Many modules should be common to more than one course, so we describe each module and link it to roles and the ISM in Annex A.

For the technical staff the aims are twofold:

- to provide a thorough grounding, and practical experience, in the use of state of the art techniques for design, development, verification, validation, etc. of software for safety-critical systems;

- to provide an understanding of the principles behind these techniques, so that attendees have a clearer understanding of the *limitations* of these techniques and therefore can make sound engineering judgements when it is necessary or desirable to limit the use of software in safety-critical systems.

The latter aim clearly is concerned with sound engineering judgement and is obviously appropriate for engineers working on such applications, whereas the former aim sounds much more like technical training. However, the working party believes that this is appropriate. In other engineering disciplines, professional engineers and technicians are registered on the basis of their ability to apply particular techniques in an effective manner. We can see no reason why this principle should not apply to software, but it is clear that the principle should be applied at the professional rather than the technician level.

It is *not* intended that the courses should cover everything that a software engineer needs to know in order to work in the development of some safety-critical system. The working party firmly believes that sound application knowledge is needed in order to develop safety-critical systems. (This is one of the classes of 'non-core' material in the ISM.) It is clear that software of itself cannot be safety-critical, it is only safety-critical when used in some particular application area in control of, or monitoring, some hazardous process. Consequently the working party believes that, in order to exercise sound engineering judgement, the engineer must have an adequate knowledge and understanding of the application domain. Consequently we expect that there may be many circumstances whereby some particular industry should choose to supplement the material that we have suggested for the syllabus with industry-specific information. In other words, we believe that the material identified in the syllabus covers those aspects of the technology for developing and evaluating software for safety-critical systems which is largely independent of application area, but we also recognise that application-specific expertise is required before a software engineer undertakes the development of safety-critical systems.

It is intended that people wishing to gain a managerial level of understanding of the topics will attend the material on principles and on the limitations of the available techniques and technology, but not attend those parts of the courses that deal in detail with the particular technologies. Nevertheless it could be useful for managerial staff to attend one of the detailed courses in order that they appreciate the technical strengths and limitations from first hand knowledge. The relationship between modules and roles *vis-à-vis* an SCS project is set out in more detail in Annex A.

3.2. Structure of the Courses

For a number of reasons it is intended that the material should be presented on a modular basis. First it is recognised that the people who would wish to attend the courses will be very busy, and can probably not be spared from their work for an extended period of time. Second it is desirable for managerial staff to be able to attend a subset of the courses. Third it may be appropriate for technical staff to attend only a subset of the courses, dependent upon how recent, and how thorough, their first-degree education was. In other words, there should be no need for someone who has recently completed a first degree in, say, software engineering to attend some of the detailed technical course units, or modules. In Annex A we distinguish background software engineering material from that which is specific to SCS. The working party initially believed that it should be most appropriate to organise modules as one-week, intensive, residential units and that modules should be attended at the rate of about one per month. Following the public meeting this conclusion was reviewed and it was concluded that a more flexible mix of residential units and distance should be appropriate. We return to this issue in sections 4 and 5, although it should be noted that the scale of the modules is still that of a one-week residential unit.

A further benefit of the modular structure is that it should be possible to set up the individual course modules at those establishments which have the appropriate expertise. This is felt to be very important because the working party recognised that no single academic or industrial site in the UK had an adequate understanding of the technical material set out in the syllabus to cover all the issues in an appropriate and effective manner. It was also felt appropriate that the course should be put on in universities and polytechnics, but that appropriately qualified industrial staff should be involved in course giving, especially where the skills are available in industry and not in academia.

Modularity gives flexibility, but it also makes examination of the participants' attainments difficult. It is intended therefore that there should be an assessment and some form of certificate for each course module. The assessment should include both written examinations and practical sessions, e.g. with verification tools, as appropriate. However, there should not be a pre-set number, or group, of course modules necessary to gain an overall qualification from the set of courses. Instead there should be a central body, probably administered by the BCS, which should determine for each individual what constitutes an appropriate set of courses. The definition of this material should take into account both the individual's previous experience and the content of undergraduate courses he has studied, and how recently these courses were taken. It was intended that some overall qualification should be awarded, and the issues of qualifications are considered in detail in the next section.

From the point of view of resources, it was considered essential that there should be two or three tutors for each one-week module. The reason for this was both practical, in terms of the presentation of the material, and in order to provide enough tutors so that course attendees can get a reasonably large amount of individual tuition. Since many of the modules would be based around the use of computer based tools, it was also recognised that adequate computing facilities would need to be provided for each module. Consequently it is expected that the resources required to put on these courses would be quite substantial, certainly much higher than those associated with normal undergraduate or postgraduate tuition.

It was felt to be appropriate that, for suitable modules, alternative forms of tuition might be made available. For example, it should be possible to make some material available via distance learning techniques. An example of such material might be the introductory course on discrete mathematics for software engineering, available on video through the IEE.

3.3. Overview of Syllabus

The courses as currently envisaged fall into seven major groups, some of these groups being several modules long. Six groups were identified in the initial report but, following the public meeting, it was decided that it was appropriate to add a further group dealing with management issues.

Part A contains introductory material giving some of the technical, economic and social background to the development of safety-critical systems. It also describes the structure and organisation of a typical safety-critical systems project, and deals with the problems and principles of achieving and evaluating safety.

Part B covers risk analysis. It covers general principles of identifying hazards and classifying risks, and then goes on to system hazard analysis and to the role of hazard analysis at the different stages in the lifecycle, and ends by explaining several key techniques in depth. These techniques include fault tree analysis.

Part C covers techniques and technology for the achievement of safety. This is the major part of the course, and should comprise a number of different modules put on by different organisations. The material covered includes basic software and systems-engineering material. It also covers requirements analysis and risk analysis techniques, formal approaches to specification and software development, and techniques for software system testing. Further techniques covered include software and hardware fault tolerance, failure modes analysis, basic psychology especially as applied to the design of interactive systems, and a treatment of implementation issues. Finally it discusses architectural issues in terms of how to determine what combination of techniques to employ in a given system. Much of this material is 'background' in that it is relevant to software and systems, and is not specific to SCS. It is included here as the working party believes that few SCS practitioners have all of the appropriate background knowledge.

Part D deals with management of SCS projects. It discusses establishment of a suitable process for developing SCS, including definition of roles. It covers planning and estimating for SCS projects. It also considers the effects of standards and certification on project management.

Part E deals with statistical evaluation techniques. In particular it covers basic probability and statistics, and gives an outline of the capabilities and limitations of current techniques for modelling software and hardware reliability.

Part F goes through a more methodological approach to the techniques for building safe systems. In essence it works through the software lifecycle giving illustrations of how to combine and deploy techniques which are effective at each of the different levels. It also discusses some issues in achieving certification against current standards.

Part G returns to the principles and problems of developing safety-critical systems and gives a number of detailed case studies. The case studies, in a sense, represent the culmination of the description of the technical material, but it is intended that they should be presented in such a way that they should be accessible to managerial staff. This module also covers social issues with regard to the deployment of safety-critical systems controlled by software.

It is intended that the first and last parts should be available, and accessible, to managerial staff and so the basic principles set out in Part A should not be repeated in Part D. The central part of the course (excluding part D) is intended to be much more detailed, and to require considerable technical expertise to complete satisfactorily. Assessment of the central technical modules should involve demonstration by the course attendees that they are capable and fluent in applying the techniques that have been described to them.

The complete set of modules is equivalent to about 20 weeks full-time tuition, although about half this material is background which many SCS practitioners *should* not need. The tuition can be provided in a phased manner corresponding to progressing through levels in the ISM. This phasing is indicated in tabular form in Annex A.

4. Items from the Terms of Reference

The main point in the terms of reference was the definition of a syllabus. The background to, and aims of, the courses were set out in the previous section, and the details of the syllabus are presented in Annex A. In this section we deal with the other items raised in the terms of reference for the working party. We give both the initial views of the working party and, where appropriate, discuss modifications to these views brought about by the public meeting.

4.1. Qualifications
4.1.1. *Initial Views*
It was agreed that it was not appropriate to give a qualification such as MSc for the courses, because the nature of the material and its assessment would be considerably different from that normally involved in an MSc course. However, the working party considered that some form of qualification, e.g. a diploma, was appropriate.

It was suggested that the systems analysis examination board of the BCS be asked to investigate the feasibility of awarding a diploma for the courses, based on a set of modules that were determined to be appropriate to a particular applicant. Each organisation giving a particular course module would be responsible for assessing the module, but the examinations board would be responsible for collating the results of the assessments, and making the overall award of the diploma.

4.1.2. *Revised Views*

After the working party produced its initial report it was realised that, if any qualification were to be awarded, then it was appropriate that it should be an Engineering Diploma (EngDip), or similar qualification, because this is based on both academic skills and practical experience. It seems appropriate to view establishment of such a qualification as a long-term objective, but it is not thought to be a viable short-term goal.

As a result of the public meeting and the ensuing discussion it was agreed that it was more appropriate to link the course modules to the ISM, rather than to think of a specific course qualification (at least in the short term). This conclusion is reflected in Annex A.

4.2. Delivery Mode

4.2.1. *Initial Views*

As indicated above it was intended that, in general, modules would be given on a one-week intensive basis at academic establishments with the appropriate expertise. Where the expertise is not all available within academic departments, the academic staff would be supplemented by staff from industry with the appropriate skills.

Much of the material to be taught demands that the attendees gain some understanding of principles, and some ideas of social responsibility. This does not seem well suited to distance learning techniques. Similarly, much of the material requires hands-on experience with state-of-the-art software engineering tools. However, certain parts of the courses, e.g. the basic discrete mathematics and basic statistics, seem much more appropriate for computer-based or distance learning techniques. As a consequence distance learning techniques should be considered for appropriate parts of the courses.

4.2.2. *Revised Views*

The public meeting confirmed the principle of having a balance of distance learning and residential tuition; there was considerable (commercially motivated) resistance to having a highly residential course. Pragmatically this means that more use of distance learning needs to be made and that residential periods need to be reduced, e.g. to two days at a time (perhaps on Friday and Saturday). It was recognised that establishing such a course would be a major problem, see section 5.

4.3. Industry-Specific Modules

4.3.1. *Initial Views*

The modular structure of the courses is such that it would be possible to augment the material with industry specific modules. The working party felt it was appropriate to leave this option open, but it did not wish to indicate what particular modules might be added for specific industry sectors. The working party felt that it was not appropriate to mandate having industry-specific material in order to gain the qualification from the BCS. There were several reasons for this, the main one being that the Society was not in a position to dictate to various industry sectors what qualifications they should accept, but it was appropriate for it to specify what software skills somebody should have when working with computer-controlled safety-critical systems.

4.3.2. *Revised Views*
The public meeting confirmed these views and it was noted that the IEE was defining a syllabus which included some aspects of system engineering which would complement the BCS syllabus.

4.4. Prerequisites
4.4.1. *Initial Views*
The working party agreed that it was appropriate that somebody attending the courses should have the equivalent experience and academic qualifications to be able to gain Chartered Engineer status. The working party did not feel that it was appropriate to mandate Chartered Engineer status as a prerequisite for the courses, because only a relatively small number of those people who would be qualified to undertake this work already have Chartered Engineer status. However, it was felt that in the long run the aim should be to require Chartered Engineer status as a prerequisite.

4.4.2. *Revised Views*
The course description has now been modified to make clear that:

- level 3 in the ISM is deemed to be a minimum level for work on SCS;

- part of the course material is viewed as being prerequisite (background) to the SCS-specific part of the course.

The structure can be seen in Annex A.

4.5. Roles of SCS Projects
4.5.1. *Initial Views*
The working party was asked to determine for which roles *vis-à-vis* a safety-critical systems project the courses would qualify their attendees. The working party was of the opinion that the courses would not, of themselves, qualify attendees for any specific role. It wishes to stress the need for application-specific knowledge before attempting work on a safety-critical system. However, the working party believes that the material in the courses is necessary for those working in the role of a chief designer or certifier/assessor of a safety-critical system with a significant software content.

4.5.2. *Revised Views*
The working party now sees the different parts of the course as relating to different levels in the ISM, and these levels corresponding to roles. The correspondence is set out in Annex A.

4.6. Course Presenters
4.6.1. *Initial Views*
The working party agreed that there was no single body with enough knowledge and experience to put on the complete set of courses. This was a major reason for the working party suggesting a modular structure to the courses. There was also general agreement that the courses should be put on at academic premises, and that the locations should be chosen to reflect local expertise. However it was recognised that some of the necessary expertise was not available amongst academics in computer science and related departments, so some of the material would have to be taught by industrial staff.

The modular structure of the courses creates some problems for arranging and assessing the quality of the individual modules. The working party thought it appropriate for the BCS to take on this role, much in the way it accredits undergraduate degree courses.

4.6.2. *Revised Views*
The working party now sees it as being much more appropriate to link the courses into the BCS Professional Development Scheme (PDS) in terms of the ISM. Specifically it seems appropriate to establish a Safety Critical Systems sub-specialisation in the Software Engineering Sub-stream.

4.7. Register of Software Engineers for Safety Critical Systems
4.7.1 *Initial Views*
The working party thought that there ought to be a register of software engineers qualified to work on safety-critical systems, although they recognised that merely being a member of such a register did not necessarily mean that a software engineer was appropriately qualified to work in any given industry. Therefore an additional selection would have to be made when it came to finding an engineer for a particular project.

The working party also thought that it was necessary for members of this register to have passed the course as defined in the enclosed syllabus, but that this was not a sufficient condition to be on the register. In particular the working party thought that some evidence of expertise with respect to a particular application domain, or domains, would be necessary before somebody was admitted as a member of the register. The working party thought that this was consistent with the rules under which the existing BCS register had been established.

4.7.2. *Revised Views*
The working party feels that the above principles are still sound, but that the register should, in effect, relate to those individuals in the relevant stream of the PDS (see also section 4.6.2). This would effectively mean that the register would define competencies for various levels in the ISM for those working on SCS.

4.8. Other Training Initiatives
4.8.1. *Initial Views*
The working party compared the proposed syllabus with the recommendations from CITI of a set of training courses for software engineers to the standards required by Def Stan 00-55. The working party believed that a much broader curriculum than that identified by CITI was appropriate. Specifically they believed that the set of topics identified by CITI is too narrow, and that the syllabus defined here was more appropriate for the education of software engineers working on safety-critical systems than that proposed by CITI.

4.8.2. *Revised Views*
The working party still hold their initial views about the level and scale of training required. Indeed they are concerned that there is a tendency amongst industrialists to minimise the need for training – but experience of real safety-critical systems indicates

that lack of adequate education or training is a major contribution to systems problems (and failures). Thus the working party see no need to change their views on this matter – despite the unpopularity of the ideas.

5. Conclusions

The working party has outlined what it believes to be a sensible syllabus for training software engineers to work on safety-critical systems. It has also addressed a number of issues about ways in which the courses can be run and assessed. It is clear from the syllabus and the other aspects of the course, e.g. its modular nature, that establishing such courses would be quite a difficult and costly exercise. These conclusions briefly look at the issues involved in establishing the courses proposed.

The working party initially believed that the BCS should take a pro-active role with regard to education and training in software engineering for SCS. In particular the working party thought it appropriate for the BCS to foster the establishment of a set of courses and to establish a mechanism for accrediting individual course modules.

Following the public meeting and further discussion of the working party it no longer seems practical for the BCS to take on this role, although the aims of establishing courses and an accreditation mechanism remain valid. The primary reasons for this decision are the absence of 'market pull' for the courses and the difficulty of securing funding for the course development and co-ordination. However, if a suitable opportunity arises, e.g. associated with a standard, then the society should seek to foster the development of courses on software engineering for SCS.

The group now concludes that the following actions should be taken:

- the syllabus should be published more widely to solicit further critical feedback, and to provide a reference for others considering developing courses in this area (this is the prime purpose of this report);

- the ideas of the training courses should be fostered through the PDS. This point is partly addressed through annex A and, if possible, the ideas in the annex should be included in future releases of the ISM for use with the PDS;

- individual members of the BCS should seek to have the notion of education and training included in international standards, as opportunities arise;

- again, as opportunities arise, an attempt should be made to set up a set of SCS courses on a European basis as this may help overcome difficulties regarding market size and initial course development costs.

The above conclusions are somewhat unsatisfactory as they do not show a clear way of addressing, in the short-term, the problems of inadequate skills in SCS development perceived by the working party. Nonetheless, they probably reflect the best that can be achieved in the current climate and it is to be hoped that the linking of the course modules to the PDS scheme will provide a normative, if not a prescriptive, standard against which SCS practitioners may be judged.

ANNEX A

DRAFT COURSE SYLLABUS

A.1. Introduction

The following draft syllabus is intended as a general guideline on course content, and should be read in conjunction with section 3 of this report. Parts A and G are described in more detail as the working party thought it essential to be clear about those aspects of the course which deal with general issues and which are not well documented in textbooks. Before establishing the courses, parts B to F would need to be amplified. Each module is intended to represent one week's intensive residential study, although other forms of presentation may be appropriate.

Section A.2 outlines the syllabus for each part of the course and section A.3 maps the modules to the ISM and roles in an SCS development project. Section A.4 briefly discusses the character and content of the course modules.

A.2. Syllabus

Part A – Introduction (also Module A)
Problem Characteristics

- Safety – no physical disasters; causes – accident, failure, malicious behaviour
- Relationships between safety, integrity and security (dependability)
- Impossibility of *guaranteeing* safety – cost/benefit and risk analysis
- Typical safety 'events' – multiple errors, complex interaction

Legal and Economic Issues

- Health and Safety at Work Act
  - reasonable care
  - reasonably practical
- Consumer Protection Act legislation
  - negligence need not be proved
  - development risks defence
- Economics of risk
  - acceptability of risk

- cost of measures vs benefits

- speed to market

Definitions/Terminology

- General

  - fault, error, failure, fault avoidance, tolerance, etc.

  - reliability, availability, etc.

  - recursive system structuring

  - formal methods/program analysis terms

  - assurance

- Safety

  - safety integrity

  - risk (analysis)

  - hazard, etc.

Typical SCS Project

- Roles

  - procurer

  - design authority

  - safety authority

  - independent assessor

  - certification agency

- Typical Process

  - requirements and hazard analysis

  - high level design and failure modes effects analysis (FMEA)

  - detailed design and FMEA

  - implementation and testing

  - assessment/evaluation

  - certification

  - installation and use

  - verification and validation issues at each stage

  - maintenance and recertification

Certification Standards

- Typical examples
- Industry variations
- Design for certification

Systems Issues

- Modelling problem domain (simulation)
- Architectural decisions/systems definition
  - critical components
  - issues when 'man in loop'
- Inter-disciplinary; software, hardware, mechanical engineering, etc.
- Application domain knowledge essential

Problems

- What is safe? – relative concept (controlled explosion)
- Fail active, not fail safe (no 'safe side')
- Risk/threat analysis – against what do we have to defend?
- How do we know we've obtained safety?
- unobtainable absolutes (10^{-9} failures per hour)

Principles of Solutions

- Methods of achieving safety
  - reduce complexity
  - systems architecture and structure
  - separation of functionality from safety mechanisms
  - minimise trust
  - containment and firewalls
  - diversity, redundancy, fault tolerance
  - independent monitoring
  - formal methods: principles and limits of the approaches
  - testing methods, fault removal
  - re-use of components and design principles

- Methods of assuring and evaluating safety
  - verification
  - validation
  - configuration management and audit trails
  - testing and test coverage
  - models of fault tolerance
  - Markov models of structural reliability
  - reliability growth
  - data collection
  - certification
  - independence in evaluation

Part B – Hazard and Risk Analysis
Module B.1. Hazard Analysis

- Risk analysis
  - concept of risk, different sorts of risk, risk vector
  - definition of hazard, accident, initiating event and idea of accident sequence
  - risk policy, acceptable risk, risk aversion (see the HSE papers), limits achievable
  - classifying risks – qualitative and quantitative schemes, examples from MOD, Nuclear, Aviation, Transport, HSE – failures per hour, failures per event
  - identifying safety-critical properties of computer systems
- System hazard analysis
  - functional analysis
  - zonal analysis
  - component failure analysis
  - operating and support hazard analysis
  - occupational health hazard analysis
  - testing and monitoring
- Safety analysis
  - hazard severity classification and probability of occurrence

- computing system and software classification

- independent assessment and safety review

- Hazard analysis and the system lifecycle

 - what is done when, from initiation through to disposal

Module B.2. Risk Analysis and Requirements

- Limits of current techniques

- Extension – environment modelling, failure analysis – completeness!

- Risk analysis – economics

- Failure analysis techniques

 - consider several key techniques, strengths, weaknesses, how they fit together, tool support

- checklists and brainstorms

- fault tree analysis

- failure modes and effects analysis (and FMECA)

- event trees

 - other techniques such as reliability block diagrams, ... and their relationship to general reliability assessment

Part C – Techniques and Technology

Module C.1. General Software and Systems Engineering Issues

- Designing the lifecycle/choosing the process

- Structured analysis and design

- Configuration management

- Quality management and control

- IPSEs and CASE tools

- Maintenance and maintainability

Module C.2. Architectural Issues

- Non-functional issues

 - timing

 - sizing, etc.

- Protection and firewalls

- Safety analysis
- Hardware/software trade-offs
- Basic discrete mathematics

Module C.3. Basic Discrete Mathematics

- set theory
- predicate calculus
- elementary algebra

Module C.4. Formal specification

- algebraic
- model-oriented
- process algebras
- temporal logics
- details of specific approaches

Module C.5. Formal Approaches: Principles and Program Verification

- Principles: soundness of logical systems
- Programming logics and proof
- Formal construction of programs
- Environments and tools for formal methods
- Limits of verification

Module C.6. Testing

- Roles of testing
  - fault location
  - evaluation
- Theory of testing
  - graph theoretic
  - testing by oracle
- Phase of testing
  - requirements
  - specification
  - design

- module

- integration

- system

- regression

- Strategies of testing

    - functional (black box)

        - partition testing, subcase evaluation

        - boundary and stress testing

        - random/environment testing

    - structural (white box)

        - statement, branch, path, function, LCSAJ (Linear Code Sequence And Jump)

- Tools for testing

    - test data-set description languages

    - test harness

    - test coverage monitors

    - test history files, journalling

- Test measurement

    - coverage (see structural testing)

    - source/object

Module C.7. Validation

- emphasis is actually on invalidation

- desk checking

- Fagan inspections

- walkthroughs, reviewers, audits

- static analyses

    - cross reference, maps, call graphs, metrics

    - data and control flow analysis

    - usage analysis

    - concurrency analysis

    - fault tree analysis

- interaction analysers
  - symbolic execution
- formal verification as a test method – dynamic analysers
  - traces
  - histograms of module/variable use
  - value ranges

Module C.8. Fault Tolerance

- Static and dynamic approaches
- Fault and error detection and isolation
- Damage assessment and management
- Systems reconfiguration
- State restoration, backward and forward recovery
- Cold and hot standby
- Recovery blocks, conversations, etc.
- Adjudication
- Design diversity
- Software control over hardware redundancy and resources
- Systems, e.g. Tandem, A320

Module C.9. Psychology – HCI

- Causes of disasters – operator error
- Problems: human failings and operational environment
- Cognitive models of systems
- Models of error – Reason, etc.; classes of error – rehearsal faults, etc.
- Design principles for interactive system (interaction styles, etc.)
- Prototyping of interfaces
- Interface evaluation

Module C.10. Implementation

- Static bounds on execution
- Verifiable (safe, secure) programming language subsets
- Unexceptional languages (NewSpeak)

- Interrupts, timing and other horrors
- Properties of assemblers and compilers
- Static analysis
- Timing Analysis

Part D – Management
Module D.1. Principles and Techniques

- Establishing a process
  - stages: technical activities
  - phases: managerial control
  - process definition
    - activities
    - resources
    - reviews
    - deliverables
- Estimating
  - parametric models
  - cost drivers and their effects
- Planning and monitoring
  - basic planning
  - PERT and Critical Path Methods
  - progress, slip and replanning
- Risk management
  - identifying major risks
  - risk reduction strategies

Module D.2. SCS Management

- Additional management problems
  - certification
  - legal constraints
  - access for independent V&V
  - conflicts between safety and corporate objectives

- personal and corporate liability
- Additional control techniques
  - hazard and fault logs
  - separation of duty (independent roles in the process)
  - using diversity of tools in the development process
  - achieving traceability
- Conformance to standards
  - defining an appropriate process
  - establishing acceptable working methods
- Management for certification
  - problem reporting procedures
  - change request procedures
  - status accounting
  - establishment of baselines

Part E – Evaluation
Module E.1. Basic Probability and Statistics

- Life distributions
- Elementary stochastic processes, particularly point processes
- Probability and statistics of repairable systems (see e.g. Ascher and Feingold book)
- Statistical inference: classical and Bayesian

Module E.2. Software reliability

- Basic reliability models
- The need for stochastic models of program failure behaviour
- Conceptual models of the failure process
- Reliability measures, predictions
- Data collection
- The main software reliability growth models
- Statistical analysis of failure data
- Methods for evaluation of accuracy of reliability measures and predictions

- Model recalibration
- Limitations of reliability growth modelling
- Limits to evaluation: the 10^{-9} problem
- Structural models: Markov, Petri nets etc
- Reliability models for fault tolerant systems
- Relationship of reliability evaluation to certification
- Work in progress; research directions
- Models for hardware and software integration: system dependability
- Process evaluation
- Testing for evaluation
- General safety arguments

Part F – Building Safe Systems
Module F.1. Integration of Techniques

Realisation – Putting it all Together

- Trade-offs – what balance of techniques
- Trade-offs – redundancy brings fault tolerance, and more faults!
- Culture – variations in industry and certification authorities
- Available technology

Requirements

- Application dependent – no general models
- Analyse environment, and failure modes of system and environment
- Requirements problem – not all failure modes known/predictable
- Example – medical, etc.

Systems Realisation – Architectural Level

- Triple Modular Redundancy (TMR), N Modular Redundancy (NMR) – principles
- Design diversity – results: Leveson et al, etc.
- Fail safe, fail active
- Distributed vs centralised systems
- Multi-disciplinary safety arguments
- Protocols, etc.

System Realisation – Detailed Level

- NMR – lane synchronisation and voting
- Diversity – lane synchronisation and voting
- Hardware verification – VIPER
- FMEA, etc. – examples

Certification

- What is required
- Common standards – RTCA DO178A(B), Def Stan 00-55

Module F.2. Examples

- Major worked examples (technical details)

Part G – Principles and Problems – Reprise (also Module G)

Problems

- Impossibility of *guaranteeing* safety
- Limits to what we can assess/evaluate
- Limitations of current technologies
- Convincing the 'layman'
  - assurance revisited
  - residual doubts

Social Issues

- Should we build computer controlled SCS?
  - when and how – economics
  - modification of requirements
  - mechanical back-ups
  - cost/benefit analyses
- Professional responsibility
- Recent legislation and prosecutions

Case Studies

- Three case studies – principles and key decisions, especially trade-offs

Future Trends

- Continued use of computers or reaction?

- Technology: improved V&V, etc

- Applications: more active safety-critical controls, 7J7

- Possible Futures: Baber, Software Reflected

A.3. Modules, Roles and PDS Levels

The purpose of this section is to relate the modules to the levels in the PDS ISM, and hence to classes of role in an SCS project. Modules C.1, C.3, C.4, C.6, C.7 and E.1 are viewed as being technical background which would normally be familiar to those at ISM Level 3 and above in the software engineering substream. This background is referred to collectively as BG in the following tables. Similarly D.1 is viewed as being managerial background.

Tables A.1 to A.3 summarise the relationship between modules, roles and levels. We believe the minimum level for work on SCS is ISM Level 3. The software engineering substream does not include Level 9 so we discuss Levels 3 to 8 inclusive.

Table A.1 Levels and Classes of Role

ISM Level	Description	Class of Role
3	Trained Practitioner	Supervised development
4	Fully Skilled Practitioner	Unsupervised development or supervised evaluation
5	Experienced Practitioner Supervisor	Unsupervised development or evaluation
6	Specialist Practitioner Manager	Authority for stage, phase or activity
7	Senior Specialist Manager	As 6, plus team leader/ workpackage manager
8	Principal Specialist Experienced Manager	Project manager, design authority or evaluation authority

The allocation of role classes against levels in Table A.1 is intended to give some flexibility, but more senior staff should be used where the level of risk is high.

We can therefore relate modules to levels, and hence role classes (Table A.2). For convenience of reference Table A.3 gives module titles. In general the level of training required increases with level of responsibility. Also the nature of the training changes with the level of responsibility. Thus at Levels 3 and 4 the emphasis is mainly on development activities whereas at Levels 5 and 6 knowledge of overall system design and hazard analysis activities is required, reflecting the design responsibilities of the associated roles.

Table A.2 Levels and Modules

Level	Modules Completed
3	BG, C.5, C.10, G
4	As 3, plus B.1, C.2
5	As 4, plus B.2, C.8, C.9, E.2, F.1, F.2
6	As 5, plus D.1, D.2
7	As 6, or *exceptionally* only A, G, D.1, D.2
8	As 7

Table A.3 Module Identifiers and Titles

Identifier	Title
A.1	Introduction
A.2	Syllabus
B	Hazard and Risk Analysis
B.1	Hazard Analysis
B.2	Risk Analysis and Requirements
C	Techniques and Technology
C.1	General Software and Systems Engineering Issues
C.2	Architectural Issues
C.3	Basic Discrete Mathematics
C.4	Formal Specification
C.5	Formal Approaches: Principles and Program Verification
C.6	Testing
C.7	Validation
C.8	Fault Tolerance
C.9	Psychology – HCI
C.10	Implementation
D	Management
D.1	Principles and Techniques
D.2	SCS Management
E	Evaluation
E.1	Basic Probability and Statistics
E.2	Software Reliability
F	Building Safe Systems
F.1	Integration of Techniques
F.2	Examples
G	Principles and Problems – Reprise

It is recognised that it is possible that management staff will come to SCS projects without relevant technical background in SCS. This is not desirable but may be unavoidable and it is suggested that it may be appropriate to establish a 'technical appreciation' course for managers of SCS projects.

The tables show a minimum of four weeks training prior to working on an SCS project for staff with suitable background education and training, e.g. an accredited first degree. This period would extend to ten weeks for those without the appropriate background. The course load expands to fourteen to twenty modules over a five- to eight-year period depending on age, previous experience and personal capabilities. This seems to be quite a tolerable burden representing, at most, 8% of staff time devoted to training.

A.4. Character and Content of the Modules

The syllabus is intended to be reasonably definitive and the working party believes it has identified an appropriate set of topics for the proposed course. However, the working party does not believe that it has necessarily identified the right balance between topics. This is an issue which would have to be reviewed when detailed contents were agreed for each module.

The stress in the modules would be on practical skills balanced by study of the principles and limitations of the techniques discussed. Thus a typical one-week course might be one third lectures and two thirds use of appropriate tools. For the first and last modules a more tutorial style of course unit would be appropriate.

ANNEX B

WORKING PARTY MEMBERS

Professor T Anderson	University of Newcastle upon Tyne
Mr R Bloomfield	Adelard
Ms G Hooper	British Computer Society
Mr A R Lawrence	Nuclear Electric
Professor B Littlewood	City University
Professor J McDermid	University of York
Professor M R Moulding	Royal Military College of Science
Mrs P Walmisley	British Computer Society

ANNEX C

REPORT OF THE ONE-DAY SEMINAR
ON THE PROPOSED SAFETY-CRITICAL SYSTEMS SYLLABUS
held at the IEE on 24 September 1990

The number of fatal incidents occurring as a direct result of the failure of computer systems could increase over the next ten years unless appropriate steps are taken. So warns Professor Cullyer, Chairman of the BCS Safety Critical Systems Task Force, in a statement echoed by all in the SCS field. Swift, but pragmatic, considered action is required – the *raison d'être* of the Task Force.

First and foremost, the issues of education and training must be addressed. Achieving excellence in these basic building blocks across all sectors of industry – and IT in particular – is crucial for sustained future success, especially when lives could be at stake.

A seminar, held at the IEE on 24 September 1990, heard that increasing reliance on computers to control nuclear developments – whether civil or military – and a whole raft of industrial processes, required that those who build and program them must work to exacting standards. As a result, the Task Force has been developing a proposal for a 'post-experience' modular course to ensure high quality SCS practitioners. The qualification would cover the principles, tools and techniques required and be aimed at software engineering practitioners of CEng or equivalent level.

Representatives from industry, academia, the military and both Western and Eastern European science heard a presentation on the role of training from Robin Bloomfield, a description of the proposed curriculum from Professor John McDermid and a description of possible methods of delivery from Professor John Buxton. The afternoon session consisted of an industry view from Jim Thomas of SD Scicon, representing the Computer Services Association, an assessment of the position of the IEE from Professor Andrew McGettrick, the European dimension from Gavin Kirkpatrick and accreditation issues from Mrs Aline Cumming.

Such a varied audience ensured lively discussions at the end of each session. While all agreed that SCS, with a current market worth £0.5 billion and growing at 20% per annum, required high-quality training and methodologies, their implementation was a much thornier problem.

Professor McDermid outlined the prerequisites of such a course. It must be post-experience and not aimed at undergraduates. Direct experience – preferably three years postgraduate experience – of the real-world techniques and trade-offs required are vital. As the needs of both managers and engineers have to be addressed, it should be modular, enabling each to take a different subset of modules depending on their requirements. This would also allow for considerable flexibility in selecting modules dependent on relevant past knowledge and experience.

The modular nature would enable the curriculum to be taught in twelve to eighteen intensive residential one-week courses – essential, as few firms would be prepared to lose key staff for a three- to four-month block. Further, as no one institution could easily furnish the skills or resources required for the entire course, it could be taught at several locations on this modular basis, with flexible industry-specific sections inserted as required.

McDermid suggested that 'Diploma of Engineering' would be a suitable qualification title for those completing the course, being in wide European use and covering both theory and practice. Most delegates agreed with this, as they did the general principles outlined and the contents of the curriculum. The six sections would entail: a general introduction; hazard and risk analysis; an ability to evaluate systems; using techniques to build systems; a review of the principles; and a review of the problems covered, including case studies.

It was made clear that the purpose of the seminar was not to present a hard and fast curriculum, but to provide concrete proposals to stimulate positive discussion. Numerous problems were envisaged by delegates, providing considerable feedback to the working party. Chief concerns were the cost of the course itself and the amount of time key staff would have to be absent. While accepting that a price cannot be put on safety, it was clear that many companies would not be willing to pay for the course as proposed. Already, military SCS standards were making it impossible for many contractors to tender. Without a cheaper course or external funding, it was clear that there might be a lack of support.

The question was also raised as to whether it was right to spend so much training a few hundred software engineers, rather than giving more general training to thousands. While not denying the need for training for all trades, the panel felt that this was a different issue – the need for intensive procedures for safety-critical computing was essential, regardless of the general level of expertise in industry.

It was also felt that such a major scheme might have difficulties in being accepted and implemented. As Professor John Buxton pointed out in his presentation on the means of delivery, the discipline of software engineering was not at present taught in an effective, structured way.

Without the support of the professional bodies it would not be possible to implement the course. Moreover, even if it was accepted, it would only be a starting point. It would require contractors to accept the need to train to such standards – a procedure that would take some time. Only when such standards were included in system specifications would the qualification take off. Once this was achieved, those who failed to implement them would be failing to apply 'reasonable care'.

It was generally felt that problems of cost and time, and therefore the content of the syllabus, required further study, even though the need to address the growth in SCS problems was recognised.

Jim Thomas, in presenting an industry view, echoed Professor Buxton in pointing out that an SCS course would also require the implementation of a more general programme that addressed the work processes in both individual organisations and the SCS industry as a whole. Not only must the costs be covered, but the implementors and procurers of systems must be prepared to accept the need for high-quality SCS training and to include these methods in the specifications. In short, both industry and the educators must agree the requirements and work in concert with the professional bodies.

The relevance of the EC General Directive on the Mutual Recognition of Professional Qualifications to SCS training was examined by Gavin Kirkpatrick. By the beginning of 1991, qualifications of an agreed standard gained in one EC state must be recognised in all others. This is of particular relevance to IT, as the growth of Informatics, increasing professional convergence and the envisaged skills shortage will all be affected by the mobility brought about by the Single Market.

All professions will have their concerns about equivalence of educational standards and basic problems such as language, terminology and resources. It is essential that the BCS and other bodies are active in promoting sensible agreements through the Council of European Professional Informatics Societies (CEPIS) and the EC Commission, particularly in areas such as SCS qualifications.

Professor McGettrick explained the remit of the IEE's SCS education working group – namely to define the IEE standpoint on SCS education. The proposals had many similarities to those of the BCS Working Party. He did point out that although the main thrust of training should be post-experience, increasing attention should be paid to SCS in undergraduate courses; a move that found favour with many delegates. He also saw a modular approach for the post-experience course, with all engineers taking basic awareness modules. Those with specific SCS responsibility would take core modules, specialised courses and an SCS project. Moreover, he believed that attention should be paid to legal liability and philosophical issues as well as to industrial involvement in connecting theory to practice.

It was unclear whether this approach would be a means of significantly reducing costs. Either way, favourable resourcing and the identification of relevant skills would be essential. It was agreed that the existing professional bodies would be able to organise an SCS qualification, and Mrs Aline Cummings pointed out that, when approved, a course could be administered by the course providers and moderated by a Certification Board. The Information Systems Examinations Board (ISEB) could take overall responsibility for the policy and finance, with an initial pilot scheme eventually becoming self-supporting through fees.

Two types of award were generally accepted – those for individual modules, with allowance made for previous experience, and an overall award, as previously proposed, of an Engineering Diploma. The separate issue of recognition would require a body with different terms of reference. It was noted that the BCS was in favour of an SCS Register, with peers assessing applications on the basis of a professional review and the qualification. Neither would be a necessary or sufficient criterion and the Register's establishment would have to be monitored very closely.

The closing general discussion served to emphasise the fears over the costs to industry that a course as proposed would entail. There was general agreement that attention had to be paid to the course content. It had to be short enough to be affordable but rigorous enough to satisfy the world at large that standards of safety were sufficient. The continually changing world of technology would require flexible criteria and content. Moreover, attention would have to be paid to the wider issues of educational standards in general and to the attitudes of managers in industry.

A professional qualification was indeed required, but was not in itself a sufficient condition to ensure safer systems. The Task Force and the wider Informatics industry will clearly have to expend considerable efforts to achieve such a goal.

A DEVELOPMENT MODEL FOR SAFETY-CRITICAL SOFTWARE

Edited by B A Wichmann

1. Introduction

This paper is concerned with the development of safety-critical software. Although such software is little different from other application software, there is a major concern that it should function in a safe manner. Hence methods of quality assurance and technical methods of detecting defects in software are particularly relevant.

There are clearly numerous different methods that could be used to develop such software, and to ensure it meets its specification. Some aspects of this process for the construction of military software were addressed in [7].

This paper attempts to draw together the views of members of the British Computer Society specialist group on safety-related computer systems. The idea behind this is to recommend a strategy for development to aid both those developing and those assessing such software. Unlike [7], it should be applicable to civil as well as military software. Even after several revisions, substantial and well-founded objections could be made to the particular approach adopted here (there is no canonical method). Hence this paper should be taken as guidance to be used in formulating one's own development model.

Inevitably, the software is only one component of a safety-critical system. This paper is only concerned with the software component and therefore does not address all the issues which impact upon the safety of the system. For some of the issues outside the software which need to be addressed to ensure safety, see [8]. One could reasonably query the use of 'safety-critical' in the title of this paper since safety is not specifically addressed. However, for software, it is thought that very careful conventional software engineering is needed, and this is the topic covered.

At least three aspects need to be addressed if an assured level of quality is to be attained:

- *Management*. Time and effort needs to be allocated to the development of any system. Moreover, with any complex system involving many staff, management skills are needed. For assured quality, a company should have a Quality Management System (QMS) such as that of ISO 9001 [13, 18]. Quality Management Systems are not covered in this paper; such a system should specify technical measures which could be the ones detailed here. The draft of the IEC standard for safety-critical software requires conformance to ISO 9001 [6].

- *Experience*. Although formal training helps, the computing industry depends upon the experience of the staff. This is natural in a young industry which has not yet had the time to develop standard procedures and practices that are the hallmark of the longer established professions. It is hoped that this paper can be used to gain insights into the development process.

- *Technical Measures*. This paper details a series of technical measures (or methods) which it is felt could give a reasonable degree of confidence in the software. It is important to note that these measures are necessarily a compromise between the practical and the theoretically possible.

This paper has arisen out of a study [2] of the UK Ministry of Defence proposals in this area [7]. It has previously been concluded that the Interim Defence Standard has much to recommend it, but that it lacks some coherence. The aim here is to outline a series of technical measures which provide a stronger model of the development process. Since Quality Management Systems and Experience are not included in this paper, the scope is somewhat less than [7].

It is assumed that the input to this software construction process is a view of the degree of criticality of the application. This is essential since the cost of performing the technical measures which give the greatest assurance is very high (especially for larger systems). As an example, for some medical applications, an increased cost of the devices could reduce their use, thus increasing the risk to life.

Some developers of safety-critical systems advocate the use of diverse redundancy and other fault-tolerant methods to reduce the dependence upon a single software component. If a system design involved a triplicated diversely redundant system with a voting system, then it is clear that the voting system would have the same criticality as the entire system, while the criticality of the diverse components would be somewhat less. The analysis of criticality levels is related to the application and the perceived risks and is not considered further here. The voting system could well be an independent re-usable component. The re-use and simplicity of the voting system could allow greater resources to be applied to its validation, perhaps to the level of formal proof of correctness of its design, though this does not remove the need for redundancy (within the device) to protect against breakdowns in service.

2. User Requirement

This is often vague since the user may only have an idea rather than a completely formulated proposal. It is important that the idea is produced in writing in a form that the main parties agree to. At this stage, some estimate must be made of the level of criticality of the system being proposed so that overall costing and planning can be undertaken.

In some industries, the systems engineer will provide a very detailed specification of the external characteristics of the system. Given experience with similar systems, translating this requirement into the Formal Specification (see below) may be relatively straightforward.

3. Requirements Analysis

This stage consists of a classical development with a detailed analysis of the idea to synthesise an informal specification of the complete system (of which the software could be quite a small part). In practice, this process can be very difficult since the user may not be familiar enough with the results of the analysis to validate the process. Also, if the User Requirement was vague and lacked detail, then the analysis will be long and detailed, again making the validation difficult for the user. If the user cannot validate the analysis, then there is a substantial risk that the software/system will not be as required. The user needs to be confident at the end of this stage that the result of the analysis is consistent with the original idea.

Included in this stage must be some form of hazard analysis in order to quantify the criticality of the system and the software components. This aspect will clearly determine the rigour of the software development process that is needed, but is not covered in this note (which is only concerned with technical measures to aid the process).

4. Natural-Language Specification

Formulation of a natural-language specification of the software component by the Systems Designer. This process involves at least a Fagan inspection [17] by the Software Engineer.

A common problem to be faced with software is that of checking a specification. Unfortunately, even simple checks are sometimes omitted with potentially disastrous consequences. In reviewing programming language specifications (which are examples of natural-language specifications), silly mistakes are sometimes found which could easily have been avoided.

4.1. Checks to be Undertaken
The following list of checks is proposed:

- *Spelling.* This is a simple check to perform on any system having a reasonable dictionary. It is necessary to check all the words not in the dictionary by hand.

- *Words.* An alphabetical list of words used should be produced, and this list examined manually to determine any irregularities. Sometimes a mis-spelt word will be in the dictionary and hence will not be found from the previous check. The ICL 2900 system which produces the list of words while undertaking a spelling check is superior to the Unix 'spell'. Glancing through the complete list of words is quite quick. A UNIX script to perform this is given in Appendix A.

- *Glossary.* Every detailed document defines its own terms in either a special section or 'in-line'. These words need to be extracted, all uses of them identified and manually checked that the uses are correct. If any term has a commonly used synonym, then either the synonym should be banned (and checked) or used as another special term.

- *Configuration Control*. It goes without saying that important documents should be controlled carefully. In practice, this depends upon the facilities offered by the computing system in use.

- *Document Control*. The document should be page numbered and dated. NAMAS requires that the total number of pages is also stated (a useful addition).

- *Modularity*. Locally used terms should not be used outside the module in which they are defined. Machine-assisted checks should be made to ensure this. In general, the scope of the definition of terms must be clearly stated.

- *List of Readers*. If a document is produced by one person in isolation, then problems are bound to arise. Merely knowing that others have reviewed a document is helpful. It would be better to use a formal review process, such as a Fagan inspection.

It is important that when the above checks have been made, this should be recorded correctly (via the QMS). Merely stating that the spelling check has been made is not adequate – at least the date (and version number) should be recorded also. A significant factor in undertaking these checks is the need to repeat them when changes are made. Also, each of the individual checks is rather weak in itself, but the combination should give good assurance that major issues have been handled correctly.

4.2. Structured Textual Specification

The fact that a specification is held as natural-language text does not mean that a degree of formalism cannot be introduced. For instance, ISO specifications are conventionally in natural-language but have a specific structure to aid their use [9]. The Standard Generalised Markup Language [10]. is a natural method of exhibiting the structure within the document itself. As an example, the new computerised Oxford English Dictionary is held in SGML.

At the National Physical laboratory (NPL), the Pascal programming language standard has been converted to an SGML-like form in order to analyse and print the standard in a more intelligent manner. This allows checks to be performed which cannot be undertaken otherwise. Several small inconsistencies have been found during this process. Another possibility is Hypertext [1].

5. Formal Specification

The next stage is the derivation of a formal specification from the natural-language specification by the Software Engineer. This derivation can use implicit specification methods. The specification should be designed to be as succinct as possible, although readability and elegance are major goals. Any faults detected in the formal specification would imply that at least the natural-language specification needs to be reviewed. If corrections to the natural-language specification are found to be necessary, then it will be necessary to review the user requirements. Following these reviews, the appropriate steps must be redone.

The formal specification can omit non-critical parts of the software, but these must be detailed in natural-language form.

The only formal specification methods which can be recommended for this are VDM [11] and Z [4], since they are reasonably mature and well understood by a significantly large enough industrial community. VDM has the advantage of being in the process of standardization by ISO. Formal specification methods which require that the specification is in an executable form cannot be regarded as ideal, but could be used. The danger of requiring an executable form is that it will be more complex in those cases in which an implicit specification is natural. (The specification of a sort routine is very different from its implementation.)

If VDM were used as the specification language, then the implicit form using pre- and post-conditions would be most appropriate. The goal is to express the specification in a succinct, simple manner which gives the greatest confidence in its correctness.

There is a school of software engineering which advocates the use of executable specification languages. This is not thought to be appropriate at the earliest stages, since in the majority of real systems, an executable specification is significantly larger than an implicit one. This makes handling and checking of the specification more complex. For this reason we do not recommend OBJ [5], since the form and complexity of an OBJ specification is little different from than of an implementation in a high-level language supporting abstract data types, such as Ada.

If the formal specification is greater than 100 lines (say), then manual checking cannot be expected to locate all potential bugs and ambiguities. This implies that some form of machine processing is needed. This shall include syntax checking and other static checks. The natural-language text should include a statement on the checking performed. Tools are currently available to perform a syntax check on VDM [15] and tools to perform a complete static check on VDM are being developed.

An important aspect of the formal specification is the degree to which it characterises the software sufficiently to *guarantee* the acceptability of the software. At one end of the spectrum, a software specification may be entirely expressible in logical functions, such as perhaps a railway signalling system. In this case, adherence to a formal specification will give a very high degree of certainty that the software will meet the user needs. At the other end of the spectrum, the acceptability of the software may depend upon aspects which cannot be characterised formally, such as some aspects of the man–machine interface. In this case, a user review of the Executable Specification would appear to be essential (see below). This review is shown as optional in Appendix B since it is not needed for all applications. A user review has clear cost implications, especially if a review reveals problems, although, of course, the non-acceptance of the final software by the user is far more expensive. The development method without the optional review has the nice characteristic that it is a two-stage process: the production of the formal specification, then the production of the final software from the formal specification. The optional user review produces a validated formal specification which is then handed over to the System Designer; but the two stages then overlap to a greater extent.

If the requirements cannot be captured completely by the application of Formal Methods, then the user review is virtually essential if only to allocate responsibilities, should the final system not be acceptable to the user.

If the Systems Designer is not familiar with VDM, the review can be of the Executable Specification. The text of this specification should not be provided to the implementation team, to avoid any implementation bias it may contain.

6. Review of the Formal Specification

This should be undertaken by the Software Engineer walking through the specification with the System Designer. Any fault implies that all the previous steps are reviewed and corrections applied as necessary. The necessity of a simple expression of the requirements is clear from such a review since one cannot expect the System Designer to be familiar with the details of VDM, or similar formal specification methods.

7. Executable Specification

The next stage is the derivation of an executable version of the formal specification. This is done by the Software Engineer using appropriate tools to ensure the closest possible correspondence with the potentially implicit version. Even if implicit specification methods are not used, it may be necessary to perform some transformations on the specification.

The Executable Specification shall contain a machine interface so that it can be executed in a convenient form. There is no requirement to interface to real hardware or to meet timing constraints.

If VDM were used in the formal specification, then the natural approach to the executable version is to use the explicit form of specification in VDM. For an example of this approach see [12]. This would imply replacing the implicit specification parts by executable equivalents. If execution tools are available for VDM, then very little needs to be added to provide the executable version. Otherwise, conversion of the text to a language like OBJ could be undertaken.

The software team needs to review the Executable Specification, taking into account those parts which are not directly derived from the formal specification.

The user could also review the Executable Specification. However, unless the user attempts to exercise this Specification comprehensively, there is a danger that a false degree of confidence will be gained. Obviously, if the user can 'sign-off' the Executable Specification so that it becomes the primary vehicle for establishing the correctness of the final system, then the position is very different. The execution is clearly advantageous in providing early feedback during the development process, but is only likely to be effective if the form that the Executable Specification takes is convenient to the user. Hence we make such a review optional (an option which is specified in advance as part of the project plan).

7.1. A Second Implementation?

It could be argued that the Executable Specification advocated here is just like another implementation. However, another diverse implementation would have the advantage that it could be used for redundancy in the final system.

The approach of a second implementation is not thought to be appropriate for the following reasons:

1. A second system would have too much in common with the primary system, giving rise to common-mode failures. In contrast, an Executable Specification would be produced in a logic language (Miranda, Prolog, LISP, etc.) which would be very different from the primary implementation.

2. An Executable Specification should be available more quickly, being a prototype, leading to feedback into the development process.

3. Since the Executable Specification is based upon the Formal Specification, it is relatively free from implementation bias and hence allows the early effort to be concentrated on the 'what', not the 'how'.

7.2. Refinement of the Executable Specification

It is possible to envisage a further refinement of an Executable Specification to aid the development process. For instance, an initial Executable Specification could be a mainframe emulation using Prolog, and a further refinement could be undertaken by moving the Prolog onto the target hardware environment. Such a refinement could be useful in aiding a review by the user. No refinement is shown in Appendix B.

8. Review of Executable Specification

The System Designer then executes the Executable Specification until sufficient confidence is gained that it embodies the agreed (natural-language) specification. During this process, the System Designer accumulates the test cases that were used to confirm this Executable Specification as being 'correct'. These test cases are not given to the Software Engineer, and must be an authoritative set of cases containing at least all boundary-value tests, see [14]. The test cases are preserved for later use.

9. Classical Implementation

The Software Engineering team then produces the Full Implementation from the formal specification. The Full Implementation shall contain a facility to execute it divorced from the target hardware environment (i.e. some form of test harness is required).

Methods for reification and the discharge of proof obligations involved in VDM are not covered here; see [11] for further information.

This classical implementation step will contain several components, such as module design and test. Each step needs to be undertaken in a rigorous manner so that the additional controls advocated here act as a safety net rather than as a debugging process. Test cases produced during the development process are noted for later use.

10. Test Harness

A software mock-up is produced so that the Executable Specification and the Full Implementation can be run in parallel and compared. (Since the Executable Specification will almost certainly not meet the timing constraints, some method is needed to overcome this.)

11. Test Data

An independent team constructs critical test data both by using random input data, black-box data, white-box data and the data collected during review of the Executable Specification, and during the development of the Full Implementation. A reasonable strategy for white-box test data would be to attempt the exercise all of the code in the system.

12. Comparison Testing

Back-to-back testing of the Executable Specification and the Full Implementation using all these data is then used to complete the dynamic testing. A failure at this point would be a serious lapse, since the testing here is supposed to be a safety net.

If a failure does arise, then the reasons for this must be established, and changes made to the procedures used so that such a failure could not recur. It would probably be best to apply the techniques appropriate to the next higher level of criticality of the software, so that additional static analysis checking would be performed.

13. Static Analysis

An agreed level of static analysis of the code is undertaken. This level would depend upon the criticality of the software. It is necessary for the appropriate level of static analysis to be taken into account in the design stage. For instance, the use of complex language features would typically render formal proof impossible.

- *Review* (always undertaken). Code walk-through. Fagan inspection against formal specification. Comments checked for completeness and coherence.

- *Defect Analysis*. Statically non-reachable code detected. Unused variables, procedures, etc. deleted. Data flow anomalies detected, and corrections made as necessary.

- *Algebraic Checks*. Algebraic checks made on critical statement sequences.

- *Formal Proof*. Formal mathematical proof of correctness produced.

It should be noted that the higher levels of static checking imply a large amount of work. In practice, Formal Proof cannot be applied to a complex system. This therefore implies that it is vital that the specification of highly critical systems is made simple enough that Formal Proof *can* be undertaken. It appears that one has to rely upon the experience of the System Designer and Software Engineer for this, since it is not possible to give a firm prediction of the complexity of the software in advance.

Review and Defect Analysis could be done early in the development, being fairly simple and inexpensive. Algebraic Checks and Formal Proof levels could be done later in the hope that no expensive rewrites will be needed. The QMS should specify how the timing/resources are managed. Errors found during static analysis must be corrected, which can be expensive, depending upon how many steps have to be redone.

The ability to perform any form of Static Analysis apart from a Review depends upon the programming language; see [3].

14. Final Acceptance

It is tempting to indicate that final acceptance is for the user and therefore show an error arrow in the diagram in Appendix B. Although formally for contractual reasons some user acceptance may be needed, it is difficult to justify this in technical terms if the user has already indicated acceptance of the Natural Language Specification (and perhaps the Executable Specification as well). Non-acceptance implies that either the Natural Language Specification is ambiguous (all too likely) or that it was incorrectly interpreted when producing the Formal Specification. A user review of the Executable Specification is obviously advantageous in reducing the risk of non-acceptance of the final software.

There are issues which could make a product which passes the Comparison Testing unacceptable. Performance is such an issue. These issue need to be identified in advance and criteria produced to reduce the risk. This is not easy, since projecting the performance of anything other than trivial systems is notoriously difficult.

15. Other Issues

15.1. Management

This paper does not detail the management issues since these will depend upon the context in which the software is developed. Software developed for MoD will need to satisfy the contractual requirements that are imposed by MoD (for instance). Quite different arrangements are likely to apply to in-house development. The role of any certification or accreditation agency needs to be considered. The independence of the various parties needs to be reviewed. This paper advocates an independent team for the back-to-back testing since this is seen as the primary method of gaining assurance which could be undermined without strict controls on its independence.

15.2. Non-critical Components

Significant problems arise with the handling of the non-critical components within the software subsystem. For instance, a non-critical component could take an excessive time, thus preventing the critical component from operating within its time constraints. In Ada, complex interactions can take place even though the non-critical and critical components are well separated. In general, it is very difficult to verify that two software components are separated if they operate within the same address space of a computer.

A built-in test facility is a common method of increasing confidence in a system. If this is implemented in software, then the non-interference and separation from the critical components may be very hard to establish.

15.3. Timing Constraints

There are obviously some issues omitted from the above. Timing constraints can be important and are not always easy to handle. Static analysis may provide acceptable upper bounds to the timing of program components so that constraints can be verified. Otherwise, the use of probes to measure actual times taken can be used. For the Executable Specification which cannot meet such constraints, pre-computed expected results should be used so that the test harness can execute in real time, if that is necessary to validate the timing constraints.

15.4. Software Maintenance

Software maintenance is defined as the set of all those activities that are undertaken after a software system is first delivered. It includes corrective maintenance (to repair errors), perfective maintenance to undertake modifications required as a result of changing user needs, and adaptive maintenance, to modify the system owing to a changed performance requirements or changed environment such as host operating system. A further possibility is preventive maintenance, where modifications are undertaken to the software in order to improve its maintainability. Surveys have shown that the major software maintenance activity is perfective maintenance, and we would anticipate that the quality assurance methods applied to safety-critical software will further reduce the effort expended in corrective maintenance. Most software evolves, and it seems that the more successful software is, the more that users will demand modifications and changes to it. Often safety critical systems are used in a real-time environment, where actuators, valves and the general interface to the outside world can also change. Much safety-critical software is also very long lived, so that maintainability must be built in from the start, and quality assurance must continue to sustain or enhance quality throughout the whole lifetime of the product. Therefore the system must be designed from the outset for maintainability, and it is important to stress that all software items, including specifications, test suites, and documentation must also evolve.

This implies clear management policy, a strong commitment to training and the appropriate technical measures in designing the system for maintainability, and undertaking subsequent evolution without degrading the maintainability of the system. A clear process model with strong procedures is essential and whole system needs to be firmly supported by configuration management and metrics to provide essential management visibility. Quality assurance must be sustained throughout the maintenance process.

15.5. Accreditation

The editor would like to see some of the above steps worked out in full detail so that an independent test house could perform the Comparison Testing under NAMAS accreditation.

16. Acknowledgements

The editor wishes to thank: N D North and G O'Neill for the UNIX script for obtaining a list of words and for being a 'reader' of this document; the members of the British Computer Society Specialist Group on Safety-Related Computer Systems; and Professor K H Bennett (University of Durham). This work has been supported by the Department of Trade and Industry as part of their programme on Software Quality.

17. References

1. J Conklin, 'Hypertext: An Introduction and Survey', *Computer*, Vol. 20 No. 9, pp. 17-41, 1987.

2. G O'Neill and B A Wichmann, *A Contribution to the Debate on Safety-Critical Software*, NPL Report DITC 126/88, September 1988.

3. W J Cullyer, S J Goodenough and B A Wichmann, 'The Choice of Computer Languages in Safety-Critical Systems', (to be published in the *Software Engineering Journal*).

4. I Hayes, *Specification Case Studies*, Prentice-Hall, 1987.

5. J A Gougen, 'Parameterized Programming', *IEEE Transactions on Software Engineering*, Vol. 10, pp. 528-543, 1984.

6. IEC SC65A/WG9 *Software for Computers in the Application of Industrial Safety-Related Systems*, 3rd draft, June 1989.

7. Interim Defence Standard 00-55, *Requirements for the Procurement of Safety Critical Software in Defence Equipment*, Ministry of Defence, undated.

8. Interim Defence Standard 00-56, *Requirements for the Analysis of Safety Critical Hazards*, Ministry of Defence, undated.

9. ISO/IEC publication, *Rules for the **drafting** and **presentation** of International Standards*, first edition, 1986.

10. ISO 8879, *Information processing – Text and office systems – Standard Generalised Markup Language (SGML)*.

11. C B Jones, *Software Development: A Rigorous Approach*, Prentice-Hall, 1980.

12. G I Parkin and G O'Neill. *Specification of the MAA Standard in VDM*, NPL Report DITC 160/90, February 1990.

13. *Quality Management Standards for Software*, DTI Report, April 1988.

14. G J Myers, *The Art of Software Testing*, Wiley, 1979.

15. 'SpecBox', Adelard, 28 Rhondda Grove, London E3 5AP.

16. *STARTS (Software Tools for Application to Large Real-Time Systems) Purchasers Handbook*, second edition, May 1989.

17. *Software Inspection Handbook*, IEE, ISBN 0 86341 225 4, 1990 (commonly known as the Fagan inspection method; see Fagan, M.E. *IBM Systems Journal*, Vol. 15 No. 3, pp182-211, 1976.)

18. *NATO Requirements for an Industrial Quality Control System* Allied Quality Assurance Publication 1, May 1984.

APPENDIX A. Producing a List of Words in UNIX

The line below produces the words in `file` in alphabetical order.

```
cat file | tr -cs A-Za-z '\012' | sort -u
```

With:

```
tr -cs A-Za-z0-9\"\' '\012'| sort -d | uniq -c
```

the filter is extended to include numbers and single/double quotes (this checks on inconsistent uses like `'C'` and `"C"`). The list is sorted in dictionary order and the frequency of each 'word' is given. The shell script can be put into an executable file, say `freq` and invoked by the command

```
freq < textfile > wordlist
```

The list in 'wordlist' can be sorted in frequency order by

```
sort -rn wordlist > newwordlist
```

APPENDIX B. Wall Chart of Development Process

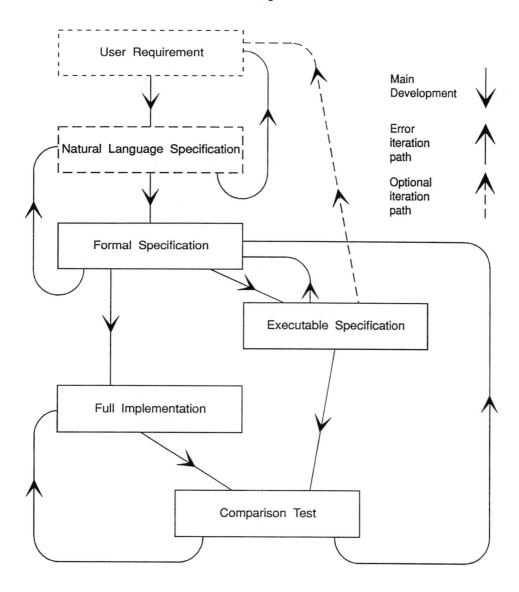

INT DEF STAN 00-55

The Procurement of Safety Critical Software in Defence Equipment

Part 1
Guidance

Part 2
Requirements

Revision of Defence Standards
Defence Standards are revised when necessary by the issue of amendments or of revised editions. **It is important that users of Defence Standards should ascertain that they are in possession of the latest amendments or editions.** Information on all Defence Standards is contained in Def Stan 00-00 (part 3) Section 4, Index of Standards for Defence Procurement — Defence Standards Index published annually and supplemented periodically by Standards in Defence News.

Defence Standards are published by and obtainable from: Ministry of Defence, Directorate of Standardization, Kentigern House, 65 Brown Street, Glasgow G2 8EX; Tel. 041-248 7890.

THE PROCUREMENT OF SAFETY CRITICAL SOFTWARE IN DEFENCE EQUIPMENT

PART 1: REQUIREMENTS

PREFACE

i This Part of the Standard introduces requirements for procedures and technical practices for Safety Critical Software (SCS). These procedures and practices are applicable to all MOD Authorities involved in procurement through the specification, design, development and certification phases of SCS generation, and maintenance and modification. This Standard is to be used by Defence Contractors as required by contract.

ii This Standard is being issued as INTERIM and is provisional in order to obtain information and experience of its application. This will then permit the submission of observations and comments from users, using DGDQA Form 0826 enclosed.

iii This Standard has been produced for MOD by a Working Group acting under the authority of the Policy Coordinating Committee on Guided Weapons and Electronics (PCCGWL). The Working Group was directed by a Steering Group comprising representatives of the three Systems Controllerates, RSRE, DGDQA and the Ordnance Board.

iv It is recognized that many of the procedures and technical practices needed to generate SCS are still being developed. The procedures and technical practices referred to in this Standard are considered to be the best currently available.

v This Standard will be one of a family of standards dealing with safety that is to be developed or adopted by MOD, taking into account international standardization activities and supporting research and development.

vi This Standard has been agreed by the authorities concerned with its use and shall be incorporated whenever relevant in all future designs, contracts, orders etc. and whenever practicable by amendment to those already in existence. If any difficulty arises which prevents application of the Defence Standard, the Directorate of Standardization shall be informed so that a remedy may be sought.

vii Any enquiries regarding this Standard in relation to an invitation to tender, or a contract, in which it is invoked, are to be addressed to the responsible technical or supervising authority named in the invitation to tender or contract.

viii This Standard has been devised for the use of the Crown and of its contractors in the execution of contracts for the Crown and, subject to the Unfair Contract Terms Act 1977, the Crown will not be liable in any way whatever (including but without limitation negligence on the part of the Crown its servants or agents) where the Standard is used for other purposes.

CONTENTS

	PAGE
Preface	1

Section One.   General

0	Introduction	4
1	Scope	4
2	Warning	5
3	Related Documents	5
4	Definitions	5
5	Requirements Enabling Competition, Use, Alteration and Support	5

Section Two.   Safety Management

6	Responsibility for Safety	7
7	MOD Safety Assurance Authority	7
8	Hazard Analysis and Safety Risk Assessment	7
9	Tenders	7
10	Support	7
11	Quality Assurance	8
12	Risk Analysis	8
13	Quality of Staff	8
14	Design Team	8
15	V&V Team	8
16	Independent Safety Auditor	9
17	Subcontracting Arrangements	9
18	Safety Plan	10
19	Safety Reviews	10
20	Code of Design Practice	11
21	Safety Records Log	11
22	Documentation	11
23	Requirements for Deliverable Items	12
24	Configuration Management	12
25	Certification and Acceptance into Service	13
26	Production	13
27	In-service	13
28	Disposal	14

Section Three.   Software Engineering Practices

29	Specification	15
30	Design	16
31	Coding	18
32	Formal Arguments	19
33	Dynamic Testing	19

34 Use of Existing Software   20
35 Validation   20
36 Tool Support   21

Annex A   Definitions   A-1
Annex B   Deliverables   B-1
Annex C   Requirements for the Configuration System   C-1
Annex D   Safety Critical Software Certificate   D-1

Index   Index i

THE PROCUREMENT OF SAFETY CRITICAL SOFTWARE IN DEFENCE EQUIPMENT

PART 1: REQUIREMENTS

Section One.   General

0   Introduction

0.1   Safety Critical Software (SCS) is software that relates to a safety critical function or system. A safety critical function or system is one in which a failure or design error could cause risk to human life; it is of the highest level of safety integrity.

0.2   This Part of the Standard addresses Safety Critical Software and describes the additional procedures necessary for specification, design, coding, production and in-service maintenance and modification of SCS that are required over and above those applied by conventionally well-managed projects to produce software of lower levels of integrity, and to which Def Stan 00-16 and Def Stan 00-31 refer. These procedures complement those applied to safety aspects of hardware and contribute to the assurance of the safety of the total equipment.

0.3   The safety integrity requirements of the software components in the equipment will have been determined by means of a hazard analysis and safety risk assessment according to Def Stan 00-56.

0.4   The Standard sets out a software development process in which verification and validation are integral parts, and achieved by using formal mathematical methods in conjunction with dynamic testing and static path analysis.

0.5   Guidance on the requirements in this Part of the Standard is contained in Part 2. However, this Standard assumes a degree of familiarity with software engineering and the conduct of MOD projects.

1   Scope

1.1   This Standard specifies requirements for all software used in Defence Equipment designated as Safety Critical. It refers only to the development of SCS and does not deal with the safety of the whole system.

1.2   The requirements of the Standard extend to tools and support software used to develop, test, certify and maintain SCS through all phases of the project lifecycle, if hazard analysis shows such tools to be safety critical.

1.3   This Standard or specified clauses thereof may also be applied to non-safety-critical software.

2 Warning

This INTERIM Defence Standard refers to a number of procedures, techniques, practices and tools that when used strictly are expected to give greater assurance that software is free from errors than if they are not used. However, compliance with this Standard in no way absolves the designer, the producer, the supplier or the user of systems containing software from statutory obligations relating to safety at any stage.

3 Related Documents

3.1 The following documents and publications are referred to in this Standard:

ISO 9000	Quality Management and Quality Assurance Standards
AQAP-1	NATO Requirements for an Industrial Quality Control System
AQAP-13	NATO Software Quality Control System Requirements
Def Stan 00-16	Guide to the Achievement of Quality in Software
Def Stan 00-31	Development of Safety Critical Software for Aircraft
Def Stan 05-57	Configuration Management Policy and Procedures for Defence Materiel
Def Stan 00-22	The Identification and Marking of Programmable Items
Def Stan 00-56	Hazard Analysis and Safety Classification of the Computer and Programmable Electronic System Elements of Defence Equipment
JSP 188	Requirements for the Documentation of Software in Military Operational Real Time Computer Systems
DEFCON 143	Software Development Questionnaire

3.2 Reference in this Part of the Standard to any related documents means, in any invitation to tender or contract, the edition and all amendments current at the date of such tender or contract unless a specific edition is indicated.

3.3 Part 2 of this Standard lists documents that, although not directly referenced in this Part of the Standard, contain detailed information that is related to the scope of this Standard.

4 Definitions

The definitions in annex A apply to this Standard.

5 Requirements Enabling Competition, Use, Alteration and Support

5.1 Competition is an essential element in defence procurement. The MOD(PE) shall be in a position to employ competition at any stage in a project lifecycle. System use, modification, enhancement, replication and in-service support during the life of a project require the unfettered availability and use of comprehensive information about software and its development environment.

5.2 It is a requirement of this Standard that MOD and subsequent owners of the system or any contractor either directly or indirectly employed by them shall be able to verify, validate, use, modify, enhance, replicate and issue software and its documentation and development environment that are the subjects of MOD(PE) funded contracts employing this Standard. These rights shall be determined before the design contract is let and shall not require subsequent approval, negotiation or additional payments.

5.3 Software or elements of the development environment for which these requirements are not satisfied, or software that is not MOD(PE) funded, or already existing software (irrespective of ownership), shall not be incorporated into the design without the prior written approval of the MOD(PE) PM. If approval is granted, suitable arrangements shall be made so that the principles behind the requirements in **5.1** and **5.2** shall not be compromised.

5.4 Contractors shall ensure that the requirements of this clause **5** apply also to subcontractors or suppliers.

Section Two.   Safety Management

6   Responsibility for Safety

The Design Authority has corporate responsibility for all aspects of the design and production of SCS. It is responsible for all safety management and shall nominate a responsible individual to sign the Safety Critical Software Certificate on its behalf.

7   MOD Safety Assurance Authority

An appropriate MOD Safety Assurance Authority is tasked by the MOD(PE) PM. The MOD Safety Assurance Authority advises the MOD(PE) PM on safety matters.

8   Hazard Analysis and Safety Risk Assessment

8.1   SCS components shall be identified as soon as practicable in the procurement of a project or equipment by means of the systematic application of Def Stan 00-56. The Design Authority shall advise the MOD(PE) PM if the equipment will or is likely to contain SCS.

8.2   Safety integrity analysis.   At each stage in the design of SCS, the Design Authority shall carry out a hazard analysis and safety risk assessment in accordance with Def Stan 00-56, in order to:

  (a) identify potential failures of the SCS that may cause new hazards or contribute to existing ones;
  (b) establish the correct level of safety integrity for each software component.

9   Tenders

In response to a tender invitation, contractors are required to provide the following:

  (a) Reasonable evidence that there is an awareness of safety throughout their organization.
  (b) A completed form DEFCON 143.
  (c) A statement identifying full compliance with this Standard, or each item of non-compliance referenced to the relevant clauses of the Standard.
  (d) A clear and detailed statement indicating how the requirements of this Standard are to be planned for and met, including areas of special risk to cost and timescales, and the deliverable items to be provided.

10   Support

The Design Authority shall ensure that the SCS will be maintainable during the required supported life. Support shall be planned for the SCS, its documentation and supporting hardware and software, including any non-deliverable items essential for maintenance.

11 Quality Assurance

11.1 The Quality Control System Requirements laid down in AQAP-1 and AQAP-13 or MOD declared equivalent shall be applied in all MOD contracts involving SCS. The use of an equivalent international standard such as those in the ISO 9000 series shall be agreed before any contract commences.

11.2 The Design Authority shall produce a Software Quality Plan for any SCS proposed before the work commences. The Plan shall be agreed between the Design Authority, the Independent Safety Auditor, the MOD Safety Assurance Authority and the MOD(PE) PM. The Plan shall require compliance with this Standard and the project Safety Plan (clause **18**).

12 Risk Analysis

The Design Authority shall undertake an analysis to demonstrate that the techniques and tools cited in the Safety Plan (clause **18**) are appropriate to the type of system being developed, and that the development can be undertaken with acceptable risk to the success of the project, and provide details to the MOD Safety Assurance Authority and the MOD(PE) PM. This analysis shall be undertaken in the earliest phases of a project, preferably in feasibility but not later than project definition, and documented in the Safety Records Log (clause **21**). The analysis shall be revised during the project if the assumptions on which it was based change.

13 Quality of Staff

The Design Authority shall demonstrate to the MOD Safety Assurance Authority and the MOD(PE) PM that the seniority, authority, qualifications and experience of the staff to be employed on the project are satisfactory for the tasks assigned to them.

14 Design Team

The Design Authority shall appoint a Design Team to specify, design, code and integrate the SCS. The Design Team is responsible for ensuring that its work has been carried out in accordance with the Code of Design Practice (clause **20**).

15 V&V Team

15.1 The Design Authority shall appoint a V&V Team, independent of the Design Team, to verify and validate the SCS.

15.2 The V&V Team shall produce a Verification and Validation Plan, and shall verify the SCS by carrying out dynamic testing and checking the correctness of Formal Arguments.

16 Independent Safety Auditor

16.1 The Design Authority shall appoint one or more named individuals to act as Independent Safety Auditor from the outset of the project. A separate contract shall be placed to cover the activities of the Independent Safety Auditor. The Design Authority, the MOD(PE) PM and the MOD Safety Assurance Authority shall be satisfied with the experience and qualifications of the Independent Safety Auditor.

16.2 Continuity of the same Independent Safety Auditor throughout the project lifecycle is desirable. Any change in the Independent Safety Auditor shall be justified.

16.3 The Independent Safety Auditor shall have the right of direct access to the MOD(PE) PM and the MOD Safety Assurance Authority.

16.4 The Independent Safety Auditor shall be commercially and managerially independent from the Design Authority so that he or she can assess the safety of the SCS without fetter and free from any possible conflicts of interest. The Design Authority shall give the Independent Safety Auditor full and unfettered access to the design and production processes and documentation.

16.5 At the start of his or her contractual involvement, the Independent Safety Auditor shall produce an Audit Plan, which shall be updated at the start of each subsequent project phase.

16.6 The Independent Safety Auditor shall oversee all aspects of the work that contribute to or influence the safety integrity of the SCS.

16.7 The Independent Safety Auditor shall periodically audit the project to check consistency and to establish conformance to this Standard and any project specific standards, guidelines or codes of practice specified in the Safety Plan. These audits shall include an examination of all the documentation produced by the Design Authority to give assurance of its veracity and completeness.

16.8 The results of the independent audits shall be recorded in an Audit Report.

16.9 The Independent Safety Auditor shall endorse the Safety Critical Software Certificate (clause **25**). However, the existence of the Independent Safety Auditor shall not release the Design Authority from its responsibilities for the safety of the SCS within the overall system.

17 Subcontracting Arrangements

The Design Authority shall ensure that the requirements of the Safety Plan (clause **18**) are met by its contractors, subcontractors and suppliers.

18   Safety Plan

18.1   A Safety Plan specifically for SCS shall be developed by the Design Authority in the earliest phases of a project and not later than project definition, showing the detailed safety planning and control measures that will be employed. This plan shall be updated at the commencement of each subsequent project phase.

18.2   The Safety Plan shall specify the management and technical procedures and practices to be applied to the development of SCS so that the requirements of this Standard are met and evidence of conformance is recorded. It shall encompass the Code of Design Practice (clause **20**) and the Configuration Plan (**24.3**).

18.3   The Safety Plan shall describe the resources and organizations required by this Standard. It shall identify key staff by name, including the leader of the Design Team, the leader of the V&V Team and the Independent Safety Auditor. Any changes shall be agreed with the MOD Safety Assurance Authority, the Independent Safety Auditor and the MOD(PE) PM prior to implementation.

18.4   The Design Authority shall rigorously apply the Safety Plan throughout the project lifecycle.

19   Safety Reviews

19.1   The Design Authority shall carry out formal reviews of the specification, design and code at planned stages agreed with the MOD Safety Assurance Authority and the Independent Safety Auditor, by means of a Review Committee constituted as follows:

- (a) the individual from the Design Authority responsible for safety certification (chairman);
- (b) members of the Design Team;
- (c) members of the V&V Team;
- (d) relevant contractors and subcontractors;
- (e) the Independent Safety Auditor;

and the following invited to attend:

- (f) the MOD(PE) PM or his/her representative;
- (g) representatives of the system users;
- (h) representatives of the MOD Safety Assurance Authority.

19.2   Attendance of any of the persons identified in items e–h above shall be without prejudice to the responsibility of the Design Authority for the safety of the SCS.

19.3   The formal reviews shall be minuted in the Safety Records Log.

20   Code of Design Practice

20.1   The Design Authority shall prepare a written Code of Design Practice that defines and justifies the specific procedures, methods and techniques to be used to meet the requirements for software engineering practices laid down in section three of this Part of the Standard.

20.2   The Code of Design Practice shall state criteria for the acceptance of each SCS component. It shall also define the procedures for dealing with unacceptable components.

20.3   If a previously existing Code of Design Practice is used, it shall be reviewed for suitability by a review team constituted as laid down in clause **19**, and reissued.

21   Safety Records Log

21.1   The Design Authority shall maintain a Safety Records Log that contains, directly or by reference to detailed project documentation under configuration control, comprehensive evidence that the required level of safety integrity of the SCS has been achieved. The Design Authority shall keep the information in the Safety Records Log accurate and up-to-date throughout the project lifecycle.

21.2   The Safety Records Log shall include:

(a) the results of hazard analysis and safety risk assessment;

(b) review minutes;

(c) definitions and results of dynamic testing;

(d) resource modelling reports;

(e) results of checking of Formal Arguments;

(f) the results of reviewing static path analysis;

(g) in-service anomaly reports and their resolution.

22   Documentation

22.1   The Design Authority shall maintain a set of documentation for the SCS that covers all lifecycle phases and that is sufficiently comprehensive for the entire SCS process to be re-established.

22.2   All SCS shall be documented in accordance with JSP 188. The documentation shall be structured to facilitate an easy transition from high level to low level documents, and identified in accordance with the configuration management plan (clause **24**). Details of the style, layout and content of the documentation, and the use of the output from software tools, shall be agreed between the Design Authority, the MOD Safety Assurance Authority, the Independent Safety Auditor and the MOD(PE) PM.

22.3   The documentation shall identify:

11

(a) all software that has been procured as a result of MOD(PE) funded work to meet the requirements of this Standard;

(b) all deliverable software;

(c) all software developed as part of the project;

(d) all software developed outside the project;

(e) all other relevant software, including the software tools used and the host development system.

23 Requirements for Deliverable Items

23.1 The Design Authority shall deliver to the MOD(PE) PM software and documentation substantially as given in annex B. Any deviations from the list in annex B shall be agreed with the MOD Safety Assurance Authority, the Independent Safety Auditor and the MOD(PE) PM.

23.2 All deliverable software and documentation shall be prepared at the appropriate time during the definition, design, development and production phases. Retrospective preparation (as opposed to updating) is not acceptable.

23.3 In cases of premature termination of development, all deliverable SCS, test and support software, and documentation relating to work carried out prior to termination shall be delivered to the MOD.

24 Configuration Management

24.1 The establishment and subsequent management of configuration control of the SCS is an essential element in maintaining the overall safety integrity of the equipment being procured. The Design Authority shall employ an effective, automated configuration control system for all phases of the project lifecycle.

24.2 The Design Authority shall establish a configuration system composed of a library of all SCS, all physical occurrences of that SCS, related documentation and information. The configuration system shall provide revision control for all configuration items and configuration objects.

24.3 The configuration system shall be described in a Configuration Plan. This plan shall name the staff responsible for configuration management and describe the procedures, tools and techniques that implement the configuration system. The plan shall be agreed with the MOD Safety Assurance Authority, the Independent Safety Auditor and the MOD(PE) PM. The configuration tool shall satisfy the criteria set out in clause **36**.

24.4 The configuration system shall be as described in annex C.

25   Certification and Acceptance into Service

25.1   Certification shall be a pre-condition for the delivery of SCS. The Design Authority shall submit a Safety Critical Software Certificate to the MOD(PE) PM prior to delivery. This certificate shall be an unambiguous, clear and binding statement by accountable signatories from the Design Authority, countersigned by the Independent Safety Auditor, that the SCS is suitable for service in its intended system and conforms to the requirements of this Standard. Certification shall be supported by the evidence in the Safety Records Log and supporting documentation. A proforma certificate is given in annex D.

25.2   The Design Authority shall prepare an Acceptance Test Schedule for approval by the MOD(PE) PM. Acceptance tests that demonstrate to the MOD(PE) PM that the SCS possesses an adequate level of safety integrity shall be carried out.

25.3   Acceptance into service of the SCS shall be based on normal procedures, acceptance tests and trials plus the Safety Critical Software Certificate.

25.4   Shortfalls against the agreed requirement that are not apparent at acceptance shall be rectified promptly, without additional cost to MOD, as soon as possible after they become apparent.

25.5   Certification and acceptance into service do not relieve the Design Authority of the legal responsibilities for the safety of the product.

26   Production

26.1   For the purposes of this Standard, *production* means the replication of an executable binary image without change.

26.2   The Design Authority shall plan for the production of binary images (including firmware) incorporating SCS in such a way as to preserve the safety integrity of the SCS. Production shall be under configuration control. The version and configuration of firmware shall be uniquely identified in accordance with Def Stan 00-22. The binary images (including firmware) shall be checked by comparison with the master copy of the image held under configuration control.

27   In-service

27.1   There shall be a Design Authority responsible in accordance with clause **6** for maintaining the Safety Records Log for SCS (see clause **21**) during the in-service phase, and for carrying out modifications to SCS in accordance with the requirements of this Standard.

27.2   Adequate resources shall be made available to preserve and support the integrity of SCS during the in-service phase.

27.3 The in-service Design Authority shall establish appropriate procedures for documenting in the Safety Records Log all reported anomalies in SCS that are discovered during in-service use whether or not they result in hazardous situations or accidents. Each report shall as far as practicable include the circumstances surrounding the discovery of the anomaly, the likely consequences and any corrective action taken.

28 Disposal

28.1 Disposal and decommissioning of the SCS shall be treated as projects in their own right. This Standard shall be applied accordingly with due consideration given to decommissioning activities. Relevant safety documentation arising from former use shall be considered. Where disposal constitutes sale to a third party, the contract of sale shall include a disclaimer of MOD responsibility for the safe use of the SCS.

28.2 If any part of the SCS is transferred to a third party, the liabilities covered by the Safety Critical Software Certificate may have to be renegotiated. Any recertification shall be to the requirements of this Standard.

Section Three.   Software Engineering Practices

29   Specification

29.1   General

29.1.1   As the first step in the design of SCS, the Design Team shall produce a Software Specification from the Software Requirements Specification. The Software Specification shall include a specification of the software using the specification notation of a Formal Method (the Formal Specification), plus a commentary on the Formal Specification in English together with engineering notations where appropriate (the English Commentary).

29.1.2   The Design Authority shall use a suitable established and standardized Formal Method for the Formal Specification. Properties that cannot be expressed using the Formal Method shall be notified to the MOD(PE) PM and a suitable, established specification method agreed.

29.1.3   The Design Authority should continue to use established structured methods where these provide practical guidance on the software specification process. However, the Formal Specification shall be as far as possible self-sufficient.

29.2   Verification

29.2.1   The Design Team shall check the Formal Specification for syntactic and type errors by means of a suitable tool in accordance with clause **36**. They shall check the English Commentary for accuracy, completeness and consistency.

29.2.2   The Design Team shall construct the Proof Obligations necessary to show that the Formal Specification is internally consistent, and discharge them by means of Formal Arguments, as laid down in **32.1**.

29.3   Preliminary Validation

29.3.1   The Design Team shall validate the Software Specification against the Software Requirements Specification by animation of the Formal Specification. Animation shall be carried out by both of the following:

(a) By the construction of Formal Arguments in accordance with **32.1** showing that the Formal Specification embodies all the safety features described in the Software Requirements Specification.

(b) By the production of an Executable Prototype derived from the Formal Specification. The minimum number of changes shall be made to the Formal Specification in the construction of the Executable Prototype; Formal Arguments shall be constructed in accordance with **32.1** to show the link between the two.

29.3.2   The Executable Prototype shall be tested by the Design Team. The aim of each

15

test and the expected results shall be determined before the test is executed. As a minimum, the tests shall exercise all the safety functions of the SCS. The results shall be recorded in the Software Specification.

29.3.3 The Design Authority shall involve the MOD(PE) PM in preliminary validation to the greatest extent practicable. Changes to the Software Requirements Specification and the Software Specification arising from the results of Preliminary Validation shall be agreed between the Design Authority, the MOD Safety Assurance Authority, the Independent Safety Auditor and the MOD(PE) PM.

29.4 Checking and review

29.4.1 The Proof Obligations constructed by the Design Team and the Formal Arguments that discharge them shall be checked and reviewed by the V&V Team as described in **32.2**.

29.4.2 The Formal Arguments showing the link between the Formal Specification and the Executable Prototype shall be checked and reviewed by the V&V Team as described in **32.2**.

29.4.3 The Software Specification shall be reviewed by a Review Committee as laid down in clause **19** before detailed design commences. The review shall consider the correctness, completeness, consistency, absence of ambiguity, general style and quality of the document, and its conformance to the Code of Design Practice. It shall establish that the Software Specification correctly interprets the requirements of the Software Requirements Specification, taking into account the results of Preliminary Validation (see **29.3**).

30 Design

30.1 General

30.1.1 Each design produced during the design process shall be documented in a Design Description. The Design Description shall include a description of the design using a Formal Method (the Formal Design) and an English Commentary. It shall include all the information required by subsequent design, coding and integration steps, and contain detailed design level diagrams in accordance with JSP 188.

30.1.2 The Design Authority shall use a suitable established and standardized Formal Method or Methods for the Formal Design. Properties that cannot be expressed using the Formal Method or Methods shall be notified to the MOD(PE) PM and a suitable, established design method agreed.

30.1.3 SCS shall be designed so that it is easy to justify that it meets its specification in terms of both functionality and performance. This requirement may restrict the length and complexity of the software and inhibit the use of concurrency, interrupts, floating point arithmetic, recursion, partitioning, and memory management.

30.1.4 The Design Team shall carry out resource modelling to establish that the design can be accommodated by the proposed hardware and that the functionality and response requirements can be met.

30.1.5 The design shall employ defensive programming techniques that, as a minimum, check data at the input to each module against the assumptions recorded in the Formal Specification or Formal Design of the module, unless the data are produced by a module that is verified by Formal Proof. The principle of defensive programming shall also apply to the interfaces between software and hardware as well as to those between software modules.

30.1.6 The design shall ensure that software configuration and version identity are confirmed according to the requirements of Def Stan 00-22.

30.1.7 The design shall employ existing software only in accordance with clause **34**.

30.1.8 The Design Authority should continue to use established structured design methods where these complement the Formal Method. However, the Formal Design shall as far as possible be self-sufficient.

30.2 Verification

30.2.1 The Design Team shall check the Formal Design for syntactic and type errors by means of a suitable tool in accordance with clause **36**. They shall check the English Commentary for accuracy, completeness and consistency.

30.2.2 The Design Team shall construct the Proof Obligations necessary to verify each Formal Design with respect to the preceding Formal Design or the Formal Specification, and discharge them by means of Formal Arguments as laid down in **32.1**.

30.3 Checking and review

30.3.1 The Proof Obligations constructed by the Design Team and the Formal Arguments that discharge them shall be checked and reviewed by the V&V Team as described in **32.2**.

30.3.2 Each Design Description shall be reviewed by a Review Committee as laid down in clause **19**. The review shall consider the correctness, completeness, consistency, absence of ambiguity, general style and quality of the document, and its conformance to the Code of Design Practice. It shall establish that it correctly implements the higher level Design Descriptions or the Software Specification, taking into account the Formal Arguments produced by the Design Team.

31 Coding

31.1 General

31.1.1 The Design Team shall work to coding standards that lead to clear source code that is analysable by Formal Arguments and Static Path Analysis.

31.1.2 SCS shall be programmed in a language, or a predefined subset of a language, which shall have the following characteristics:

(a) A formally-defined syntax.

(b) A means of enforcing the use of any subset employed.

(c) A well-understood semantics and a formal means of relating code to the Formal Design.

(d) Block structured.

(e) Strongly typed.

31.1.3 Language translators (e.g. compilers and interpreters) shall satisfy the criteria set out in clause **36**.

31.2 Verification

31.2.1 The Design Team shall construct the Proof Obligations that verify the source code with respect to its Formal Design, and discharge them by means of Formal Arguments, as laid down in **32.1**.

31.2.2 Using a suitable tool, the Design Team shall carry out Static Path Analysis of the source code, which shall include the following analyses:

(a) control flow analysis, including checks for redundant code;

(b) data use analysis;

(c) information flow analysis;

(d) where a restricted subset of an implementation language is employed, analysis of the program constructs used to ensure that the subset has been adhered to.

31.3 Checking and review

31.3.1 The Proof Obligations and Formal Arguments produced by the Design Team shall be checked and reviewed by the V&V Team, as described in **32.2**.

31.3.2 The V&V Team shall review the results of Static Path Analysis and satisfy themselves that no reported anomaly is due to an error. If defects are discovered, the Design Team shall take appropriate corrective action.

31.3.3   When Static Path Analysis has been completed, the V&V Team shall carry out dynamic testing of the code, as described in clause **33**.

31.3.4   The source code shall be reviewed by a Review Committee as laid down in clause **19**. The review shall consider its conformance to the Code of Design Practice. It shall establish that it correctly implements the Design Description, taking into account the Formal Arguments of verification, Static Path Analysis and results of dynamic testing. If defects are discovered, the Design Team shall take appropriate corrective action.

32   Formal Arguments

32.1   Construction of Formal Arguments

32.1.1   Formal Arguments shall be constructed using Formal Proofs or Rigorous Arguments. Formal Proofs shall be used unless the Design Authority, the Independent Safety Auditor, the MOD Safety Assurance Authority and the MOD(PE) PM are satisfied that, taking into account the safety risk from failure of the SCS, Rigorous Arguments offer a sufficient degree of assurance.

32.1.2   Formal Arguments shall be made available to the V&V Team, the MOD(PE) PM and the Independent Safety Auditor in machine readable form.

32.2   Review of Formal Arguments

32.2.1   The V&V Team shall establish that Formal Arguments produced by the Design Team include the discharge of all the necessary Proof Obligations.

32.2.2   The V&V Team shall scrutinize all Rigorous Arguments produced by the Design Team for correctness and completeness. If found to be unsatisfactory, they shall be returned to the Design Team for elaboration or correction.

32.2.3   The V&V Team shall check Formal Proofs for correctness and completeness using a diverse tool from any employed by the Design Team in the discovery of the proof.

33   Dynamic Testing

33.1   The V&V Team shall carry out dynamic testing on all individual modules, partly integrated groups of modules and the integrated SCS. The test set shall exercise all safety functions of the SCS. The test set shall include checks on timing constraints, numerical accuracy and stability, and reliance on system components where appropriate. Each test set shall be concealed from the Design Team until the tests have been carried out.

33.2   Tests shall be monitored with a test coverage monitor. Testing shall continue until at least the following have been exercised:

(a) All statements.

(b) All branches for both true and false conditions, and case statements for each possibility including 'otherwise'.

(c) All loops for zero, one and many iterations, covering initialization, typical running and termination conditions.

33.3 The integrated SCS shall be tested in a test harness that enables the results to be compared with the Executable Prototype. During these tests, the SCS shall be run on the target hardware or on an emulator that has been shown by Formal Arguments to be equivalent to the target hardware.

33.4 The results of tests on individual modules shall be compared with the behaviour calculated in advance from the appropriate Design Description.

34   Use of Existing Software

34.1   The Design Authority shall ensure that existing library or other software developed outside the project that is to be used in the final delivered equipment conforms to the requirements of this Standard. Such software shall be used only with the agreement of the MOD Safety Assurance Authority, the Independent Safety Auditor and the MOD(PE) PM.

34.2   Where existing software is shown by hazard analysis and safety risk assessment in accordance with Def Stan 00-56 to be safety critical, but where such software has not previously been produced as required by this Standard, the Design Authority shall carry out verification during the appropriate project phases by means of a Formal Specification, Formal Design, Formal Arguments of verification, dynamic testing and Static Path Analysis that are compliant with this Standard.

34.3   The Design Authority shall provide as deliverable items documents relating to the existing software that correspond to the Software Specification, Design Description and Safety Records Log as defined in this Standard.

35   Validation

35.1   The V&V Team shall perform validation testing of the SCS to establish that it conforms to the Software Requirements Specification. These tests shall be carried out, preferably with a representative of the In-Service Authority present, with the integrated SCS in its final environment, or where that is not practicable, using a simulator.

35.2   Validation testing shall be carried out to an extent that gives the best practicable estimate of the achieved safety integrity of the SCS. The extent of testing shall be agreed with the MOD Safety Assurance Authority, the Independent Safety Auditor and the MOD(PE) PM.

35.3   The test schedule shall provide the following:

(a) coverage of each function;

(b) coverage based on the expected input domain, including boundary values, singularities, special values, out of range and erroneous values;

(c) coverage of the states of each individual output.

35.4 Each test set shall be concealed from the Design Team until the tests have been carried out.

35.5 The results shall be checked for:

(a) correct functionality;

(b) correct action on error, including the action of the fault tolerant features;

(c) correct timing;

(d) conformance to the requirements for non-functional properties.

36 Tool Support

36.1 All tools and support software used in the development of the safety critical software shall have sufficient safety integrity to ensure that they do not jeopardize the safety integrity of the SCS.

36.2 The safety integrity requirements for the tools and support software shall be established by a hazard analysis and safety risk assessment implemented by the systematic application of Def Stan 00-56. This analysis shall define the safety integrity required of each tool in view of the role of the tool in the project. Criteria shall be defined for the assurance and evaluation of tools and support software for each level of safety integrity used in the project, either by direct definition or by reference to existing standards.

36.3 Compilers shall meet the following requirements:

(a) They shall be validated with an approved international or national validation certificate. The Design Authority shall demonstrate that the certificate relates to the version and use intended in the project.

(b) They shall be verified to the extent indicated from the hazard analysis and safety risk assessment. As a minimum they shall have been developed within a recognized Quality Control System (e.g. AQAP-1/13 or the ISO 9000 series).

(c) If the object code is not shown by Formal Arguments to be equivalent to the source code, the compiler shall be classified as safety critical and shall have been developed to the requirements of this standard.

36.4 The selection of tools and support software should also consider their costs, benefits, performance, maturity, usability, interoperability and maintenance.

36.5 The safety assessment of the tools and support software and the evaluation of their safety integrity shall be documented in the Safety Records Log. Any pragmatic considerations that led the Design Authority to use a tool or support software of a lower safety integrity than that indicated by the hazard analysis and safety risk assessment shall also be recorded in the Safety Records Log and noted on the Safety Critical Software Certificate.

36.6 The requirements of this clause **36** apply also to tools and support software introduced during the course of the project and to the upgrade of existing tools. The impact of any change to the tools or support software shall be analysed in advance by the Design Authority, and the results documented in the Safety Records Log.

Definitions

A.1 Definition of Terms

A.1.1 Accident. An unintended event or sequence of events that causes death, injury, environmental or material damage.

A.1.2 Animation. The process by which the behaviour defined by a formal specification is examined and validated against the informal requirements.

A.1.3 Code. The representation of particular data or a particular computer program in a symbolic form, such as source code, object code or machine code.

A.1.4 Component. A discrete structure within the total SCS, such as a module, considered at a particular level in the design.

A.1.5 Concurrency. Pertaining to the occurrence of two or more events or activities within the same specified interval of time.

A.1.6 Configuration Control. Activity to ensure that any change, modification, addition or amendment is prepared, accepted and controlled by set procedures.

A.1.7 Configuration Item. An item that may be stored by a computer designated for configuration management.

A.1.8 Configuration Management. Technical and administrative procedures to:

  (a) identify and document functional and physical characteristics of any part of the system;
  (b) control changes to these, and their interfaces;
  (c) record and report change, its process and implementation.

A.1.9 Configuration Object. A physical configuration item (e.g. a paper document, an EPROM etc.). Configuration objects are not necessarily unique; however, identical versions must be identical copies.

A.1.10 Configuration System. The collective term for the library, procedures and configuration tools for manipulation of the library.

A.1.11 Defence Equipment. Includes ships, aircraft, vehicles, weapons systems, surveillance/detection systems, communications systems, ammunition or main components forming part of systems and also ancillary support items such as training aids, tools etc.

A.1.12 Defensive Programming. Writing programs that detect erroneous input and output values and control flow. Such programs prevent propagation of errors and recover by software where possible.

A.1.13   Design Authority. The approved firm, establishment or branch responsible within the terms of the contract or other formal agreement for all aspects of the design of a system, sub-system or item of equipment to approved specifications, and authorized to sign a certificate of design or to certify drawings.

A.1.14   Design Description. A detailed formulation, in document form, that provides a definitive description of a stage in the design of the SCS for the purpose of developing and verifying the system. The Design Description contains a Formal Design and an English Commentary.

A.1.15   Documentation. The management of documents, which may include the actions of identifying, acquiring, processing, storing and disseminating them. A collection of documents on a given project.

A.1.16   Dynamic Testing. Execution of a program with test data and the analysis of the results.

A.1.17   Engineering Change Proposal. The formal documentation of a proposal for an engineering change.

A.1.18   English Commentary. That part of the Software Specification or Design Description written in English and appropriate engineering notations.

A.1.19   Executable Prototype. An executable form of a Formal Specification, produced by making the minimum changes to it, that is used to validate the Software Specification.

A.1.20   Failure. The inability of an equipment or component to fulfil its operational requirements.

A.1.21   Firmware. Computer logic that is either hardwired or in a state that cannot readily be modified.

A.1.22   Formal Arguments. Formal proofs or rigorous arguments.

A.1.23   Formal Design. The part of the Design Description written using a Formal Method.

A.1.24   Formally Defined Syntax. A syntax defined in a formal notation, such as Backus Naur Form (BNF).

A.1.25   Formal Method. A software specification and production method, based on a mathematical system, that comprises: a collection of mathematical notations addressing the specification, design and development phases of software production; a well-founded logical inference system in which formal verification proofs and proofs of other properties can be formulated; and a methodological framework within which software may be developed from the specification in a formally verifiable manner.

A.1.26 <u>Formal Proof</u>. The discharge of a proof obligation by the construction of a complete mathematical proof.

A.1.27 <u>Formal Specification</u>. The part of the Software Specification written using the specification notation of a Formal Method.

A.1.28 <u>Hazard</u>. A physical situation, often following from some initiating event, that can lead to an accident.

A.1.29 <u>Interrupt</u>. A suspension of a process, such as the execution of a computer program, caused by an event external to that process, and performed in such a way that the process can be resumed.

A.1.30 <u>Module</u>. A separately identified part of a computer program that performs a specific function.

A.1.31 <u>Nondeterminism</u>. The situation where a specification does not distinguish between alternative behaviours, e.g. the order in which two actions are to be performed.

A.1.32 <u>Project lifecycle</u>. The sequence of phases through which defence equipment projects pass during their lifecycle. The phases are: concept formulation; feasibility; project definition; full development; production; in-service; and disposal.

A.1.33 <u>Proof Obligations</u>. Mathematical statements arising during a formal design and development process that must be proved in order to verify the design or development step.

A.1.34 <u>Rigorous Argument</u>. An outline of the way in which a proof obligation can be discharged, which presents the main steps but does not supply all the intervening detail.

A.1.35 <u>Risk</u>. The combination of the frequency, or probability, and the consequence of an accident.

A.1.36 <u>Safety Critical Software</u>. Software, including firmware, used to implement a function or component of the highest level of Safety Integrity.

A.1.37 <u>Safety Features</u>. The features that are required to remove unacceptable safety risks and constrain the other risks from the Defence Equipment to a tolerable level.

A.1.38 <u>Safety Integrity</u>. The likelihood of a safety critical system, function or component achieving its required safety features under all the stated conditions within a stated measure of use.

A.1.39 <u>Safety Requirements</u>. The requirements for safety features to be met by Safety Critical Software.

A.1.40 <u>Software</u>. All instructions and data that are input to a computer to cause it to function in any mode; the term includes operating systems, supervisory systems, compilers and test routines as well as application programs. The word embraces the documents used to define and describe the program (including flow charts, network diagrams and program listings) and also covers specifications, test plans, test data, test results and user instructions.

A.1.41 Software Specification. A detailed formulation, in document form, that provides a definitive description of the software for the purpose of developing, verifying and validating the system. The Software Specification contains a Formal Specification and an English Commentary.

A.1.42 Static Path Analysis. The use of a software tool to detect control flow, data use and information flow anomalies.

A.1.43 Strongly typed. A programming language that has the property that applying a procedure, function or operator to a value of an inappropriate type gives rise to a reported error. (See also **A.1.51.**)

A.1.44 Support Software. Software used in the process of specifying, designing, coding, testing, verifying, validating, executing, integrating, downloading and controlling the configuration of software.

A.1.45 Systematic failure. A failure that is due to faults in the specification, design, construction, software coding, operation or maintenance of the system or its components. Systematic failures cause the system to fail under some particular combinations of inputs or under some particular environmental conditions.

A.1.46 Target Hardware. Computer hardware upon which the delivered software is to be executed.

A.1.47 Test Case. A set of inputs, execution conditions and expected results.

A.1.48 Test Coverage. A measure of how far a test exercises the specified requirements of a system, module or component.

A.1.49 Test Coverage Monitor. A software tool to measure test coverage.

A.1.50 Test Harness. Software or a test driver used to invoke a module, and to provide test input, and to monitor and report test results.

A.1.51 Type Errors. A violation of the typing discipline (or typing rules) of a formal language. This typing discipline specifies how to assign types (such as integer or boolean) to expressions and defines well-formedness of a composite construct in relation to its components' type values. For example, adding an integer expression to a boolean $(1 + true)$ results in a type error. (See also **A.1.43.**)

A.1.52 Under-specification. The situation where a specification deliberately does not address certain properties of the system, e.g. the colour of parts of a display.

A.1.53 Validation. The test and evaluation of the integrated computer system (hardware and software) and its specification to ensure that it carries out its intended purpose.

A.1.54 Verification. The process of determining whether or not the product of each phase of the computer system development process is an accurate realization of the one before.

A.2 Definition of Abbreviations

A.2.1 A&AEE. Aeroplane and Armaments Experimental Establishment

A.2.2 IPSE. Integrated Project Support Environment.

A.2.3 ISO. International Standards Organization

A.2.4 SCS. Safety Critical Software.

A.2.5 V&V Team. Verification and Validation Team

Deliverables

This annex lists the deliverable software and documents produced in accordance with this Standard. It gives the project phase and the organization principally responsible for each.

B.1 General

(a) Contents list.
Produced by: Design Authority. Project phase: feasibility or project definition and updated at subsequent phases.
A list of all SCS and its documentation, identified in accordance with the configuration system.

B.2 Planning

(b) Safety Plan.
Produced by: Design Authority. Project phase: feasibility or project definition and updated at subsequent phases. (Refer to clause 18)
The management and technical procedures and practices to be applied to the development of SCS.

(c) Software Quality Plan.
Produced by: Design Authority. Project phase: feasibility or project definition. (Refer to clause 11)
The plan for implementing the software quality control system for the SCS.

(d) Code of Design Practice.
Produced by: Design Authority. Project phase: feasibility or project definition. (Refer to clause 20)
The specific procedures, methods and techniques to be used by the Design Authority to meet the requirements for software engineering practices.

(e) Configuration Plan.
Produced by: Design Authority. Project phase: feasibility or project definition. (Refer to clause 24)
The description of the configuration system.

(f) Audit Plan.
Produced by: Independent Safety Auditor. Project phase: start of contractual involvement and updated at subsequent phases. (Refer to clause 16)
The plan for the audit and overseeing activities of the Independent Safety Auditor.

(g) Verification and Validation Plan.
Produced by: V&V Team. Project phase: project definition or full development. (Refer to clause 15)
The plan for the V&V Team, specifying their role in dynamic testing and the verification of formal arguments.

(h) Target Downloading Specification.
Produced by: Design Authority. Project phase: full development.

The specification of the procedure for downloading the SCS to the target hardware, including:

(1) precise identification of all tools to be used;

(2) user instructions for downloading the SCS.

B.3 System-level documents

(i) Statement of Technical Requirements.
Produced by: MOD. Project phase: feasibility and project definition.
The top level definition of the function, operational features and performance required by the equipment. It should be updated where necessary during the project to reflect changes and concessions.

(j) System Elements Analysis.
Produced by: Design Authority. Project phase: project definition.
A breakdown of the structure and an analysis of the overall system in response to the Statement of Technical Requirements.

(k) System Implementation Plan.
Produced by: Design Authority. Project phase: project definition.
A plan of the system design resulting from the System Elements Analysis.

B.4 Software documents

(l) Software Requirements Specification.
Produced by: Design Authority. Project phase: project definition.
The expansion of the Statement of Technical Requirements, following from system elements analysis and implementation planning, to define the specific requirements for SCS.

(m) Software Specification.
*Produced by: Design Authority. Project phase: full development. (Refer to clause **29**)*
A detailed specification of the SCS that includes:

(1) A specification of the SCS using the specification notation of a Formal Method (the Formal Specification).

(2) A commentary on the Formal Specification in English together with engineering notations where appropriate (the English Commentary).

(3) The results of checking the Formal Specification for syntactic and type errors, and the English Commentary for accuracy, completeness and consistency.

(4) The discharge of the Proof Obligations necessary to show that the Formal Specification is internally consistent.

(5) The results of the application of any structured methods employed.

(6) The results of Preliminary Validation.

(n) Design Description.
*Produced by: Design Authority. Project phase: full development. (Refer
to clause 30)*
A description and justification of the design of the SCS that includes:

(1) A description of the design using a Formal Method (the Formal Design),
including the program structure and partitioning.

(2) A commentary on the Formal Design (the English Commentary).

(3) The results of checking the Formal Design for syntactic and type errors, and
the English Commentary for accuracy, completeness and consistency.

(4) The discharge of the Proof Obligations necessary to verify each Formal Design
with respect to the preceding Formal Design or the Formal Specification.

(5) The discharge of the Proof Obligations that verify the source code with respect
to its Formal Design.

(6) The results of the application of any structured methods employed.

(7) The results of Static Path Analysis of the code.

(8) Analysis of the degree of isolation between the SCS and other equipment
functions.

(9) Resolutions of non-determinism and options in the Software Specification.

(10) Justification for the algorithms used including their stability and performance.

(11) The results of resource modelling.

(12) Analysis of response time, throughput and capacity of the design.

(13) Analysis of the amount of storage required for operation of the system as a
function of time and quantity of input.

(14) Memory organization and sizing information.

(o) Configuration Record.
*Produced by: Design Authority. Project phase: project definition and updated at
subsequent phases. (Refer to annex C)*
The detailed and certified changes to the SCS during its lifecycle.

(p) Acceptance Test Schedule.
*Produced by: Design Authority. Project phase: full development. (Refer
to clause 25)*
Test that demonstrate to the MOD(PE) PM that the SCS possesses an adequate
level of assurance.

(q) Safety Records Log.
*Produced by: Design Authority. Project phase: project definition and updated at
subsequent phases. (Refer to clause 21)*
Comprehensive evidence that the required level of assurance of the SCS has been
achieved.

(r) Audit Report.
Produced by: Independent Safety Auditor. Project phase: periodically throughout the project. (Refer to clause 16)
The Independent Safety Auditor's report.

(s) Safety Critical Software Certificate.
Produced by: Design Authority and Independent Safety Auditor. Project phase: full development. (Refer to clause 25)
The certificate shown in annex D.

(t) User Manuals.
Produced by: Design Authority. Project phase: full development.
These provide instructions for operating the SCS during in-service use in such a way that its safety integrity is not compromised.

(1) The function and limitations of the software.

(2) The loading, initialization and running of the software.

(3) Any safety override functions.

(4) The manual procedures needed for safe operation.

(5) The procedures for and format of any parameters or data to be entered manually.

(6) Examples of the use of the software.

(7) Explanation of all error messages and advice on correction.

(u) Maintenance Procedures.
Produced by: Design Authority. Project phase: full development.
These include the requirements for configuration control, support hardware, software tools, test harnesses and rigs and safety management in the in-service phase.

(v) Development Environment Specification.
Produced by: Design Authority. Project phase: project definition and full development. (Refer to clause 36)
The precise identification of the hardware and software used for a host or development machine, including software design aids, emulators, target downloading and the compiler if used.

(w) Special tools.
Produced by: Design Authority. Project phase: project definition and full development. (Refer to clause 36)
The description of any tools not covered elsewhere, including specially developed tools.

B.5 SCS code

(x) Source Code.
Produced by: Design Team. Project phase: full development. (Refer to clause 31)
The complete source code listings, with a master and backup copy.

(y) Object Code.

*Produced by: Design Team. Project phase: full development. (Refer to clause **31**)*
The executable code, with a master and backup copy.

Requirements for the Configuration System

C.1 Configuration control shall be maintained throughout the project lifecycle.

C.2 All items and objects shall be subject to configuration control upon their creation.

C.3 Project specific conventions for the following shall be agreed by the Independent Safety Auditor and documented in the Configuration Plan:

(a) definition of a configuration item;

(b) definition of master items;

(c) item and object naming conventions;

(d) maintenance of data compatibility of the project tool set.

C.4 The configuration system shall have the following attributes:

(a) It shall meet the requirements of Def Stan 05-57.

(b) All configuration items shall be uniquely identified with a version number and an item code or name. The version and configuration of firmware shall be uniquely identified in accordance with Def Stan 00-22.

(c) All configuration objects shall be identified with a version number and an item code or name.

(d) The current location and person responsible for a configuration object shall be recorded.

(e) Only authorized personnel shall create, modify or extract configuration items; reasonable steps shall be taken to protect against malicious acts.

(f) The quality plan and the safety plan under which the configuration item was developed and maintained shall be recorded.

(g) The configuration system shall maintain the status of configuration items.

(h) The environment in which configuration items have been built shall be recorded.

(i) All safety critical configuration items and configuration objects shall be identified as safety critical.

(j) The configuration system shall ensure that a configuration item is released for change to only one user at any given time.

(k) The configuration system shall ensure that only approved versions are made available for use.

(l) Control of safety critical configuration items shall be maintained by an automatic tool (see clause **36**).

C.5 A defined method of change control shall be provided such that:

(a) The impact of any change shall be assessed and reviewed for its effect on safety before the change is implemented.

(b) Any changes to the safety requirements or to SCS shall result in the re-application of this Standard in its entirety from project definition onwards.

(c) No in-service modification to SCS shall be made to installed equipment without the written authorization of the MOD(PE) PM. All in-service changes shall be under the control of the Design Authority and subject to its approval. All work shall meet the full requirements of this Standard and shall be documented in the Safety Records Log.

(d) The re-commissioning of a system after maintenance shall include checks and produce evidence that the integrity of the SCS has not been compromised. Re-certification shall be carried out.

C.6 All documentary configuration items shall be capable of issue in hard copy form to the MOD(PE) PM.

C.7 The configuration system shall include arrangements for disaster protection and protection from subversion and sabotage of the configured items.

C.8 Firmware shall be checkable by comparison with the master copy of the executable code that is held under configuration control.

Safety Critical Software Certificate

PROCUREMENT EXECUTIVE, MINISTRY OF DEFENCE

CERTIFICATE OF DESIGN

For Safety Critical Software System/Subsystem

Certificate Number   [*unique identification issued by MOD(PE)*]

Parent System/Subsystem Identification   [*name*]

Parent System/Subsystem Configuration
Version/Mark/Model/Build Standard   [*version number*]

Safety Critical Software Identification   [*name*]

Safety Critical Software Configuration
Version/Mark/Model   [*version number*]

Contract Number   [*contract reference*]

We the designers of the above hereby certify that :

(a) The above complies with :

    (1) Defence Standard 00-55 issue [*issue number*] as implemented in the:

        (i) Safety Plan [*document reference and issue number*].

        (ii) Quality Plan [*document reference and issue number*].

    (2) System/Subsystem Specification [*document reference and issue number*] with the exception of the authorized deviations and nonconformances detailed in [*document reference and issue number*].

    (3) Defence Standard 00-56 [*certificate number*].

(b) Compliance is documented in Safety Records Log [*document reference and issue number*].

(c) Is suitable for use as defined in [*reference and issue number of document describing system use to which the hazard analysis relates*] subject to the restrictions as documented in [*document reference and issue number*].

(d) The requirement, hazard analysis, design, methods employed and standard of work carried out, with a specific regard to safety meet the satisfaction of the Independent Safety Auditor.

Signatories:

System Design Authority

Software Design Authority

Software Developer (if different)

Independent Safety Auditor

GUIDANCE

The Parent System/Subsystem refers to the equipment within which the Safety Critical Software will operate. The Parent System/Subsystem configuration includes the hardware and Safety Critical Software.

Instructions for completion are given in *italics*.

Index

Principal entries are underlined.

acceptance   clause **25**
   criteria   **20.2**
Acceptance Test Schedule   **25.2, B.4**
animation   **29.3**
AQAP-1   **11.1, 36.3**
AQAP-13   **11.1, 36.3**
Audit Plan   **16.5, B.2**
Audit Report   **16.8, B.4**

certification   clause **25**
Code of Design Practice   clause **14,**
   18.2, clause **20, 29.4.3, 30.3.2,**
   31.3.4, B.2
   existing   **20.3**
coding   clause **31**
   standards for   **31.1.1**
competition   **5.1**
compiler   **31.1.3, 36.3**
compliance   clause **9**
concurrency   **30.1.3**
configuration control   clause **24,**
   annex C
configuration item   clause **24**, annex C
configuration object   clause **24**
Configuration Plan   **18.2, 24.3, B.2,**
   C.3
Configuration Record   **B.4**
configuration system   clause **24**
configuration tool   **24.3, C.4**
conformance   **18.2**
Contents list   **B.1**
contractors   **5.4,** clause **9,** clause **17,**
   19.1

Def Stan 00-16   **0.2**
Def Stan 00-22   **26.2, 30.1.6, C.4**
Def Stan 00-31   **0.2**
Def Stan 00-56   **0.3, 8.1, 8.2, 34.2,**
   36.2
Def Stan 00-57   **C.4**
DEFCON 143   clause **9**

defensive programming   **30.1.5**
definitions   annex A
deliverable items   clause **9,** clause **23,**
   annex B
design   clause **30**
Design Description   **30.1.1, 31.3.4,**
   33.4, B.4
   review   **30.3.2**
design team   clause **14, 18.3, 19.1,**
   29.1.1, 29.2, 29.3, 30.1.4,
   30.2, 31.1.1, 31.2, 31.3.2,
   31.3.4, 32.2.2
development environment   clause **5,**
   22.3
Development Environment Specification
   B.4
documentation   clause **22**
dynamic testing   **0.4, 15.2, 21.2,**
   29.3.2, 31.3.3, 31.3.4,
   clause **33**
   for validation   clause **35**

English Commentary   **29.1.1, 29.2.1,**
   30.1.1
errors
   syntactic   **29.2.1, 30.2.1**
   type   **29.2.1, 30.2.1**
Executable Prototype   **29.3, 29.4.2,**
   33.3

firmware   clause **26, C.8**
floating point arithmetic   **30.1.3**
Formal Arguments   **15.2, 21.2, 29.2.2,**
   29.3.1, 29.4.1, 29.4.2, 30.2.2,
   30.3.1, 30.3.2, 31.1.1, 31.2.1,
   31.3.1, 31.3.4, clause **32, 33.3,**
   36.3
   construction   **32.1**
   review   **32.2**
Formal Design   **30.1, 31.1.2, 31.2.1**
   review   **30.3**

verification **30.2**
Formal Method **0.4, 29.1.1, 29.1.2,**
  30.1.1, 30.1.2
Formal Proofs **30.1.5, 32.1.1, 32.2.3**
Formal Specification **29.1, 30.1.5,**
  30.2.2
  animation **29.3**
  Preliminary Validation **29.3**
  review **29.4**
  verification **29.2**

hardware **0.2, 30.1.5**
hazard analysis **0.3, 1.2,** clause **8,**
  21.2, 34.2, 36.2, 36.5

in-service anomaly reports **21.2, 27.3**
In-Service Authority **35.1**
Independent Safety Auditor **11.2,**
  clause **16, 18.3, 19.1, 22.2,**
  23.1, 24.3, 25.1, 29.3.3,
  32.1.1, 32.1.2, 34.1, 35.2, B.2,
  B.4, C.3, annex D
interpreter **31.1.3**
interrupts **30.1.3**
ISO 9000 **11.1, 36.3**

JSP 188 **22.2, 30.1.1**

Maintenance Procedures **B.4**
memory management **30.1.3**
MOD Safety Assurance Authority
  clause **7, 11.2,** clause **12,**
  clause **13, 16.1, 16.3, 18.3,**
  19.1, 22.2, 23.1, 24.3, 29.3.3,
  32.1.1, 34.1, 35.2
MOD(PE) **5.1, 5.2, 5.3**
MOD(PE) PM **5.3,** clause **7, 8.1,**
  11.2, clause **12,** clause **13, 16.1,**
  16.3, 18.3, 19.1, 22.2, 23.1,
  24.3, 25.1, 25.2, 29.1.2,
  29.3.3, 30.1.2, 32.1.1, 32.1.2,
  34.1, 35.2, B.4, C.5, C.6

Object Code **B.5**

partitioning **30.1.3**
planning clause **9**

Preliminary Validation **29.3, 29.4.3**
programming language
  characteristics **31.1.2**
  subset **31.1.2**
project lifecycle **18.4, 22.1,** annex B
  disposal clause **28**
  feasibility clause **12**
  in-service clause **27, C.5**
  production clause **26**
  project definition clause **12, 18.1**
project phase **18.1, 22.1,** annex B
project risk clause **9,** clause **12**
Proof Obligations **29.2.2, 29.4.1,**
  30.2.2, 30.3.1, 31.2.1, 31.3.1,
  32.2.1

quality assurance clause **11**

recursion **30.1.3**
resource modelling **21.2, 30.1.4**
review **20.3, 21.2**
Review Committee **19.1, 29.4.3,**
  30.3.2, 31.3.4
Rigorous Arguments **32.1.1, 32.2.2**

safety
  awareness of clause **9**
  responsibility for clause **6**
Safety Critical Software Certificate
  clause **6, 16.9,** clause **25, 28.2,**
  36.5, B.4, annex D
safety integrity **0.1, 0.3, 8.2, 21.1,**
  35.2, clause **36**
safety integrity analysis **8.2**
Safety Plan **11.2,** clause **12, 16.7,**
  clause **18, B.2, C.4**
Safety Records Log clause **12, 19.3,**
  clause **21, 25.1,** clause **27, 36.5,**
  36.6, B.4, C.5
safety reviews clause **19**
safety risk assessment **0.3,** clause **8,**
  21.2, 34.2, 36.2, 36.5
Scope clause **1**
software
  existing **5.3, 30.1.7,** clause **34**
  documentation of **34.3**

verification of   **34.2**
    library   clause **34**
    non-safety-critical   **1.3**
Software Quality Plan   **11.2, B.2, C.4**
Software Requirements Specification
    29.1.1, 29.3.1, 29.3.3, 29.4.3,
    35.1, B.4
Software Specification   **29.1.1, 29.3.1,**
    29.3.3, 30.3.2, B.4
    review   **29.4.3**
source code   clause **31, B.5**
    review   **31.3**
    verification   **31.2**
Special tools   **B.4**
specification   clause **29**
staff
    quality of   clause **13**
Statement of Technical Requirements
    B.3
static path analysis   **0.4, 21.2, 31.1.1,**
    31.2.2, 31.3.2, 31.3.4
structured methods   **29.1.3, 30.1.8**
subcontractors   **5.4**, clause **17, 19.1**
suppliers   **5.4**, clause **17**
support   clause **10**
support software   **1.2**, clause **36**
system
    safety of   **1.1**
System Elements Analysis   **B.3**
System Implementation Plan   **B.3**

Target Downloading Specification   **B.2**
target hardware   **33.3**
tenders   clause **9**
tools   **1.2, 22.3, 29.2.1, 30.2.1,**
    31.2.2, 32.2.3, clause **36**
    configuration control   **C.4**
    quality system requirements   **36.3**
    safety integrity   clause **36**
    simulator   **35.1**
    test coverage monitor   **33.2, 33.3**

unacceptable components   **20.2**
User Manuals   **B.4**
users   **19.1**

validation   clause **35**

test coverage   **35.3**
verification and validation   **0.4**
Verification and Validation Plan   **15.2,**
    B.2
V&V team   clause **15, 18.3, 19.1,**
    29.4.1, 29.4.2, 30.3.1, 31.3,
    32.1.2, 32.2, 33.1, B.2

THE PROCUREMENT OF SAFETY CRITICAL SOFTWARE IN DEFENCE
EQUIPMENT

PART 2: GUIDANCE

PREFACE

i   This Part of the INTERIM Defence Standard contains guidance on the requirements contained in Part 1. This guidance serves two functions: it elaborates on the requirements in order to make conformance easier to achieve and assess; and it provides technical background.

ii   The area of software engineering addressed by the Standard is one of rapid development. Some methods and techniques that would be desirable in the development of SCS are not yet proven by widespread application; however, as the technology matures, this Part may be reissued to include developments that will increase the assurance of SCS.

iii   This Standard is being issued as INTERIM and is provisional in order to obtain information and experience of its application. This will then permit the submission of observations and comments from users, using DGDQA Form 0826 enclosed.

iv   This Standard has been produced for MOD by a Working Group acting under the authority of the Policy Coordinating Committee on Guided Weapons and Electronics (PCCGWL). The Working Group was directed by a Steering Group comprising representatives of the three Systems Controllerates, RSRE, DGDQA and the Ordnance Board.

v   This Standard will be one of a family of standards dealing with safety that is to be developed or adopted by MOD, taking into account international standardization activities and supporting research and development.

vi   This Standard has been agreed by the authorities concerned with its use and shall be incorporated whenever relevant in all future designs, contracts, orders etc. and whenever practicable by amendment to those already in existence. If any difficulty arises which prevents application of the Defence Standard, the Directorate of Standardization shall be informed so that a remedy may be sought.

vii   Any enquiries regarding this Standard in relation to an invitation to tender, or a contract, in which it is invoked, are to be addressed to the responsible technical or supervising authority named in the invitation to tender or contract.

viii   This Standard has been devised for the use of the Crown and of its contractors in the execution of contracts for the Crown and, subject to the Unfair Contract Terms Act 1977, the Crown will not be liable in any way whatever (including but without limitation negligence on the part of the Crown its servants or agents) where the Standard is used for other purposes.

CONTENTS   PAGE

Preface   1

Section One.   General

0   Introduction   4
1   Scope   4
2   Related Documents   4
3   Definitions   5

Section Two.   Guidance Articles

4   Lifecycles   6
5   Requirements Enabling Competition, Use, Alteration and Support   6
6   Responsibility for Safety   6
7   MOD Safety Assurance Authority   6
8   Hazard Analysis and Safety Risk Assessment   6
9   Tenders   7
10 Support   8
11 Quality Assurance   8
12 Risk Analysis   8
13 Quality of Staff   8
14 Design Team   8
15 V&V Team   8
16 Independent Safety Auditor   9
17 Subcontracting Arrangements   10
18 Safety Plan   10
19 Safety Reviews   11
20 Code of Design Practice   12
21 Safety Records Log   13
22 Documentation   13
23 Requirements for Deliverable Items   14
24 Configuration Management   14
25 Certification and Acceptance into Service   15
26 Production   16
27 In-Service   16
28 Disposal   16
29 Specification   16
30 Design   21
31 Coding   25
32 Formal Arguments   28
33 Dynamic Testing   29
34 Use of Existing Software   31
35 Validation   31
36 Tool Support   32

Annex A   Bibliography   A-1

Index   Index i

3

THE PROCUREMENT OF SAFETY CRITICAL SOFTWARE IN DEFENCE EQUIPMENT

PART 2: GUIDANCE

Section One. General

0 Introduction

This Part of the INTERIM Defence Standard provides guidance on the requirements in Part 1. From clause **5** onwards, it is organized by the main clause headings used in Part 1; however, subclauses do not necessarily correspond to the subclauses in Part 1. Where a clause in the guidance is applicable to more than one clause in Part 1, it is given under the heading of the first clause to which it relates and references provided from the others.

1 Scope

1.1   This Part of the Standard provides information and guidance on the procurement of Safety Critical Software (SCS).

1.2   Examples of specific tools, techniques and methods are included to illustrate the text. Often, one example is used in each illustration; the choice of an example neither implies that it is suitable in a particular instance nor that other tools, techniques or methods are unsuitable.

1.3   It should be emphasized that safety is a system property. Achieving and maintaining safety requires attention to all aspects of the system including its human, electronic and mechanical components. This Standard addresses one important component—SCS; the achievement of safety targets by overall design, and in particular whether particular safety features are to be controlled by hardware, software or manual procedures, are not addressed. A systems approach to hazard analysis and safety risk assessment is explained in Def Stan 00-56 [22]; some guidance and an introduction to this area is given in [75]; and design safety requirements for particular equipments are given in relevant standards, such as Def Stan 00-970 [23], Def Stan 08-3 [25] and Def Stan 08-5 [26].

2 Related Documents

2.1   The documents and publications referred to in this Part of the Standard are listed in annex A.

2.2   Reference in this Standard to any related documents means, in any invitation to tender or contract, the edition and all amendments current at the date of such tender or contract unless a specific edition is indicated.

2.3   Documents that may be found useful during the development and use of SCS are also listed in annex A.

3   Definitions

The definitions in Part 1 apply also to this Part of the Standard.

Section Two.   Guidance Articles

4   Lifecycles

4.1   The Standard makes reference to lifecycle phases. The lifecycle referred to is the MOD(PE) *project* lifecycle; its phases are concept formulation, feasibility, project definition, full development, production, in-service and disposal.

4.2   In order to manage and control the software development process, contractors may employ an explicit *software* lifecycle. There are a number of different software lifecycles in use, including the classic waterfall and the prototyping approaches; a typical example is that in the Starts guide [79]. Their advantages and disadvantages are not as important as their common property of describing development phases that order a progressive refinement from requirements to product, and that have defined and documented inputs and outputs. Contractors may use their customary lifecycle when developing the Safety Plan, but should relate it to the project lifecycle.

5   Requirements Enabling Competition, Use, Alteration and Support

No guidance required.

6   Responsibility for Safety

No guidance required.

7   MOD Safety Assurance Authority

Staff from various organizations may be employed as MOD Safety Assurance Authority depending on the application, technology, and statutory and legal requirements. The organizations may include the Ordnance Board, A&AEE or other formal and independent body competent to advise the MOD(PE) PM on matters related to safety.

8   Hazard Analysis and Safety Risk Assessment

8.1   Software does not suffer from random failure, that is failure that is due to physical change and whose probability can be predicted to a reasonable degree of accuracy. Instead, the failure of software is due to *systematic* failure, that is failure due to errors in the specification, design or coding. If an error exists in the software, a systematic failure will occur whenever a certain sequence of inputs is encountered. Since the number of distinct combinations of inputs is very large, testing provides no assurance of finding all systematic errors; indeed, even in use such errors may remain hidden for a considerable period of time. Furthermore, because the failure rate depends on the inputs and not on the physical properties of the software, prediction of the failure rate is difficult.

8.2   For these reasons, it is usual to distinguish the requirements of the equipment for resistance to systematic failure and resistance to random failure. The overall failure requirements are conventionally expressed as a failure rate in terms of time or demands; the specific systematic failure requirements are, however, expressed as *safety integrity levels* that are related to techniques judged to give an adequate protection against systematic failure. The limits of these techniques are expressed as *claim limits*, which place bounds on the failure rate that can be claimed for equipment built to a certain safety integrity level.

8.3 The determination of safety integrity requirements is addressed in detail in Def Stan 00-56 [22], and application of that standard should commence early in the project lifecycle. The techniques in INTERIM Def Stan 00-55 will then be applied to software components identified as being of the highest safety integrity level.

8.4 Clearly consideration should also be given to the feasibility of achieving the required safety integrity, and of assuring that it has been achieved. This latter point is considered further in the discussion on validation testing in clause **35**.

8.5 The equipment should be designed so that the SCS is isolated as far as practicable. This will minimize the quantity of software that, though it does not itself implement safety features, has to be developed to the highest level of safety integrity because of the possibility that it may, if it fails, interfere with SCS.

8.6 Generally, the design should aim to minimize the quantity of all types of SCS. This reduction should preferably be carried out by removing hazards, or if that is not practicable, by using simple hardware devices (e.g. interlocks) to provide the necessary safety features. However, implementing a complex safety critical function in hardware logic merely to avoid the development of SCS is likely to add little to the safety integrity of the equipment.

9 Tenders

9.1 In order to expedite the evaluation of tenders, the Standard calls for both general and specific evidence of the ability of a tendering contractor to fulfil the requirements. It calls for evidence of an established safety culture, and also, by means of the Software Development Questionnaire DEFCON 143, for details of the contractor's experience with the methods and techniques for the production of SCS. It also seeks evidence of proper planning of the management and technical procedures required by the Standard, which should include:

(a) Details of any areas of high risk that may unduly or unpredictably influence the cost or duration of the development of the SCS.

(b) The Software Quality Plan.

(c) The Safety Plan (see clause **18**).

(d) The programme for the development of the SCS, showing module and sub-system dependencies.

(e) A statement of the methods, language, automated tools and IPSE to be used.

(f) A statement of the methods to be adopted to maintain the SCS throughout its support life (see clause **10**).

(g) The proposed list of deliverable items and the media on which they are to be delivered, relating planned delivery to the programme phases.

(h) Curricula Vitae (CVs) of the proposed key development staff.

10   Support

10.1   The maintenance of SCS may be required at any time during the life of the equipment in which it is installed, which may be up to thirty years. The support life should be determined early in the project by the Design Authority in consultation with the MOD(PE) PM; the MOD(PE) PM will review the equipment periodically, and decide when support for it may cease.

10.2   Support is necessary for all items needed to maintain the SCS. The support plan should address which items will be held in an operational state and which will be re-activated when required.

10.3   The plan for support should take into account the expected life of the hardware on which the SCS is installed, in order to achieve an acceptable lifetime for the equipment as a whole.

11   Quality Assurance

No guidance required.

12   Risk Analysis

No guidance required.

13   Quality of Staff

No guidance required.

14   Design Team

No guidance required.

15   V&V Team

15.1   It is extremely important that verification and validation are carried out independently of design, both to preserve objectivity and to minimize pressure for premature acceptance. Such independence also introduces worthwhile diversity into the software production process, and helps enforce adequate documentation. The Design Authority should therefore set up a V&V Team composed of a team leader and personnel who are not otherwise involved on the project, and which is independent up to senior management level. Verification and validation will be carried out more efficiently if good lines of communication at working level exist between the Design Team and the V&V Team, but these should be set up in such a way that independence is not compromised. The arrangements for V&V should be included in the Safety Plan.

15.2 The V&V Team should base their judgement on the design documentation (which should include the Formal Arguments prepared by the Design Team), augmented by critical reviews with the Design Team. They are responsible for the following:

(a) checking the Formal Arguments produced by the Design Team to discharge the Proof Obligations for each design step;

(b) checking the Static Path Analysis carried out;

(c) specifying and implementing the tests on individual and partly integrated modules and the integrated SCS;

(d) specifying and implementing the validation tests.

15.3 The Standard does not prohibit the testing of SCS by the Design Team in addition to that carried out as described above; planning for such testing is a matter for the Design Authority.

16 Independent Safety Auditor

16.1 Selection

16.1.1 The technical and managerial independence of the Independent Safety Auditor from the Design Authority can best be achieved by using an independent company, but an independent division of the prime contractor may be acceptable if adequate technical and managerial independence can be shown at Director or Board level. The Independent Safety Auditor may be part of an Independent Safety Audit Team appointed by the Design Authority to assess the safety of the overall equipment; and, especially for projects involving large quantities of SCS, the Independent Safety Auditor role may be taken by several people.

16.1.2 Appropriate qualifications for the Independent Safety Auditor would be Chartered Engineer status and a minimum of five years experience of SCS and its implementation in systems. He or she should be trained and experienced in the methods, tools and procedures that the Design Authority proposes to apply.

16.2 Activities.   The Independent Safety Auditor should assess and audit all the activities related to SCS. The programme and scope of work to be carried out by the Independent Safety Auditor should be defined in the contract between the Design Authority and the MOD. The activities of the Independent Safety Auditor should include:

(a) Production of an Audit Plan.

9

(b) Assessing the adequacy of the Safety Plan.

(c) Checking that the software has been specified, designed and coded in accordance with this Standard.

(d) Auditing the adequacy of the verification and validation carried out by the V&V Team.

(e) Auditing the veracity and completeness of the Safety Records Log.

(f) Preparation of audit reports in accordance with the agreed plans.

(g) Confirming that the results of the audit have been satisfactory by signing the Safety Critical Software Certificate.

17 Subcontracting Arrangements

No guidance required.

18 Safety Plan

18.1 The Safety Plan is produced by the Design Authority during the earliest practicable phase of the project, and subsequently updated at the start of each new phase. It deals specifically with the methods, techniques and organization required by this Standard. The Code of Design Practice and the Configuration Plan are specific procedures referenced by the Safety Plan.

18.2 The safety plan for the production of SCS should contain the following:

(a) A definition of the purpose and scope of the plan, including those safety goals that are expected to be achieved by adherence to it.

(b) Definitions and references.

(c) Details of the management of the production of SCS, including:

  (1) the identification of the organizations and key personnel required by this Standard, including:
    (i) Design Authority;
    (ii) Review Committee;
    (iii) member of Design Authority responsible for signing Safety Critical Software Certificate;
    (iv) Design Team;
    (v) V&V Team;
    (vi) MOD Safety Assurance Authority;
    (vii) Independent Safety Auditor;
    (viii) relevant subcontractors or suppliers;

  (2) a description of the interfaces between the MOD(PE) PM, the Independent Safety Auditor, the Design Authority, the MOD Safety Assurance Authority and their respective subcontractors;

(3) the definition of the circumstances under which matters concerning safety integrity should be referred between the Design Authority or its subcontractors, the Independent Safety Auditor, the MOD(PE) PM and the MOD Safety Assurance Authority;

(4) details of adequate resource planning, including, but not limited to, finance, personnel, equipment and tools;

(5) details of the way in which evidence of application of the plan is to be recorded throughout the project lifecycle;

(6) details of the deliverable items to be produced;

(7) reference to the Configuration Plan (see clause **24**);

(8) details of the organization and CVs of individuals who will produce the SCS;

(9) specification of the qualifications required of key staff;

(10) details of the certification process;

(11) specification of the criteria for tool approval and limitations on the use of certain tools;

(12) the procedures for evaluating the safety integrity of previously developed or purchased systems.

(d) Details of the procedures and practices to be undertaken, including:

(1) reference to the Code of Design Practice (clause **20**);

(2) details of the safety review procedures.

19 Safety Reviews

19.1 Formal reviews.   Where formal reviews are conducted on the documentation, such techniques as Fagan Inspections [30] could be used in addition to the mathematical checks carried out where appropriate.

19.2 Checks on English documents.   The English Commentary cannot be checked to the same extent as the Formal Specification. Nevertheless, many typographical and some more serious errors can be avoided by carrying out the following checks which, although weak in themselves, give a reasonable degree of assurance when used in combination.

19.2.1 Spelling checks.   An automated spelling check should be carried out.

19.2.2 Examination of words.   In order to identify some of the errors that result in valid English words that are acceptable to the spelling check, a list of words used should be produced, preferably in alphabetical order. This should be checked for unexpected words.

19.2.3 Local definitions.   All usages of words defined within the document should be identified and checked with their definitions. Commonly used synonyms for these words should either be defined in the document, or their use should be banned and checked for by the preceding check (**19.2.2**).

20   Code of Design Practice

20.1   The Code of Design Practice is a key element of the Safety Plan. It is identified as a separate document because it is likely to be an existing company manual containing the Design Authority's interpretation of the software engineering practices required by the Standard. It should specify, referencing other standards and guidelines where appropriate, the procedures, methods and techniques used by the Design and V&V Teams, including:

(a) the Formal Method to be used for the specification notation;

(b) the methods to be used for animation of the specification;

(c) the Formal Method or Methods to be used for design, and the way in which these Method or Methods are to be formally related to the specification;

(d) the implementation language or subset language, and the way in which this is to be formally related to the design;

(e) the policy on whether Formal Arguments will be presented as Rigorous Arguments or Formal Proofs;

(f) guidance on the production of the English Commentary;

(g) the structured method or methods to be used in the specification or design process, both to provide practical guidance on specification and design and to cover properties that cannot be described in terms of a Formal Method;

(h) the tools to be used:

    (1) to support the Formal Method or Methods;

    (2) in constructing and checking Formal Arguments;

    (3) for Static Path Analysis;

    (4) for dynamic testing during verification and validation;

    (5) to support any structured methods employed;

(i) the strategy for the generation of test cases;

(j) the policy for the application of defensive programming measures;

(k) the criteria for acceptance for each SCS item, and the procedures for dealing with unacceptable components;

(l) the way in which adequate integrity of tools and supporting software is to be identified and achieved.

20.2   Justification for the choices should also be included.

20.3   The acceptance criteria for SCS, item (k) above, should distinguish between errors in Formal Arguments and discrepancies found during dynamic testing. The criteria should include the maximum number of errors found by the V&V Team in Formal Arguments or during Static Path Analysis beyond which the item will be redeveloped from scratch. Errors found by dynamic testing in properties verified by Formal Arguments are particularly serious, and would generally lead to non-acceptance of the application.

21   Safety Records Log

21.1   The Safety Records Log is a living document in which much of the evidence for the safety of the equipment is recorded. All the work of the V&V Team is documented in it.

21.2   The Safety Records Log is a key document in the support for certification of the equipment.

21.3   Anomaly reporting

21.3.1   The Design Authority for the in-service phase should set up procedures so that defect data relating to SCS is recorded and analysed. The mechanism for achieving this will depend on the equipment and its location: for example, a separate defect log could be kept with each equipment on board a ship; alternatively, in cases where space is limited, a single log might be kept at the equipment's base. In either case, a system for periodically collecting this data and entering it in the Safety Records Log will be required.

21.3.2   Each anomaly report should:

(a) give the personnel concerned and the date;

(b) describe the configuration of the equipment and the version number of the SCS;

(c) state the problem and conditions that produced it, including whether the SCS was being operated within its design envelope;

(d) assess the likely consequences;

(e) describe the corrective action taken.

22   Documentation

*See also Review and Checking of Documents (clause **19**).*

22.1   The Design Authority should produce a set of documentation that, comprehensively and cost-effectively, covers the specification, design, integration, verification and validation, and in-service support of the SCS. Each document should be well structured with a glossary of locally defined terms, and be identified in accordance with the Configuration Plan. A higher level of assurance can be obtained by using a method such as Standard Generalized Markup Language [46] to structure the documents; use of a defined, restricted vocabulary may also be beneficial. Representative examples of the proposed documentation should be agreed between the Design Authority, the MOD Safety Assurance Authority, the Independent Safety Auditor and the MOD(PE) PM at the start of the project.

22.2   The documentation should enable the complete development environment to be re-established by another contractor for the purposes of maintaining the SCS. It should therefore identify the precise versions of support software and hardware, and give all necessary details such as the job control commands used to start building the SCS.

22.3   The documentation should include a copy of the relevant parts of the Software Requirements Specification and provide details of any amendments and concessions.

23   Requirements for Deliverable Items

No guidance required.

24   Configuration Management

24.1   The Standard imposes requirements for a Configuration Management System in addition to those in Def Stan 05-57 [24]. These requirements refer to the SCS and not to the configuration of the equipment being produced.

24.2   Access to configured items should be restricted and controlled by an authorization procedure to prevent accidental corruption of the product configuration. The Design Authority should also take all reasonable steps to protect against malicious acts.

24.3   It is important that both SCS in the form of computer files (configuration items) and physical objects (configuration objects) such as discs, tapes, etc. are controlled. It should be noted that items and objects may not necessarily be directly related. An object such as a disc may contain many items; similarly there may be many copies of the object such as a ROM containing the same item.

24.4   Items and objects should be subject to configuration control as soon as possible. It is not acceptable for configuration control to be applied at the end of a task.

24.5   The status of an item should be readily available (e.g. under development, subject to V&V or frozen).

24.6   Ideally an Integrated Project Support Environment should be used to develop SCS. However, the current state of tool technology makes the use of an IPSE unlikely. In such a situation tool compatibility will be a problem. Hence, there is a need for project specific definitions and procedures as described below:

(a) In a poorly integrated project environment, the time of creation of an item may be unclear. Hence, a project specific definition and associated status should be provided. For example, an item may be deemed to exist when a work item is identified and the personnel to carry it out are identified.

   A problem may arise when tools such as Ada compilers are used that perform a degree of configuration control. The mechanism for controlling such items as Ada libraries and object code should be defined.

(b) It may not be possible to exert full control on a configuration item when it is external to the tool that created it. For example, consider a design tool that is capable of exporting a design description. However, the design description is interpreted in the context of a data dictionary that cannot be exported. The configuration item is only completely controlled if both the description and the data

14

dictionary are controlled. In such a scenario, the configuration plan should clearly define the procedures for tool control and define exactly what constitutes a configuration item and which instance of the configuration item constitutes the master copy. Hence the definition of a configuration item given in annex A of Part 1 may require project-specific interpretation.

(c) The same configuration item may concurrently exist on several different tools. It is likely that the different tools will have different naming conventions. The problem can be resolved for text files by including the identity within the file. However, this may not be the case for object code and binary files, although executable programs should where practicable identify themselves. In such situations the mapping of configuration item identities on different tools should be declared in the configuration plan.

(d) The policy for ensuring tool compatibility and support continuity or migration path should be defined in the configuration management plan. Tool hardware and SCS upgrades should not render configuration items irretrievable. In order to ensure compatibility, it is important that the names and versions of all software tools and any relevant host hardware details are recorded.

24.7 All safety critical source code should be identified as safety critical and be clearly distinguished from non-safety-critical code in the configuration list. Safety critical configuration objects should be visibly or electronically identifiable as safety critical.

24.8 Ideally all configuration items should be included within the automated configuration system.

25 Certification and Acceptance into Service

25.1 Certification is the formal process of recording that the Safety Requirements have been met, that in the opinion of the Design Authority the SCS is of adequate safety integrity and that all the work associated with the creation and provision of the SCS has been diligently carried out in accordance with the requirements of this Standard.

25.2 The Safety Critical Software Certificate should contain the following:

(a) certification of conformance to this Standard;

(b) identification of the system for which SCS was developed;

(c) reference to the documentary evidence of conformance;

(d) reference to the hazard analysis and safety risk assessment applied;

(e) identification of the equipment use for which hazard analysis and safety risk assessment was applied;

(f) specification of the equipment version, mark, model or applicable identifier to which the certificate refers;

(g) specification of the SCS version, mark, model or applicable identifier to which the certificate refers;

(h) reference to an accurate record of any allowed deviations or nonconformities;

(i) reference to any requirement for restrictions on use;

(j) reference to any exceptions or limitations recommended by the MOD Safety Assurance Authority, without prejudice to MOD;

(k) certificate identity (to record against a MOD master record);

(l) signatures from responsible and accountable personnel:

    (1) System Design Authority;

    (2) Software Design Authority;

    (3) Software Developer (if different);

    (4) Independent Safety Auditor.

25.3 A proforma for the Safety Critical Software Certificate is given in Part 1.

25.4 The MOD(PE) PM may consult the MOD Safety Assurance Authority, the MOD Equipment Sponsor and the In-Service Authority for advice on certification.

26 Production

No guidance required.

27 In-Service

See Anomaly reporting (21.3).

28 Disposal

No guidance required.

29 Specification

See also Documentation (clause 22).

29.1 Formal Method: selection

29.1.1 In order to be suitable for safety critical applications, a Formal Method should meet the following criteria:

(a) It should contain a formal notation for describing specifications and designs in a mathematically precise manner. This notation should have a formally defined syntax and a semantics in terms of generally understood mathematical concepts.

(b) It should have a proof theory for the verification of design steps.

(c) It should provide guidance on good strategies for building a verifiable design.

(d) It should be accessible in the public domain.

(e) Case studies published in the open literature should demonstrate its successful industrial use.

(f) It should be suitable for design as well as specification, either on its own or in combination with another Formal Method.

(g) Courses and textbooks should be available.

(h) A recognized standard version should exist. This should preferably be an international or national standard or published draft standard.

(i) It should be supported by industrialized tools.

29.1.2   Relatively mature Formal Methods that are understood by a sizeable industrial community exist for describing and reasoning about sequential properties (e.g. VDM [49] or Z [78]). Formal Methods for reasoning about concurrent and communicating systems also exist (e.g. Lotos [47]) but they have not achieved the same level of acceptance.

29.2   Non-functional properties

Formal Methods do not currently address very well the verification and validation of non-functional properties of SCS. These are properties of the system such as usability, maintainability, response time, numerical accuracy and numerical stability. These properties should continue to be addressed using established methods. Criteria for acceptance should be specified whenever possible; for example, a criterion for the acceptance of a human/computer interface might be expressed in terms of the number of errors per 1,000 data entries (see **35.5**).

29.3   Checking the Formal Specification

29.3.1   The Formal Specification, and the Formal Design developed from it, are mathematical objects constructed according to certain formal rules. Because of this, it is possible to carry out checks on them in addition to those that are possible on a specification written in English (**19.2**). One important class of check is concerned with validation by means of animation, which is discussed in some detail in **29.6**; however, it is also possible to carry out mechanical checks for consistency with the formally defined syntax and semantics of the Formal Method employed.

29.3.2   It is possible to ensure that the syntax of the Formal Specification and Formal Design is correct in two ways. The first is by entering the specification by means of a structure editor; this is a tool that constrains the input to that which is syntactically correct, and thus prevents errors in the first place. The alternative is to check the specification after it is written, by using a tool equipped with a parser that accepts input from a separate or built-in text editor.

29.3.3   Semantic checking detects the presence of errors, such as type errors, in syntactically correct specifications. These checks resemble, but are generally more extensive than, the checks carried out by a good compiler for a high level language.

29.3.4 Syntactic and semantic checkers for various Formal Methods are now on the market (e.g. Specbox for VDM [31] and Fuzz for Z); these sometimes incorporate other features, such as typesetting for the mathematical symbols employed.

29.4 Proof Obligations

29.4.1 Each step in a formal design and coding gives rise to a number of Proof Obligations. These are logical properties that are expected to hold of the current design step, and assert that each aspect of the current step implements some aspect of the previous one. They are known as Proof Obligations because, in order to provide assurance for the design step, the designer should establish by Formal Arguments that they could be discharged.

29.4.2 The Proof Obligations arising from the design steps may be obtained from the published definition of the Formal Method in use. However, a more assured method is to use a Proof Obligation generator, which is a tool that embodies the proof theory for the method and that will produce the Proof Obligations automatically when provided with the Formal Design. At the present time, however, Proof Obligation generators are available for only a small number of Formal Methods (e.g. the Mural specification support tool for VDM [50]), and they produce only some classes of Proof Obligations.

29.4.3 The Proof Obligations arising from the coding step can similarly be derived from the published definition of the proof theory for the implementation language (or subset) in terms of the Formal Method. However, Proof Obligation generators (e.g. Spade [17] and Gypsy [33]) are more widely available for the coding step; they take the Formal Design in the form of annotations to the code, and derive the Proof Obligations from them. Proof Obligation generators for this step are also known as verification condition generators. It is necessary to show by Formal Argument that the annotations are equivalent to the Formal Design.

29.5 Structured methods. The Design Authority's established procedures may include the use of structured methods (e.g. Core and Jackson Structured Design). These methods can give considerable assistance with specification and design, and their use should normally be retained. However, the expression of each design step and its correctness argument in the Formal Method should not depend upon informal or structured methods.

29.6 Preliminary Validation

29.6.1 General

29.6.1.1 The Standard places emphasis on validation of the Formal Specification against the Software Requirements Specification. It is in general impossible to prove mathematically that the Formal Specification matches the Software Requirements Specification because the latter is not formalized. However, because the Formal Specification is a mathematical model of the behaviour of the SCS, the technique of *animation* can be employed—in addition to reviews—to validate the Formal Specification against expectations.

29.6.1.2 Animation is concerned with exploring the properties of the Formal Specification; it is carried out by using Formal Arguments (see clause **32**) to show that the required properties hold, and by the production of an Executable Prototype directly from the Formal Specification, which can be tested using example inputs.

29.6.1.3 Animation is principally carried out by the Design Authority. It is concerned with requirements capture rather than verification (see clause **33**), and the test sets for the Executable Prototype are therefore produced by the Design Team. However, where it is practicable within the guidelines in **29.6.2** and **29.6.3** below, an Executable Prototype that the MOD(PE) PM, and preferably the In-Service Authority as well, can examine should be produced.

29.6.1.4 Just as with dynamic testing, preliminary validation is not an exhaustive validation of the SCS. Further validation of the integrated SCS is necessary, and is addressed in clause **35**.

29.6.1.5 The Executable Prototype should be preserved for use during verification of the integrated SCS, as explained in **33.4.3**.

29.6.2 <u>Objectives of animation.</u>   Animation should be used in the following ways:

(a) To explore and assess with the MOD(PE) PM and the In-Service Authority the completeness and consistency of an implementation deriving from the specification, and in particular to identify:

    (1) functions or parts of functions that have been omitted;

    (2) poorly defined functionality (for example, specifications that do not cover all expected cases);

    (3) errors in the specification that lead to inconsistent states, failure conditions or erroneous results.

(b) To demonstrate that undesirable action does not occur.

(c) To establish the behaviour at the boundaries of the specification.

(d) To show the preservation of data type invariants by compositions of operations (this can be achieved only by Formal Argument).

(e) To explore and assess extensions and improvements that can be obtained without extensive modification by building on what is already specified.

29.6.3 <u>Use of Formal Arguments.</u>   Formal Arguments should be constructed to show that the safety features laid down in the Software Requirements Specification hold of the Formal Specification. Other properties of particular importance may also be addressed. This aspect of animation should be carried out with the support of:

(a) proof checkers and editors, e.g. the Spade Proof Checker [67];

(b) semantics-based tools, e.g. the Concurrency Workbench for CCS [60];

(c) symbolic execution tools.

29.6.4 Production of an Executable Prototype

29.6.4.1 An Executable Prototype may be produced from the Formal Specification by means of:

(a) an executable subset of the specification method, e.g. Objex for OBJ [32];

(b) translation into a logic programming language, e.g. Prolog [19];

(c) translation into a procedural or functional programming language with support for the abstract data types used in the specification, e.g. Pascal or Standard ML [39].

29.6.4.2 Prototyping by means of a procedural language will generally involve more effort than the use of executable subsets or direct translation into a declarative language, and may also present problems with the adequacy of the support for the abstract data types that are a fundamental feature of Formal Methods: for example, Pascal limits the type of elements of sets to enumerated types.

29.6.4.3 The clearest and most abstract specifications may not be directly executable (the implicit definition of a square root function is a simple example); in such cases, the minimum development to achieve an executable form should be carried out. Operations may be intentionally under-specified or specified nondeterministically in order to allow latitude during the design or development phases. There is a danger that this nondeterminism may be resolved differently in the animation from the final implementation, and all options that arise from this cause should be explored and clearly documented.

29.6.4.4 The Executable Prototype should be produced to examine and investigate particular aspects of the specification that have been identified in advance, with particular emphasis on the safety features. It is likely to be a partial model in that it will be deficient in certain of the other properties required of the system (for example, response time or satisfactory human-computer interface). It is neither technically desirable nor cost effective for the Executable Prototype to represent the entire SCS, since the production of such a program would amount to a final implementation that prejudged many design decisions. A useful analogy is provided by the wind-tunnel models of aircraft used to obtain information about the aerodynamic performance; different models have to be used to investigate other aspects, such as the design of the cockpit.

29.6.4.5 The Executable Prototype should contain a machine interface that enables it to be executed in a convenient form. This may need to be more elaborate if the MOD(PE) PM or In-Service Authority is involved in the animation.

29.6.4.6 Formal Arguments should be constructed to justify the link between the Executable Prototype and the Formal Specification, in the same way that the design steps are justified (see clause **32**). These should be reviewed by the V&V Team.

30   Design

*See also Documentation (clause **22**), Formal Method: selection (**29.1**), Non-functional properties (**29.2**), Checking the Formal Specification (**29.3**), Proof Obligations (**29.4**), Structured methods (**29.5**).*

30.1   Approach of the Standard

30.1.1   The approach of the Standard is to require a software development process in which verification is an integral part. At each stage in the software lifecycle, the Design Team should produce a design and also the arguments for its correctness with respect to its specification. The correctness arguments should be constructed using a Formal Method. These arguments should be checked by the V&V Team, and the whole process audited by the Independent Safety Auditor.

30.1.2   Additional verification is also carried out by means of the more traditional techniques of Static Path Analysis and dynamic testing.

30.1.3   This approach shifts the emphasis towards the early stages of the software production lifecycle and away from coding; although operational software will start to be produced later in the project than conventionally, an assured design step is a more solid measure of project progress than some code with a lower level of assurance.

30.2   Formalisms for design

30.2.1   The objective of the design phase is to make a commitment to particular control and data structures. Whereas the Software Specification defines the properties that should be satisfied by the implementation, the design determines how the properties should be achieved. The use of Formal Methods for design enables both types of design step to be verified by Formal Arguments.

30.2.2   The most commonly used ways of expressing a Formal Design are as follows:

(a) By the use of design constructs in the Formal Method, e.g. Z's refinement calculus [62].

(b) By combining formal specifications by means of constructs from the implementation language, e.g. the specification in place of code technique of VDM [49].

(c) By means of a separate design notation, e.g. Malpas IL.

30.2.3   Transformational and constructively correct approaches also exist, and may be acceptable upon review [66].

30.2.4   The Formal Design should also address the refinement of the data structures from the abstract data types of the Formal Specification (e.g. sets and maps) to the data structures of the implementation language (e.g. arrays and records).

30.2.5   The Design Authority should justify the approach taken, and explain how the transformations between notations, if used, are to be verified; if Formal Proof is being used, a proof theory relating the notations will be required (see **31.1.1**).

30.2.6   The technique of animation, as discussed in **29.6**, can be used in the design phase to explore properties of the design. However, its use here is as a design aid rather than a validation tool, and it is not a requirement of the Standard.

30.3   Analysability

30.3.1   Once the requirements have been captured in the Formal Specification, correctness becomes the principal objective in the development of SCS. However, some design options will make correctness hard to assure; this will be reflected in Proof Obligations that are difficult to discharge.

30.3.2   The Design Authority should consider the requirement for analysability very early in the project, and should balance the design options against the ease of verification, bearing in mind the availability of methods and tools. As part of this process, the open literature should be studied to assist in judging the feasibility of any particular approach. Some of the issues that may arise are discussed in the following sub-clauses.

30.3.3   Modularity.   Comprehension of the SCS may be assisted if the design is broken into a hierarchy of modules such that each module is small enough to be understood as a whole. However, the interface between the modules requires careful attention, as too many small modules may lead to a complex data flow that is itself hard to follow.

30.3.4   Concurrency.   Designs should be avoided in which concurrency becomes particularly difficult to analyse due to the increase in complexity arising from the interleaving of processes. However, in some other systems the concurrency can be hidden and the system modelled by sequential operations; and in others, such as communication protocols, there are special techniques that can be employed (e.g. Lotos [47]).

30.3.5   Length.   Individual designs that may lead to more than about 5,000 lines of code should on the whole be avoided. However, far larger systems can be built in certain circumstances (e.g. those of many loosely coupled components); conversely, small portions of code are not always easily reasoned about.

30.3.6   Interrupts.   The use of interrupts can lead to problems during analysis because of the complexity of the control flow. Designing the system to simplify the use of interrupts should improve the ease of analysis. Present Formal Methods and Static Path Analysis methods cannot readily cope with the use of interrupts, although Formal Proofs about systems that use interrupts have been carried out [6].

30.3.7 Partitioning.   The unpredictable behaviour of software when errors are encountered should lead to designs in which SCS is separated physically from non-safety-critical software. Where this is not possible, for example because of weight and space constraints, the separation could be enforced by software implemented mechanisms. Formal Arguments should be produced to show that the mechanisms are effective during both normal operation and fault conditions. The criticality of these mechanisms should be assessed and if, as is normally the case, they are safety critical, they should be implemented to the requirements of this Standard. Guidance can be found in the literature on security kernels and their application to safety [1,72].

30.3.8 Floating point arithmetic.   The issue of whether to use floating point arithmetic is one which involves a number of trade offs between functionality and complexity, and between the respective integrities of hardware and software. These considerations are strictly outside the scope of this Standard and should logically be addressed in a computer system design guideline or standard. In the absence of these supporting standards it should be noted that the floating point coprocessors are not generally of the integrity required for safety critical hardware. Floating point arithmetic should therefore be avoided unless assurance can be given of the integrity of the supporting hardware, for example by means of formal verification [4]. In the longer term, language independent arithmetic standards will emerge [83] that will facilitate this assurance. The implications for the software design of not using floating point are those of increased complexity: integer versions of floating point algorithms are typically 3–4 times the length, with a consequential impact on analysability and feasibility.

30.3.9 Recursion.   Recursion will often be used in the Formal Specification and the Formal Design. However, recursion should be avoided in the implementation unless strict bounds can be proven on the depth of recursion and the consequent memory usage.

30.4 Design Description.   In addition to the requirements in Part 1, the Formal Design and the English Commentary between them should contain the following information where appropriate to the design technique or implementation language:

(a) A description of the program control flow and data flow.

(b) Data and control interfaces between software partitions and between software and hardware.

(c) Lists of all the module inputs and outputs, containing for each parameter the definition, program mnemonic, scaling, allowable range and units.

(d) Lists of all constants and their values used within the module.

(e) Lists of all procedures called within the module and the variables passed.

30.5 Resource modelling

30.5.1 Performance analysis

30.5.1.1 Analysis of response time, throughput and capacity should take place once the features of the design such as data structures and control flow have been sufficiently well defined. Further performance analysis should be carried out after coding is complete, when all the actual module execution times are known. Once the design has reached a stage where performance issues can be analysed, it is important to monitor the consequences of later design decisions upon this analysis.

30.5.1.2 The straightforward architectures produced according to the requirements for analysability of this Standard, with little or no concurrency and deterministic (i.e. predictable and fair) scheduling, greatly simplify performance analysis. Each system action should consist of a well-bounded sequence of primitive actions, each of which is of well-bounded duration (possibly dependent upon values of variables). This permits performance analysis to proceed by tracing events through each processing activity to obtain estimates for the time elapsed.

30.5.1.3 The following should be investigated:

(a) the overall response time from stimulation of input to the generation of output;

(b) the maximum and minimum execution times of each module;

(c) the activation rate of each module, and the time taken for context switching between modules running on a single processor;

(d) the way execution time depends upon processor loading;

(e) the response time of sensors, actuators and displays;

(f) the consistency of digital filter frame lengths;

(g) the maximum and minimum access times for any databases employed;

(h) the possibility of deadlock or livelock between communicating components;

(i) the maximum and minimum communication delays between separate processors, and the possibility of communication channel saturation.

30.5.1.4 The peak loading of processors and communication links should generally not exceed 50%.

30.5.2 Memory management

30.5.2.1 The bounds on the amount of storage required for normal operation of the system will need to be analysed; this may be difficult where the storage depends on the inputs, and particularly where it depends on the frequency of the inputs.

30.5.2.2 The storage requirements that should be analysed to show that they do not exceed their limitations include:

(a) stack sizes

(b) buffer and queue sizes

(c) static memory allocation

(d) dynamic (i.e. heap) allocation

(e) temporary file or memory usage

30.5.2.3 Dynamic storage allocation techniques that include the use of garbage collection may be particularly hard to analyse.

30.5.2.4 Peak memory utilization should generally not exceed 50%.

30.6 Defensive programming

30.6.1 Resilience may be added to the software by systematically adding code to check data values at boundaries between modules or processes and taking appropriate action if anomalies are detected. These checks should cover the assumptions under which the Formal Arguments for the design are constructed, and address:

(a) pre-conditions of the modules or processes;

(b) data type invariants;

(c) type information.

30.6.2 These checks should be added according to a coherent plan; the Standard adopts the approach that inputs from a module with the highest level of assurance do not require checking, but those from any module that was developed to a lower level should be checked. If an error is detected, the software should take action in accordance with the fault containment strategy for the module decided during the system and software design stages. The checks performed should be documented in the Design Description.

30.6.3 Note that the Standard does not address fault detection and fault tolerance at the system level; the strategy for such matters as the detection of erroneous inputs and failed hardware, data recovery, error correction and fail safety should be contained in the Software Requirements Specification.

31 Coding

*See Proof Obligations (**29.4**).*

31.1 Implementation language.

31.1.1 Well-understood semantics

31.1.1.1 Any programming language used for the implementation of SCS should have a formally-defined syntax. However, in order for the code to behave as expected, there needs to be a link between the Formal Design and the execution of statements in the implementation language. This link is provided by a formal *semantics* for the language, which ideally is shown to be consistent with both the rules for carrying out Formal Proofs about the code (the proof theory) and the design of the compiler.

31.1.1.2   These requirements are now attainable for languages of modest size; in fact, they have been met by very small languages in research publications for over a decade. But no existing full language (e.g. ISO-Ada) meets it, and the most satisfactory approach at the present time is to define *subsets* of languages (e.g. Spark Ada). These subsets are based on the full language, but have dangerous but non-essential constructs excised; dangerous constructs are those that may be ambiguous, hard to analyse, or difficult to implement in a compiler; examples are the use of functions and procedures as parameters, and variant records. If a subset is used, conformance to it should be checked during Static Path Analysis.

31.1.1.3   At the present time, the link between the Formal Design and the code should be achieved by selecting an implementation language or language subset such that:

(a) *either* it has a published formal semantics and proof theory in terms of the Formal Method in use;

(b) *or* it has an implicit formal semantics and proof theory embodied in a Proof Obligation generator (see **29.4**).

31.1.1.4   Compilers are discussed in clause **36**.

31.1.2   Assembly language.   The use of assembly language should be minimized. However, it may be impracticable to avoid the use of assembly language inserts in certain configuration specific areas; each insert should however be limited to around 20–50 lines.

31.1.3   Unconventional languages.   SCS should normally be programmed in a conventional procedural language. The onus is on the Design Authority to show both the appropriateness and correctness of any logic, functional or object-oriented language, although the simplicity of the semantics of these languages may make them attractive candidates for formal verification.

31.2   Structured programming.   The need to produce correctness arguments for every design step will tend to enforce a specific structure on programs produced by Formal Methods. Nevertheless, the coding standard in the Code of Design Practice should embody the principles of structured programming, to encourage programs that are both easy to analyse and easy to maintain. Viewed narrowly, the rules of structured programming can be summarized as follows:

(a) Each module should have a single entry and exit.

(b) Control structures should be of the type 'if ... then ... else', 'case' (with a default alternative), 'for' loops (ascending with unit increment through a discrete interval), 'while' and 'repeat'; unconditional branching (e.g. 'goto') should be avoided.

(c) Jumps into loop bodies are forbidden.

(d) Program statements and data structure definitions should be clearly distinguished.

(e) The code should be indented to show its structure.

(f) The program should be decomposed into a hierarchy of modules and atomic modules; the listing of each module should generally occupy at most two pages, although over-modularization should be avoided as it leads to complex interfaces between modules.

(g) The code should be clearly and informatively commented.

(h) Variable names should be meaningful within the application domain, and explained by means of comments accompanying variable declarations.

31.3 Static Path Analysis

31.3.1 The Design Team should use an appropriate tool to check the code for the following:

(a) control flow analysis, that is analysis of the possible paths through the code;

(b) data use analysis, that is analysis of the sequence in which variables are written to and read from;

(c) information flow analysis, that is the dependencies between input and output;

(d) where a restricted subset of an implementation language is employed, analysis of the program constructs used to ensure that the subset has been adhered to.

31.3.2 The results of Static Path Analysis should be documented in the Safety Records Log. Sometimes minor modifications have to be made to the code before it can be analysed by Static Path Analysis tools, and these should be documented and a justification provided as to why these modifications do not affect the level of assurance.

31.3.3 The V&V Team should review the results of Static Path Analysis in the following manner:

(a) the control flow should be examined for anomalies such as unintended loops, unreachable code, loops with no exits or loops with multiple entries;

(b) the data use should be examined for variables that can be used before being set or set and not used;

(c) a judgement should be made of the control flow and data flow complexity in order establish that software is neither over-modularized nor unduly monolithic, and that the module interfaces are reasonably simple;

(d) the information flow should be examined for unwanted or missing dependencies.

31.3.4 Not all the anomalies reported by a Static Path Analysis tool will be due to errors; for example, a variable that is set and not used may simply represent a particular coding style. However, the V&V Team should satisfy themselves that no reported anomaly is due to an error.

32 Formal Arguments

32.1 General

32.1.1 Formal Arguments can be constructed in two ways: by Formal Proof or Rigorous Argument.

32.1.2 A Formal Proof is a strictly well-formed sequence of logical formulae such that each one is entailed from formulae appearing earlier in the sequence or as instances of axioms of the logical theory. Formal Proofs are often highly intricate. They proceed by simple matching of syntactic structure and as such are strongly dependent upon the form of syntactic categories such as formulae and terms.

32.1.3 The highest degree of assurance in the design can be obtained by providing all supporting proofs and checking them with a *proof checker*. A proof checker can be a relatively simple program and thus can itself be verified by Formal Proof; proof checkers are discussed in more detail in **32.2** below.

32.1.4 Creation of such proofs will, however, consume a considerable amount of the time of skilled staff. The Standard therefore also envisages a lower level of design assurance; this level is known as a Rigorous Argument. A Rigorous Argument is not a Formal Proof and is no substitute for it. It is at the level of a mathematical argument in the scientific literature that will be subjected to peer review: it is a high-level sketch of how a Formal Proof could be constructed, indicating the general form of the deduction in terms of the main steps and any auxiliary lemmas that are required, whose details could be filled in if required. The key criterion for the acceptability of a Rigorous Argument is that it can be converted to a Formal Proof by the addition of detail. Thus the specification must itself be written in a notation whose formal semantics is recorded; the design step must be recorded in a similarly supported language; and any Proof Obligation on whose correctness the step depends must be in a mathematical notation. If such a Rigorous Argument was called into question, it would be clear what further formal work would be required to settle the doubt.

32.1.5 A Rigorous Argument also has a role in providing a commentary on intricate Formal Proof, to facilitate review by the Independent Safety Auditor and the V&V Team [73].

32.1.6 In summary, the practical options for Formal Arguments of verification, in decreasing level of assurance, include:

(a) machine generated Formal Proof, checked by an independent proof checker;

(b) manually generated Formal Proof, checked by an independent tool;

(c) Rigorous Argument, checked by review.

32.1.7 The balance between these options should be decided at the contractual stage, with the involvement of the MOD Safety Assurance Authority.

32.2 Proof checkers

32.2.1 In practice, it is very unlikely that Formal Proofs of any size will be created by hand. Instead, they will be developed using *theorem proving assistants*, which are interactive programs that carry out symbol manipulation under the guidance of a human operator. But theorem proving assistants are large programs whose correctness cannot readily be demonstrated by Formal Proof. It is, however, possible to remove the reliance on the correctness of the theorem proving assistant from the case for correctness of an application by arranging that a version of the final proof (omitting all history of its construction) is passed from the theorem proving assistant to a proof checker. For reasonable languages, such a proof checker could be a very simple program (perhaps ten pages in a functional programming language) that could be developed to the highest level of assurance.

32.2.2 The input to the proof checker would be the Formal Proofs to be checked. Ideally, a proof checker could be designed which coped with the output from a range of theorem proving assistants. Unfortunately, the sort of standardization work on which this would depend is nowhere in hand.

32.2.3 In the short term it is therefore likely that a separate proof checker would be associated with each theorem proving assistant. Such a proof checker would be based on a formalized proof theory, the consistency of which would have to be established. The proof checker should be verified against this proof theory.

33 Dynamic Testing

33.1 <u>Objectives.</u> The direction in which the Standard moves is towards greater reliance on auditable correctness arguments in design. However, there are still clearly identifiable uses for test cases as part of verification. The main ones are as follows:

(a) Testing can be used as an independent way of assessing if logic errors are present in components verified by Formal Arguments. Errors located by tests designed for this purpose could result in non-acceptance of the application (see **20.3**); test cases should never be used to 'debug' an application.

(b) Where Formal Proof has not been used in development, some assessment by testing will be necessary.

(c) Testing can be used to investigate conformance to requirements that are not normally the subject of Formal Proof, such as:

  (1) 'clean termination' (e.g. avoidance of overflow of computer fixed point numbers);

  (2) reliance on system components;

(3) performance.

(d) Testing also checks the software production process, e.g. configuration control.

33.2 Test coverage

33.2.1 Verification testing is carried out by the V&V Team on individual modules, partly integrated modules and the integrated SCS.

33.2.2 Testing should be undertaken in a test harness that includes a coverage monitor. Testing continues until complete coverage of all the statements and all the branches is achieved; although normally such coverage includes only a tiny proportion of the total paths.

33.3 Derivation of tests

33.3.1 Test cases are compiled by the V&V Team, and are kept concealed from the Design Team, at least until the tests have been carried out. This prevents the designers 'debugging' round the test cases and producing a design that is specifically tailored to pass the tests; experience has shown that such designs are prone to failure in service.

33.3.2 Production of enough test cases to provide the required coverage is potentially very time consuming. Random testing is an effective way of generating a large number of tests relatively cheaply; where necessary, additional test cases are supplied to address specific requirements for the behaviour during hazardous conditions. If random testing is found not to be achieving the required coverage, the design of the software may need to be examined to generate specific test cases to complete the coverage.

33.3.3 The validation test cases for the Executable Prototype should be included in the tests of the integrated SCS. However, since they are known to the Design Team, the required coverage should be achieved without them.

33.3.4 The test harness should include a means of verifying safety critical timing constraints.

33.3.5 Unless the tests are to be checked against an Executable Prototype (see **33.4.3**), the expected outcomes of the test cases should be deduced at the same time as the tests are designed.

33.4 Implementation of tests

33.4.1 The tests on individual modules, except possibly for input/output modules, will be carried out on the host computer, and an emulator for the target processor will be required. Input/output module testing and integration testing will be carried out on the target hardware, although the test harness on the host will be used to monitor the tests.

33.4.2 The tests should be checked for the following:

(a) correct functionality;

(b) action on error;

(c) timing.

33.4.3 Because of the large number of tests, manual checking will often be very time consuming. The tests on the integrated SCS are therefore checked against an Executable Prototype, using an appropriate harness. If the Executable Prototype does not meet timing constraints, the results are pre-computed and compared with the SCS in real time.

34   Use of Existing Software

No guidance required.

35   Validation

35.1   Although final validation is a system issue, the Standard addresses it because of the lack of other guidance and because of the crucial role of software in the fitness for purpose of the system.

35.2   The integrated computer system should be subjected by the V&V Team to a series of validation tests to establish that it meets the Software Requirements Specification. These tests may be carried out in conjunction with the controlled system in the final environment, or, where that is not practicable, by means of a simulator. A simulator for a complex system and its environment may be more complicated than the software under test, but in many cases (e.g. reactor protection systems or flight controllers) their use is unavoidable; the possibility of error in the simulator must be kept in mind, and if a discrepancy occurs, both the simulator and the software under test should be examined (clause **36** addresses the trustworthiness of tools). Some tests should be carried out that simulate the most demanding environmental conditions identified in the Software Requirements Specification.

35.3   Sufficient testing should be carried out to obtain a statistically significant measure of the achieved reliability of the system. The number of tests required can be calculated from the formulae in [54,68]. Difficulties may arise either because of the cost implications (the Design Authority should be aware that validation testing can represent a significant portion of the project costs), or because the duration of the testing exceeds what is practicable.

35.4   Validation solely by running a replacement system in parallel with the one that it will supersede is not recommended for systems where the frequency of operation is low (e.g. a trip system), as the evidence provided is inadequate.

35.5   As well as the functional behaviour of the system, validation testing should address conformance of the implementation to so-called non-functional requirements, where these are specified appropriately (see **29.2**).

35.6 The test specification amounts to a diverse specification of the computer system, and should be derived by the V&V Team directly from the Software Requirements Specification and agreed with the Independent Safety Auditor. The test schedule should be set up to provide the following:

(a) coverage of each function;

(b) coverage based on the expected input domain, including boundary values, singularities, special values, out of range and erroneous values;

(c) coverage of the states of each individual output.

35.7 The results should be checked for:

(a) correct functionality;

(b) correct action on error, including the action of the fault tolerant features;

(c) correct timing;

(d) conformance to the requirements for non-functional properties.

36 Tool Support

36.1 Although the Design Authority has the overall responsibility for selecting tools, certain classes of tool are required for the efficient application of this standard. These tools are for: automated configuration management; checking of specification and design documents; Static Path Analysis; dynamic testing; and tools that subsequently manipulate the object code.

36.2 The Design Authority should address the matching of tools to the members of the Design Team as this has an important effect on productivity and quality, and hence assurance.

36.3 Clearly the tools used should not compromise the final safety integrity of the SCS. However at the present time the Design Authority may find that many of the tools it wishes to use have a level of safety integrity significantly below that required of the SCS itself. This clause addresses the way in which the safety integrity requirements of the tools can be determined, and offers guidance on how the requirements for different classes of tools can be approached in the short term.

36.4 Integrity levels

36.4.1 The Design Authority should carry out a hazard analysis and safety risk assessment in accordance with Def Stan 00-56 [22] on the tools used to develop the SCS that is identical in principle to the analysis of the equipment of which the SCS is a part. The analysis should treat the software development process itself as a function that produces the code from the specification. This function will have to be modelled as a combination of development phases and verification functions, and suitable hazard analysis techniques, e.g. fault tree analysis, applied.

36.4.2 The analysis should assign integrity requirements for tools used in development depending on their configuration and role, that is what their function is in achieving safe software and systems, and what other tools or functions mitigate the consequence of failure. Since Def Stan 00-56 contains an inheritance scheme for safety integrity that enables a high-level function of a certain integrity to be implemented by components of certain lower integrities, tools of lower integrity than the overall requirement are allowed when additional safeguards, such as diverse checks and reviews, are employed. Projects will need to carry out a cost-benefit analysis to decide on the combination of tools to use.

36.4.3 Tools of the highest integrity level will have to be developed to the requirements of this Standard. The Design Authority should define lower standards of development for tools of other integrity levels; the following table outlines one possible scheme, where T4 represents the highest level of tool integrity and T1 the lowest (see also [75]).

Level	Definition
T4	To this Standard
T3	As T2 + formal specification.
T2	As T1 + structured methods and Static Path Analysis.
T1	Appropriate quality system.

36.4.4 In situations where combinations of tools are being used to achieve a higher combined safety integrity, human intervention may be involved in the combining function. Such a function should be as simple as possible and cross-checked to avoid human error.

36.5 Validation and evaluation

36.5.1 Validation and evaluation of tools should be carried out by an approved third party using an internationally recognized test suite, acceptance criteria and test procedures, taking into account the operational experience with the tool. In cases where these services are not available (e.g. for clerical tools) the Design Authority should undertake, or commission, an evaluation and validation and provide arguments that the tools meet a required integrity level.

36.6 Classes of tool

36.6.1 In addition to classifying tools according to the required integrity, it is also advantageous to consider classes of tools: this assists in the development of general arguments that can be applied to a range of projects.

36.6.2 Transformation tools. Transformation tools are those tools (e.g. compilers) that take an input text at one level of abstraction and transform it into another, normally lower, level. This often involves a transformation between two different languages. A transformation tool for SCS whose output is used without further review should be assigned to the highest integrity level. The requirements for the tool can be reduced by including an independent review of its function.

36.6.3 V&V tools.   Verification and validation tools include Static Path Analyzers, test coverage monitors and theorem proving assistants. Verification to the highest integrity level can be achieved by a single tool to the requirements of this Standard, or by a combination of tools that includes one at a lower level; the theorem proving assistant and proof checker combination is an example of this (see clause **32**).

36.6.4 Clerical tools.   Clerical tools are those used to produce, modify, display and print the objects of the system design and assessment. They include editors, printer drivers, print spoolers, terminal drivers and window management software. Because their output is checked by independent V&V, their integrity requirements are relatively low. Although they are unlikely to be subjected to in-depth V&V, the large amount of operational experience increases their assurance.

36.6.5 Infrastructure tools

36.6.5.1 Infrastructure tools include operating systems, public tools interfaces (VMS, UNIX, DOS, CAIS-A, PCTE, etc.) and version control tools. They are a potential source of common-mode failure, as they may interfere with several other tools or corrupt the output from a design step.

36.6.5.2 Infrastructure tools can be categorized into those that change the semantics of the objects they are dealing with and those that do not. If the semantic information is preserved, a variety of techniques (checksums, encryption etc.) can be used to ensure that redundant information is encoded and any changes detected and corrected. Some of these techniques can be added to existing environments.

36.6.5.3 If the tools change the semantics of the object under consideration (e.g. by incrementing a version number), additional checks will be required. These include the use of validation to check for omissions and the defences provided by downstream verification against any inconsistencies that may have been introduced.

36.7 Availability of tools.   In some cases, the strict requirements for tools that follow from the hazard analysis and safety risk assessment cannot be met at the present time. In these cases, where the Design Authority judges the benefits of the tools are such that on balance the risks from using tools of lower integrity are acceptable, a systematic approach may be adopted to the weakening of the requirements; the Design Authority should pay particular attention to its responsibility for safety when making such judgements. An example approach is a phased application in which the requirements are reduced by two integrity levels for the first phase and one for the second.

Bibliography

The references given in this annex are from the open literature. Entry in the bibliography implies no bias towards any particular product for use by the MOD. Omission from the bibliography implies no bias against any particular product that could be demonstrated to meet MOD requirements. Exceptionally, the MOD may declare a preference, for example in the use of Ada.

[1] *Information Technology Security Evaluation Criteria (ITSEC)*. Version 1 (draft), 2 May 1990. Harmonised Criteria of France, Germany, the Netherlands, the United Kingdom.

[2] J R Abrial. Programming as a mathematical exercise. In C A R Hoare and J C Shepherdson, editors, *Mathematical Logic and Programming Languages*, pages 113–139, Prentice-Hall International, 1985.

[3] R C Backhouse. *Program Construction and Verification*. Prentice-Hall International, 1986.

[4] G Barrett. *Formal methods applied to a floating point number system*. Monograph PRG-58, Programming Research Group, Oxford University, UK, 1987.

[5] H Bekič and C B Jones (ed.). *Programming Languages and Their Definition*. Volume 177 of *Lecture Notes in Computer Science*, Springer-Verlag, 1984.

[6] William R Bevier, A Hunt Warren Jr., and William D Young. *Toward verified execution environments*. Technical Report, Computational Logic Inc., February 1987.

[7] D Bjørner, C A R Hoare, and H Langmaack, editors. *VDM'90: VDM and Z – Formal Methods in Software Development*. Volume 428 of *Lecture Notes in Computer Science*, Springer-Verlag, Berlin, 1990.

[8] D Bjørner, C B Jones, M Mac an Airchinnigh, and E J Neuhold, editors. *VDM – A Formal Method at Work*. Volume 252 of *Lecture Notes in Computer Science*, Springer-Verlag, 1987.

[9] D Bjørner and C B Jones. *Formal Specification and Software Development*. Prentice Hall International, 1982.

[10] D Bjørner and C B Jones, editors. *The Vienna Development Method: The Meta-Language*. Volume 61 of *Lecture Notes in Computer Science*, Springer-Verlag, 1978.

[11] R S Boyer, M W Green, and J S Moore. *The use of a formal simulator to verify a simple real time control programme*. Technical Report ICSA-CMP-29, University of Texas at Austin, 1982.

[12] R S Boyer and J S Moore. Proof checking the RSA public key encryption algorithm. *American Mathematical Monthly 91.3*, 181–189, 1984.

[13] Robert S Boyer and J Strother Moore. *A Computational Logic Handbook*. Volume 23 of *Perspectives in Computing*, Academic Press, 1988.

[14] Michael J D Brown. Rationale for the development of the UK defence standards for safety critical computer software. Compass 7, June 1990.

[15] BS 5887: 1987. Testing of computer based systems.

[16] R M Burstall and J Goguen. An informal introduction to specifications using Clear. In R S Boyer and J S Moore, editors, *The Correctness Problem in Computer Science*, Academic Press, 1981.

[17] B A Carré, I M O'Neill, D L Clutterbuck, and C W Debney. SPADE – the Southampton program analysis and development environment. In I Sommerville, editor, *Software Engineering Environments*, Peter Pereginus, 1986.

[18] G B Clemmensen and O N Oest. *Formal specification and development of an Ada compiler—a VDM case study*. Technical Report, Dansk Datamatik Center, 1983.

[19] W F Clocksin and C S Mellish. *Programming in Prolog*. Springer-Verlag, third edition, 1987.

[20] Avra Cohn. The notion of proof in hardware verification. *Journal of Automated Reasoning*, 1989.

[21] D Craigen. *A Technical Review of Four Verification Systems: Gypsy, Affirm, FDM and Revised Special*. Technical Report, I P Sharp Associates Ltd, August 1985.

[22] Def Stan 00-56. Hazard Analysis and Safety Classification of the Computer and Programmable Electronic System Elements of Defence Equipment.

[23] Def Stan 00-970. Design and Airworthiness Requirements for Service Aircraft.

[24] Def Stan 05-57. Configuration Management Policy and Procedures for Defence Equipment.

[25] Def Stan 08-3. Ordnance Board Safety Guidelines for Munitions.

[26] Def Stan 08-5. Design Requirements for Weapon Systems (Guided Weapons, Torpedoes and Airborne Armament Stores).

[27] E W Dijkstra. *A Discipline of Programming*. Prentice-Hall, 1976.

[28] M Dyer. The IBM clean room experiment. In *Centre for Software Reliability Symposium, Bristol, 1987*, Blackwell, Oxford, UK, 1987.

[29] H Ehrig and B Mahr. *Fundamentals of Algebraic Specification 1: Equations and Initial Semantics. EATCS Monographs on Theoretical Computer Science*, Springer-Verlag, 1985.

[30] M E Fagan. Advances in software inspections. *IEEE Trans. Software Engineering*, 744–751, July 1986.

[31] P K D Froome, B Q Monahan, and R E Bloomfield. Specbox – a checker for VDM specifications. In *Proceedings of Second International Conference on Software Engineering for Real Time Systems, Cirencester, UK*, IEE, 1989.

[32] J A Goguen and Tardo J J. An introduction to OBJ: a language for writing and testing formal algebraic program specifications. In *Proceedings of the Conference on Specifications of Reliable Systems, Cambridge, Massachusetts*, 1979.

[33] D I Good. A proof of a distributed system in Gypsy. In Elphick M J, editor, *Formal Specification: The proceedings of the joint IBM/University of Newcastle-upon-Tyne seminar, University Computing Laboratory, Newcastle-upon-Tyne*, 1983.

[34] M Gordon. *HOL: a machine oriented formulation of higher order logic.* Technical Report Technical Report no. 104, University of Cambridge Computing Laboratory, University of Cambridge, UK, 1985.

[35] M Gordon, R Milner, and C Wadsworth. *Edinburgh LCF.* Volume 78 of *Lecture Notes in Computer Science,* Springer-Verlag, 1979.

[36] David Gries. *The Science of Computer Programming.* Springer-Verlag, 1981.

[37] F K Hanna and N Daeche. Specification and verification of digital systems using higher-order predicate logic. *IEE proceedings,* 01 133 Part E(5), September 1986.

[38] F K Hanna, M Longley, and N Daeche. Formal synthesis of digital systems. In *Applied Formal Methods for Correct VLSI Design, Belgium, November 1989,* North Holland, to be published.

[39] R Harper, R Milner, and Tofte M. *The Definition of Standard ML.* MIT Press, 1990.

[40] I Hayes, editor. *Specification Case Studies.* Prentice-Hall International, London, UK, 1987.

[41] P Henderson. Functional programming; formal specifications and rapid prototyping. *IEEE Transactions on Software Engineering,* SE-122:241–50, 1986.

[42] C A R Hoare. An axiomatic basis for computer programming. *Communications of the ACM,* 12(10):576–80, 583, October 1969.

[43] C A R Hoare. *Communicating Sequential Processes.* Prentice-Hall International, London, UK, 1985.

[44] C A R Hoare and C B Jones. *Essays in Computing Science.* Prentice Hall International, 1988.

[45] IEC TC 65, SC 65A. *Draft: Software for computers in the application of industrial safety-related systems.* IEC 65A(Secretariat)94, August 1989.

[46] ISO 8879. Information processing – Text and office systems – Standard Generalized Markup Language (SGML).

[47] ISO DIS 8807. Information processing systems – Lotos – a formal description technique based on the temporal ordering of observational behaviour.

[48] C B Jones. *Software Development: A Rigorous Approach.* Prentice Hall International, 1980.

[49] C B Jones. *Systematic Software Development using VDM.* Prentice-Hall International, London, UK, second edition, 1990.

[50] C B Jones, K D Jones, P A Lindsay, and R Moore, editors. *Mural: A Formal Development Support System.* Springer-Verlag, 1991. To be published.

[51] C B Jones and R C F Shaw, editors. *Case Studies in Systematic Software Development.* Prentice Hall International, 1990.

[52] H B M Jonkers. *An Introduction to COLD-K.* Technical Report METEOR/t8/PRLE/8, Philips Research Labs, Eindhoven, July 1988.

[53] D E Knuth. *Sorting and Searching.* Volume III of *The Art of Computer Programming,* Addison-Wesley Publishing Company, 1975.

[54] B Littlewood. Limits to evaluation of software dependability. In Bev Littlewood and Norman Fenton, editors, *Software Reliability and Metrics, Proceedings of 7th CSR Annual Workshop (Garmisch-Partenkirchen, September 1990)*, Elsevier, 1991. To be published.

[55] Zhaohui Luo, Robert Pollock, and Paul Taylor. *How to Use Lego (A Preliminary User's Manual)*. Department of Computer Science, University of Edinburgh, October 1989.

[56] Gordon M. *A proof generating system for higher order logic.* Technical report 103, University of Cambridge Computing Laboratory, January 1987.

[57] L S Marshall. *A Formal Description Method for User Interfaces.* PhD thesis, University of Manchester, October 1986.

[58] M A McMorran and J E Nicholls. *Z User Manual.* Technical Report 12.274, IBM UK Laboratories, Winchester, July 1989.

[59] C A Middelburg. *Syntax and Semantics of VVSL A Language for Structured VDM Specifications.* PhD thesis, PTT Research, Department of Applied, Department of Applied Computer Science, September 1990.

[60] Robin Milner. *Communication and Concurrency.* Prentice Hall International, London, UK, 1989.

[61] J S Moore. *Piton: A verified assembly-level language.* Technical report CLI-22, Computational Logic Inc, June 1988.

[62] C Morgan. *Programming from Specifications.* Prentice Hall International, 1990.

[63] Louise E Moser and M Mellar-Smith. Formal verification of safety-critical systems. *Software practice and experience*, 20(8):799–821, August 1990.

[64] G J Myers. *The Art of Software Testing.* Wiley, 1979.

[65] T Nipkow. Non-deterministic data types: models and implementations. *Acta Informatica*, 22:629–661, 1986.

[66] J N Oliviera. A reification calculus for model-oriented software specification. *Formal Aspects of Computing*, 2(1):1–23, January–March 1990.

[67] I M O'Neill. *Logic Programming Tools and Techniques for Imperative Program Verification.* PhD thesis, University of Southampton, 1987.

[68] David L Parnas, John van Schouwen, and Shu Po Kwan. Evaluation of safety-critical software. *Communication of the ACM*, 33(6):636–648, June 1990.

[69] L C Paulson. *Logic and Computation: Interactive Proof with Cambridge LCF.* Cambridge University Press, 1987.

[70] J C Reynolds. *The Craft of Programming.* Prentice Hall International, 1981.

[71] B Ritchie. *The Design and Implementation of an Interactive Proof Editor.* PhD thesis, University of Edinburgh, 1988.

[72] J M Rushby. Kernels for safety? In *CSR Symposium on Safety and Security*, Elsevier, 1989.

[73] John Rushby and Frieder von Henke. *Formal Verification of a Fault Tolerant Clock Synchronization Algorithm*. NASA Office of Management, Scientific and Technical Information Division, June 1989. NASA contractor report 4239.

[74] SafeIT 1. Overall approach. Department of Trade and Industry, 1990. A Government consultation document of the safety of computer-controlled systems.

[75] SafeIT 2. Standards framework. Department of Trade and Industry, 1990. A Government consultation document of the safety of computer-controlled systems.

[76] D T Sannella. *Semantics, Implementation and Pragmatics of Clear, A Program Specification Language*. PhD thesis, Department of Computer Science, University of Edinburgh, July 1982. Available as a Technical Report – no. CST-17-82.

[77] D A Schmidt. *Denotational Semantics: a Methodology for Language Development*. Allyn & Bacon, 1986.

[78] J M Spivey. *The Z notation—a Reference Manual*. Prentice-Hall International, London, UK, 1988.

[79] Starts Guide. Starts (Software tools for application to large real-time systems) purchasers handbook. May 1989. Second edition.

[80] R D Tennent. *Principles of Programming Languages*. Prentice-Hall International, 1981.

[81] P H J van Eijk, C A Vissers, and M Diaz. *The Formal Description Technique Lotos*. Elsevier Science, 1989.

[82] A Hunt Warren Jr. *A verified microprocessor*. Technical Report, University of Texas at Austin, 1985.

[83] B A Wichmann. Scientific processing in ISO-Pascal: A proposal to get the benefits of mixed precision floating point. *Sigplan notices*, 01:20–22, June 1989.

Index

Principal entries are underlined.

acceptance   clause **25**
    criteria   **20.1, 20.3**
Ada   **24.6, 31.1.1**
analysability   **30.3**
animation   **29.6**
    of design   **30.2.6**
assembly language   **31.1.2**
Audit Plan   **16.2**
A&AEE   clause **7**

CAIS-A   **36.6.5**
certification   **18.2**, clause **25**
claim limits   **8.2**
clerical tools   **36.6.4**
Code of Design Practice   **18.1, 18.2,**
    clause **20**
coding   clause **31**
concurrency   **30.3.4**
configuration control   clause **24**
configuration item   clause **24**
configuration object   clause **24**
Configuration Plan   **18.1, 18.2, 22.1,**
    24.6
configuration system   **24.8**
conformance   **25.2**
Core   **29.5**
curricula vitae   **9.1, 18.2**

Def Stan 00-56   **1.3, 8.3, 36.4**
Def Stan 00-970   **1.3**
Def Stan 05-57   **24.1**
Def Stan 08-3   **1.3**
Def Stan 08-5   **1.3**
DEFCON 143   **9.1**
defensive programming   **20.1, 30.6**
deliverable items   **9.1, 18.2**
design   clause **30**
Design Description   **30.4, 30.6.2**
Design Team   clause **15, 18.2, 20.1,**
    30.1.1, 33.3.1, 33.3.3, 36.2
documentation   clause **22**

DOS   **36.6.5**
dynamic testing   **15.2, 20.1, 30.1.2,**
    clause **33**

English Commentary   **19.2, 20.1, 30.4**
    examination of words   **19.2.2**
    local definitions   **19.2.3**
    spelling check   **19.2.1**
errors   **29.6.2**
    human   **36.4.4**
    syntactic   **29.3.2**
    type   **29.3.3**
evaluation
    of tools   **36.5.1**
Executable Prototype   **29.6, 33.3.3,**
    33.3.5, 33.4.3

Fagan Inspections   **19.1**
failure
    prediction   clause **8**
    random   clause **8**
    requirements   **8.2**
    systematic   clause **8**
fault tree analysis   **36.4.1**
floating point arithmetic   **30.3.8**
Formal Arguments   **15.2, 20.1, 20.3,**
    29.4, 29.6, 30.2.1, 30.6.1,
    clause **32, 33.1**
Formal Design   **30.2, 30.4, 31.1.1**
    verification   **29.3**
Formal Method   **20.1, 29.4, 30.1.1**
    for design   **30.2**
    selection   **29.1**
Formal Proofs   **20.1, 30.2.5, 31.1.1,**
    clause **32, 33.1**
Formal Specification   **29.6, 30.2.4**
    verification   **29.3**

hazard analysis   clause **8, 25.2, 36.4**

implementation language   **20.1, 31.1**
in-service anomaly reports   **21.3**

In-Service Authority   **25.4, 29.6.1,
    29.6.2, 29.6.4**
Independent Safety Audit Team
    16.1.1
Independent Safety Auditor   clause **16**,
    **18.2, 22.1, 25.2, 30.1.1,
    32.1.5, 35.6**
infrastructure tools   **36.6.5**
integrity levels
    of tools   **36.4**
interrupts   **30.3.6**
IPSE   **9.1, 24.6**
isolation of SCS   **8.5**

Jackson Structured Design   **29.5**

length of code   **30.3.5**
lifecycles   clause **4**
Lotos   **29.1.2**

Malpas IL   **30.2.2**
memory management   **30.5.2**
minimization of SCS   **8.6**
MOD Equipment Sponsor   **25.4**
MOD Safety Assurance Authority
    clause **7**, **18.2, 22.1, 25.2, 25.4,
    32.1.7**
MOD(PE) PM   clause **7**, **10.1, 18.2,
    22.1, 25.4, 29.6.1, 29.6.2,
    29.6.4**
modularity   **30.3.3**

non-functional properties   **29.2, 35.5**

Ordnance Board   clause **7**

partitioning   **30.3.7**
Pascal   **29.6.4**
PCTE   **36.6.5**
performance analysis   **30.5.1**
Preliminary Validation   **29.6**
project lifecycle   **4.1**
    in-service   **21.3**
Prolog   **29.6.4**
Proof Obligations   **15.2, 29.4, 30.3.1,
    31.1.1, 32.1.4**

recursion   **30.3.9**

resource modelling   **30.5**
resource planning   **18.2**
Review Committee   **18.2**
Rigorous Arguments   **20.1**, clause **32**

Safety Critical Software Certificate
    16.2, 18.2, clause **25**
safety integrity   clause **8**, **25.1**
    of existing systems   **18.2**
    of tools   clause **36**
Safety Plan   **9.1, 15.1, 16.2**,
    clause **18**, **20.1**
Safety Records Log   **16.2**, clause **21**,
    21.3.1, 31.3.2
safety reviews   **15.2, 18.2**, clause **19**
    formal   **19.1**
safety risk assessment   clause **8**, **25.2**,
    36.4
Software Design Authority   **25.2**
Software Developer   **25.2**
software lifecycle   **4.2**
Software Quality Plan   **9.1**
Software Requirements Specification
    22.3, 29.6.1, 29.6.3, 35.2, 35.6
Spark Ada   **31.1.1**
specification   clause **29**
spelling check   **19.2.1**
staff qualifications   **18.2**
    Independent Safety Auditor
    16.1.2
Standard Generalized Markup Language
    (SGML)   **22.1**
Standard ML   **29.6.4**
Starts guide   **4.2**
Static Path Analysis   **15.2, 20.1, 20.3,
    30.1.2, 31.1.1, 31.3, 36.6.3**
structured methods   **20.1, 29.5**
structured programming   **31.2**
subcontractors   **18.2**
suppliers   **18.2**
support   **9.1**, clause **10**
System Design Authority   **25.2**

tenders   clause **9**
tools   **9.1, 18.2, 20.1**, clause **36**
    Concurrency Workbench   **29.6.3**

configuration control   **24.6**

emulator   **33.4.1**

Fuzz   **29.3.4**

Gypsy   **29.4.3**

integrity   **20.1**

Mural   **29.4.2**

Objex   **29.6.4**

parser   **29.3.2**

proof checker   **32.1.3, 32.1.6, 32.2, 36.6.3**

simulator   **35.2**

Spade   **29.4.3**

Spade Proof Checker   **29.6.3**

Specbox   **29.3.4**

structure editor   **29.3.2**

symbolic execution   **29.6.3**

test harness   **33.2.2, 33.4.1**

theorem proving assistant   **32.2.1, 32.2.2, 32.2.3, 36.6.3**

verification condition generator **29.4.3**

transformation tools   **36.6.2**

UNIX   **36.6.5**

validation   clause **35**

of tools   **36.5.1**

VDM   **29.1.2, 30.2.2**

verification and validation   **15.1**

VMS   **36.6.5**

V&V Team   clause **15**, **18.2, 20.1, 20.3, 21.1, 29.6.4, 30.1.1, 31.3.3, 31.3.4, 32.1.5, 33.2.1, 33.3.1, 35.2, 35.6**

V&V tools   **36.6.3**

Z   **29.1.2, 30.2.2**